COMMUNICATING WITH
GRAMMAR 3
Skills for Life

Mohammad Hashemi

OXFORD
UNIVERSITY PRESS

OXFORD
UNIVERSITY PRESS

Oxford University Press is a department of the University of Oxford.
It furthers the University's objective of excellence in research, scholarship,
and education by publishing worldwide. Oxford is a registered trade mark of
Oxford University Press in the UK and in certain other countries.

Published in Canada by
Oxford University Press
8 Sampson Mews, Suite 204,
Don Mills, Ontario M3C 0H5 Canada

www.oupcanada.com

First Published 2014

Library and Archives Canada Cataloguing in Publication

Hashemi, Mohammad, 1969–, author
Communicating with grammar : skills for life. 3 / Mohammad
Hashemi.

ISBN 978-0-19-900334-1 (pbk.)

1. English language--Grammar.   2. English language--Textbooks
for second language learners.   I. Title.

PE1112.H38 2014   428.2'4   C2012-905797-5

Cover image: © Gunter Marx/Alamy

Oxford University Press is committed to our environment.
Wherever possible, our books are printed on paper
which comes from responsible sources.

Printed and bound in Canada

7 8 9 — 20 19 18

AUTHORS

Author

Mohammad Hashemi, BA, MA, is a teacher, editor, translator, and author. He has been coordinating and teaching English for more than 20 years, formerly at Carleton University and Algonquin College. He currently teaches at La Cité collégiale in Ottawa, Ontario. For more information about Mohammad visit his website at www.mohammadhashemi.com.

Series Team

The whole author team created the approach, the topics covered, and the chapter structure for the three-level series *Communicating with Grammar: Skills for Life*. Though each level has its specific lead author or authors, the team worked collaboratively in the development of these publications.

Alice Johnston-Newman, BA, MA, CTESL, is a language teacher, writer, and translator with close to 30 years' experience teaching English as a first and second language to Canadians, new Canadians, and international students. She is currently a professor at La Cité collégiale in Ottawa and has taught at Algonquin College, Carleton University, and abroad. During her professional career, she has created and adapted teaching material and student workbooks for ESL, enriched level, as well as specialized, career-oriented English courses.

Silvija Kalnins, BA, CTESL, has been teaching and coordinating English for the past 10 years at La Cité collégiale. This is her third career. As the eldest daughter of Latvian immigrants, she has experienced first-hand the difficulties of English language acquisition, which has sensitized her to the needs and challenges that her students face.

Julita Milewski, BA, M.Ed., has been an ESL teacher for the last 13 years. Her desire to teach ESL started as she herself was learning English as a second language when she first immigrated to Canada as a teenager. Her teaching experience includes working with adolescent and adult learners, international students, and immigrants. She has taught at the University of Ottawa, Carleton University, and various private language schools. She is currently an ESL professor at La Cité collégiale in Ottawa.

Jaklin Zayat, BA (Modern Languages), M.Ed., has been teaching ESL and academic writing for over 20 years. She speaks five languages and is recognized for her knowledge of the construction of many other languages. She currently teaches at La Cité collégiale and the University of Ottawa. A co-author of *Famous Canadian Authors*, she also enjoys writing stories for future publications.

Acknowledgements

From the Author

I would like to thank my colleagues and acknowledge their invaluable contribution as follows:

Alice Johnston-Newman and Julita Milewski for Chapters 1, 2, and 6
Peter Beckingham for Chapter 3
Jaklin Zayat for Chapter 4
Silvija Kalnins for Chapter 5
Omid Ghahreman for reading the whole manuscript and making valuable suggestions

Special thanks to the excellent editorial and publishing team at OUP Canada for their advice, encouragement, and tremendous support during the writing of this book.

Reviewers

Oxford University Press Canada would like to express appreciation to the instructors and coordinators who graciously offered feedback on *Communicating with Grammar* at various stages of the developmental process. Their feedback was instrumental in helping to shape and refine the series.

Gill Atkinson	Camosun College
Roisin Dewart	Université du Québec à Montréal
Susan Drolet	Cégep Garneau
Barbara Fraser	Collège Ahuntsic
Daniela Geremia	
Brandie Glasgow-Spanos	Niagara Catholic District School Board: St. Ann Adult Learning Centre
Emrah Görgülü	Simon Fraser University
Therese Gormley Hirmer	Humber College Institute of Technology & Advanced Learning
Kristina Gryz	Red River College
Corinne Hamel-Taylor	S.U.C.C.E.S.S.
Eva Ing	George Brown College
Rob Inouye	Simon Fraser University
Maureen Kelbert	Vancouver Community College
Kristibeth Kelly	Fanshawe College
Kara King-Barratt	Catholic Crosscultural Services
Izabella Kojic-Sabo	University of Windsor
Claire La Fleur	The Centre for Skills Development & Training
Anita Lemonis	Vancouver Community College
Sandra Madigan	Southeast Regional College
Corinne Marshall	Fanshawe College
Lara McInnis	Humber College
Jennifer Peachey	VanWest College
Mark Rankin	
Brett Reynolds	Humber College
Cheri Rohloff	The University of Winnipeg
Wilfried Schuster	Toronto District School Board: Adult Ed
Adrianna Semerjian	City Adult Learning Centre
Marti Sevier	Simon Fraser University

CONTENTS

Chapter 12
Adverb Clauses of Condition   239

Part 2 Review
Self-Study   259

Appendices   267

Glossary   275

INTRODUCTION

Welcome to Communicating with Grammar!

Communicating with Grammar: Skills for Life is a Canadian series for ESL and EFL students looking to improve their understanding of English grammar. Offering grammar instruction through the use of the four skills—reading, writing, listening, and speaking—the series helps students internalize concepts for better use in all their communication. Students improve their command of English grammar through a broad spectrum of activities that set them up for further study or work in an English-speaking environment.

The *Communicating with Grammar* series employs a task-based and communicative methodology. Using a "learn–practise–use in context" approach, the books deliver the essential grammar concepts via practical exercises and activities, helping learners become functional in English as quickly and efficiently as possible. The communicative activities then help students internalize the grammar in context.

Series Features

This Canadian series guides student learning by combining a communicative task-based approach with discrete grammar instruction using traditional exercises. It provides warm-up activities, explicit grammar teaching, considerable use of practical example sentences, and a combination of mechanical and interactive exercises. The more traditional exercises allow students to practise each concept, while engaging communicative activities further reinforce the grammar being studied. Moreover, the target grammar is embedded in the reading, listening, and writing sections that follow, facilitating further grammar use in context. Additionally, review units provide, at regular intervals, an opportunity for students to practise the material and solidify the key aspects of their learning. The books have the additional advantage of providing flexibility for those learners who thrive on extra challenge while maintaining the intended level of the target material.

Chapter Structure

Chapters are logically organized into an overview, a series of grammar topics with practice, a cumulative section incorporating all four skill areas, and a summary. Grammar is treated as a necessary component of all four skill areas, and students are encouraged to use the focal grammar topic with each of these skills in every chapter.

Overview

Each chapter opens with a very brief explanation of the chapter's grammar topic, followed by a **Warm-up** activity that engages students and provides an opportunity to start thinking about and using the target grammar in context. Given a real-life task, students are encouraged to use the new grammar concept to communicate with their classmates.

Grammar

The chapter's target grammar is divided into logical and manageable parts, each of which uses a learn–practice–use in context approach.

The grammar instruction starts with a **Formation** (learn) section that offers a clear explanation of the grammar topic, often by using tables and charts, and illustrates the mechanics in context.

Exercises (practice) follow the grammar explanation. A series of traditional drills gives students controlled exposure to the language structures and deals with common difficulties faced by most learners. The exercises are varied and include sentence completion, sentence construction, matching, ordering, error correction, transformation, multiple choice, fill in the blanks, and more.

Further practice through interactive **Communicative Activities** (use in context) allows students to apply the new grammar topic in a practical manner. These engaging tasks, which include class, pair, and group activities, enable learners to communicate in an authentic way by using the grammar they have learned.

Bringing It All Together

This key section at the heart of the chapter provides an opportunity for students to bring together all the chapter's grammar parts and apply them in a more authentic context. It includes a number of additional **Communicative Activities** that challenge students to incorporate all aspects of the chapter's grammar. The **Reading** section contains both a reading passage and comprehension questions, requiring students to apply the chapter's grammar points. The audio clips and comprehension questions in the **Listening** section again facilitate input and output of the target grammatical structures. In the **Writing** section, students are provided with another productive opportunity to apply the grammar, this time in a longer piece of writing.

Chapter Review

Each chapter's review section opens with a helpful **Summary** of all aspects of the grammar taught in the chapter; students can check their learning through a complete and convenient chapter grammar reference. The traditional **Exercises** that follow are designed to give additional straightforward practice for students to work on independently in class or for homework.

Appendices and Glossary

To supplement and support the learning, each book ends with quick-reference appendices, with additional information on grammar points or usage, and a glossary of all key vocabulary from the chapters' Readings.

Three Levels

Level 1 is designed for students with basic English who still need to build a solid foundation of the major verb tenses and sentence structure. Students learn to formulate more accurate sentences and questions through the grammar lessons and exercises. They expand their English vocabulary through the Reading and Listening components. This level also focuses on targeting the common basic grammatical errors students may still need to learn how to correct.

Level 2 is designed for students who have completed Level 1 or who have enough grammar and a basic understanding of the four skills to formulate questions in English and construct more-complex sentences. At the entry into this level, students can usually clearly communicate their intentions to others but still make frequent errors in structure, tense, and usage that may slow comprehension. Level 2 focuses on improving grammar in the four skills areas to an exit level at which students will have more fluency, a larger vocabulary, and the ability to express themselves by using more complicated sentence structures.

Level 3 is the bridging level to fluency in English usage. This level completes all the perfect verb tenses and has chapters on the active and passive voice and reported speech. It further develops students' ability to construct more-complex sentences with the study of clauses. Reading and Listening components are from authentic sources, preparing students for real-world communication. At the completion of this level, students will have the confidence to communicate with native speakers academically or professionally.

Additional Series Components

- Class audio is available for each level in the series. It contains either authentic or constructed listening clips, depending on the level and grammar topic.
- The **online Teacher Resource** contains teaching notes and aids, additional communicative activities and exercises to be used as practice or in a test setting, audio transcripts, and an answer key for the exercises and the reading and listening comprehension questions.

Review of Verb Tenses

OVERVIEW

- The three time frames for verb tenses in English—past, present, and future—each has three main tenses or aspects of tenses: simple, progressive, and perfect. The perfect progressive tenses combine both the perfect and the progressive aspects.

- Most English verbs are regular, and the verb tenses are formed by adding the endings -s, -ed, and -ing to the base form of the verb. (The base form is the word—such as *talk* or *work*—that you look up in the dictionary.) Combining different verb forms and using appropriate auxiliary verbs allow you to create the different tenses.

- This chapter reviews the simple and progressive tenses.

Warm-up

Interview two students in your class. Ask them the following questions, and record their answers in the chart. At the end of the exercise, share your findings with the rest of the class.

	How do you come to school every day?	How did you go home yesterday?	How will you go home today?
1			
2			

	What are you doing right now?	What were you doing at 9:00 last night?	What will you be doing at 9:00 tomorrow night?
1			
2			

SIMPLE TENSES

Formation

	Positive	Negative	Question
Simple Present	He **plays** soccer every weekend.	He **does not** (doesn't) **play** soccer every weekend.	**Does** he **play** soccer every weekend?
Simple Past	He **played** soccer last weekend.	He **did not** (didn't) **play** soccer last weekend.	**Did** he **play** soccer last weekend?
Simple Future	He **will play** soccer next year.	He **will not** (won't) **play** soccer next year.	**Will** he **play** soccer next year?

I will play   *I will played*

USE

The simple tenses are used to indicate single or repeated actions.

The **simple present tense** indicates

- routine actions in the present (She brushes her teeth every day.)
- facts or things that are accepted as true (The earth circles the sun.)
- permanent or semi-permanent characteristics (She wears glasses.)
- scheduled future events with a time signal. (The train arrives at 9:00 AM.)

- In the simple present, don't forget to add -s or -es at the end of the verb in the third-person singular form. (You run. but He runs.)

- Add *do* or *does* to create questions and negatives. (Do you run? / Does he run?)

The **simple past tense** indicates single or repeated actions completed in the past.

He ran in the marathon in Spain last year. (single action)

He ran in four marathons every year until he was 50. (repeated action)

The **simple future tense** indicates simple future actions. You can usually use *will* and *be going to* to indicate future actions.

Use *will* for spontaneous or probable actions. (Raj will get angry when he hears the news.)

Use *be going to* with planned or intended future actions. (Amit is going to take his time before he reacts to the news.)

EXERCISE 1

Fill in the blanks with the correct form of the simple tense of the verbs in parentheses.

Canada 1 _has been_ (be) a constitutional monarchy and a parliamentary democracy. The duties of head of state and head of government are distinct. Canada's Parliament 2 _consists_ (consist) of three parts: the Queen, represented by the governor general; the Senate; and the House of Commons.

Four hundred years ago, Samuel de Champlain, who 3 _was_ (be) a French explorer and became known as the father of New France, the French part of Canada, 4 _carried_ (carry) out several duties and responsibilities. Those tasks 5 _were_ (be) later the tasks of the governors of New France. When Confederation 6 _took_ (take) place in 1867, they 7 _were_ (be) the tasks of the governors general of Canada.

The governor general has many responsibilities. One of the most important 8 _is_ (be) to ensure that Canada always has a prime minister and a government in place—a government that has the confidence of Parliament. Additionally, the governor general 9 _represents_ (represent) Canada during state visits abroad and 10 _hosting_ (host) royal visitors, foreign heads of state, and ambassadors.

Furthermore, the governor general 11 _has_ (have) a major role in promoting our national identity and fostering national unity. The governor general 12 _travels_ (travel) often across Canada and 13 _takes_ (take) part in a variety of events to meet Canadians, listen to their problems, and discuss issues.

The governor general also 14 _presents_ (present) medals, honours, and awards to recognize people's excellence, courage, volunteerism, and exceptional achievements. Any person or group is welcome to nominate a deserving individual as a candidate for appointment to the Order of Canada or as a candidate for the Decoration for Bravery, the Meritorious Service Decoration, or the Governor General's Caring Canadian Award. If you visit the governor general's website, you 15 _will find_ (find) more information there. As well, you 16 _will learn_ (learn) about the dates of the next year's ceremonies and other events.

PROGRESSIVE TENSES

Formation

	Positive	Negative	Question
Present Progressive	I **am eating** supper now.	I **am not** (I'm not) **eating** supper now.	**Are** you **eating** supper now?
Past Progressive	I **was eating** supper last night at 8:00.	I **was not** (wasn't) **eating** supper last night at 8:00.	**Were** you **eating** supper last night at 8:00?
Future Progressive	I **will be eating** supper tomorrow night at 8:00.	I **will not be** (won't be) **eating** supper tomorrow night at 8:00.	**Will** you **be eating** supper tomorrow night at 8:00?

USE

The progressive tenses are used to indicate **temporary actions** or **continuing actions** over a **specific time** and to **create a link** between two or more actions within a **limited time** frame.

The **present progressive tense** indicates

* actions going on at the moment (I am doing the laundry right now.)
* an expected immediate future action (I'm going out with friends tonight.)

The **past progressive tense**

* indicates actions during a specific time in the past (I was studying for the exam between 7:00 and 8:00 last night.)
* creates a link between two or more actions happening simultaneously (While he was cooking in the kitchen, she was doing the laundry in the basement.)
* indicates a continuing action being interrupted by a simple action (While I was taking a shower, the lights went out.)

The **future progressive tense**

* indicates actions during a specific time in the future (I will be studying all night for tomorrow's exam.)
* usually creates a link to other actions in a future or present time (I will be driving home when you get this message.)

We often use a progressive tense after *while* and use a simple tense after *when*.

Restrictions

The progressive tenses normally **cannot** be used with verbs describing beliefs, knowledge, emotions, the senses, possession, or existence. You cannot limit or apply a specific time to these kinds of actions without changing their meaning. Review the chart of non-progressive (stative) verbs in Appendix A.

I **believed** you.

We **understand** your reasons.

I really **like** to play music.

The food **smells** great.

She **will have** five courses next semester.

They **seemed** to be happy.

EXERCISE 2

Fill in each blank with the correct form of one of the progressive tenses of the verb in parentheses.

Since 1999, Ontario high school students have had to complete 40 hours of volunteer work as part of their requirements for graduation. Many teens 1 *are discovering* (discover) the rewards gained from helping others through these activities. In addition, they 2 *will be increasing* (increase) their involvement in their communities. That was and is one of the main goals of the program. Since then, the opportunities for youth volunteers have expanded, and now, many more volunteer organizations 3 *are embracing* (embrace) the involvement of high school students in their activities.

Volunteering can benefit everyone. While the teen volunteers 4 *are working* (work) with senior citizens or food banks or other community organizations, they 5 *are expanding* (expand) their awareness of their community and of the needs of others, and they 6 *will be learning* *are learning* (learn) about respect. Teens realize that while they 7 *are giving* (give), they 8 *are receiving* (receive) as well. They 9 *are gaining* (gain) valuable experience while they 10 *are becoming* *becoming* (become) more engaged in their communities.

Most high school graduates 11 _will be going_ (go) on to college or university. In many cases, their volunteer experience in high school will help them choose an area of interest for their career. For example, while a student 12 _is helping_ (help) at an animal shelter, she might discover that she wants to be a veterinarian. Another might decide to become a social worker while he 13 _is volunteering_ (volunteer) at a youth drop-in centre.

Ideally, having benefited from their volunteer experience, young people will continue to participate in their community through volunteer work throughout their lives.

EXERCISE 3

Change each of the following positive sentences into the negative. Then change each positive sentence into a yes / no question. Review the formation charts if you need to.

Sentence: He won many awards in his last year of high school.

Negative: He didn't win many awards in his last year of high school.

Question: Did he win many awards in his last year of high school?

1. They will get more involved in their community this summer.

   Negative: _____

   Question: _____

2. Sergeant Canes received a medal for bravery at the ceremony.

   Negative: _____

   Question: _____

3. He knows a lot about virtual volunteering.

   Negative: _____

   Question: _____

4. Children who volunteer are likely to continue volunteering as adults.

   Negative: _____

   Question: _____

5. It was difficult to find free time to help those in need.

    Negative: _____

    Question: _____

6. They were doing their best to help those in need.

    Negative: _____

    Question: _____

7. We have a greater love for those we support than those who support us.
    —Eric Hoffer

    Negative: _____

    Question: _____

8. He did some good work as a volunteer.

    Negative: _____

    Question: _____

EXERCISE 4

Change the following sentences to information questions. The information you want to ask about is underlined. Review the formation charts if you need to.

Sentence: Volunteering is a very rewarding experience.

Question: What is a very rewarding experience?

1. I admire firefighters and police officers because they often sacrifice their lives for others.

    _____?

2. The volunteers were very happy to see the smiles on the kids' faces.

    _____?

3. Next summer, she will go abroad to participate in a humanitarian project.

    _____?

4. Carlos prepared 50 sandwiches for tomorrow's breakfast program at his son's school.

    _____?

5. We are going to teach our children to be compassionate toward others.

    _____?

6. Darnella is completing her volunteer hours <u>at a seniors' residence</u>.

   _____?

7. <u>Franklin</u> was helping children with disabilities when he decided to study education.

   _____?

8. My sister will be starting her volunteer work at the hospital <u>next week</u>.

   _____?

9. Five students <u>are helping in the kitchen</u> at the homeless shelter.

   _____?

10. Emilio was volunteering at the immigration centre <u>because he wanted to help newcomers feel welcome</u>.

   _____?

EXERCISE 5   Denisse Reyes Betancourt

Fill in the blanks with the correct tense of the verbs in parentheses.

A. The Runner (simple present or present progressive)

Every time, just before I take off in the race, I always ₁ __feel__

(feel) like I'm in a dream, the kind of dream you have when you

₂ __get__ (be) sick with fever and feel all hot and weightless. I

dream I ₃ __am flying__ (fly) over a sandy beach in the early morning

sun; I ₄ __am kissing__ (kiss) the leaves of the trees as I fly by. And there's

always the smell of apples, just like in the country when I was little. And all the time

I am dreaming this, I ₅ __am getting__ (get) lighter and lighter until I

₆ __am flying__ (fly) over the beach again, I ₇ __get__

(get) blown through the sky like a feather that ₈ __weighs__ (weigh)

nothing at all. But once I spread my fingers in the dirt and crouch over the Get on

Your Mark, the dream ₉ __goes__ (go) and I am solid again and

am telling myself, Squeaky, you must win, you must win.

Adapted from "Raymond's Run" by Toni Cade Bambara.

Denisse Reyes Betancourt

B. The Crime (simple past or past progressive)

He described this woman as tall and fair, with big blue eyes and very good-looking. He certainly ₁ _____had_____ (have) no suspicions. She ₂ ____sat____ (sit) down and ₃ ____began____ (begin) talking about his play and said she was anxious to do it. While they ₄ ____talked____ (talk), cocktails were brought in, and Mr Faulkener had one as a matter of course. Well—that's all he remembers—having this cocktail. When he ₅ ____woke____ (wake) up, or ₆ ____came____ (come) to himself, or whatever you call it—he ₇ __was lyeing__ (lie) out in the road, by the hedge. He felt very shaky—he just ₈ ____got____ (get) up and staggered along the road not quite knowing where he ₉ ____went____ (go). He just walked along without quite knowing what he ₁₀ __was doing__ (do). He ₁₁ ____came____ (come) to himself when the police arrested him.

Adapted from "The Thirteen Problems" by Agatha Christie.

C. The Workout (simple future or future progressive)

In Phase 2, you ₁ __will become__ (become) stronger and more flexible, ready for an even more challenging workout. And once you've mastered Phase 3, you ₂ __are going to know__ (know) how to work your body in a safe, healthy way, and you ₃ __will be__ (be) able to integrate the concepts of the program into your own fitness regimen.

During the days when you're not doing Interval Walking, you ₄ __are going to do__ (do) the Total Body Workout for 20 minutes, or longer. These exercises are designed to work several muscle groups simultaneously. For example, at the same time that you're working your upper arms or raising your legs, you ₅ __will hold__ (hold) in your abdominal muscles and you ₆ __will keep__ (keep) your butt tight. That's why we call it a Total Body Workout.

Adapted from _The South Beach Diet Supercharged: Faster Weight Loss and Better Health for Life_ by Arthur Agaston.

COMMUNICATIVE ACTIVITY 1

Simple Q&A

Work in pairs. Each student makes five questions out of the jumbled words in his or her box and poses the question to the other student to respond to.

> Example: at / usually / get / what time / you / up / do
>
> Student A: What time do you usually get up at?
>
> Student B: I usually get up at 7 AM.

> **Student A**
> were / you / where / born
> some / your / what / of / life principles / are
> right now / thinking / I / about / am / what
> will / be / you / at this / doing / tomorrow / time / what
> younger / your / when / what / you / favourite activity / were / was

> **Student B**
> do / study / why / you / English
> are / do / what / after / you / this / going to / class
> you / will / when / your / call / friend
> what / when / you / the teacher / doing / were / came in
> does / what / father / living / for a / your / do

COMMUNICATIVE ACTIVITY 2

My Happy Place

Work in pairs. Some people have a happy place in their imagination. When the real world gets too tough, they close their eyes and imagine themselves in their happy place. Where is your happy place? What does it look like? Close your eyes. Go to your happy place, and describe it in detail to your partner. Use only simple present and present progressive tenses. Describe what the place looks like, what you are doing, what you are wearing, and who else is there with you. Give as much detail as you can. Once you are done, switch roles. This time, your partner goes to her or his happy place and describes it.

BRINGING IT ALL TOGETHER

COMMUNICATIVE ACTIVITY 3

In The News

Work in pairs. Your teacher will give you a newspaper. Search the headlines and try to find all the verb tenses you reviewed in this chapter. Write the headline you found next to each verb tense.

Simple present: _____

Simple past: _____

Simple future: _____

Present progressive: _____

Past progressive: _____

Future progressive: _____

 ## COMMUNICATIVE ACTIVITY 4

A Story

Work in small groups. Look at the picture below. Imagine that it's a frame from a movie, and the movie has been paused. Orally, create a short story based on the picture. Share your story with the rest of the class.

In your story try to

- describe the people in the picture: how old they are, what their relationship is
- explain what is happening now
- include what happened before this scene
- foretell what is going to happen next or in the future

COMMUNICATIVE ACTIVITY 5

Mini Oral Presentation

Work with a partner. Do Internet research on a non-profit organization or a local volunteer organization. Prepare a short oral presentation for the rest of the class.

Reading

Read the passage and answer the questions that follow.

NATIONAL VOLUNTEER WEEK

April 15, 2012
Online message from His Excellency the Right Honourable David Johnston, Governor General of Canada, on the Occasion of National Volunteer Week.

OTTAWA—National Volunteer Week in Canada is an opportunity for all of us to celebrate our volunteers, to honour their efforts and to reflect on what it means to give.

Canada is a caring country; Canadians give generously of their time and resources to improve the lives of those around them.

But on the occasion of National Volunteer Week, we are reminded that we cannot be <u>complacent</u>. Many Canadians volunteer, but there are others who do not. The future strength of volunteerism in Canada will rely on the <u>frankness</u> of our dialogue on the challenges that face us.

And so, let us ask the questions that will fuel our discussions: What are the barriers to volunteering? How can we innovate and adapt to the changing needs of our communities? Can we make volunteering <u>compatible</u> with our busy, demanding lives? Can we restore lost hope to those in need?

During National Volunteer Week, I will be visiting and speaking with volunteers, exploring these issues, reinforcing how vital giving is in our everyday lives, and discovering what drives us to volunteer and what prevents us from doing so.

It is also with pride that I will present, for the first time during my <u>mandate</u>, the Caring Canadian Awards. The stories of the award recipients—from across the country, and of all ages—are inspirational and show that volunteering can take many forms.

I look forward to honouring the many Canadians who work in their communities without the expectation of recognition.

This week, I would like to challenge you to tell your own story of volunteering, and encourage others to do the same. By doing so, we can inspire others to take up a cause dear to them. Our stories are powerful, and we can do so much by showing others how much we care. And I encourage you to nominate a special volunteer hero or <u>heroine</u> for a Caring Canadian Award.

We can create a smarter, more caring nation—one step at a time. I wish all Canadians a wonderful National Volunteer Week.

—David Johnston

Johnston, David. "National Volunteer Week." *www.gg.ca/document.aspx?id=14467*. Office of the Secretary to the Governor General, 2012-04-15. Web. 2014-02-03. Adapted with the permission of the Office of the Secretary to the Governor General of Canada, (2013).

COMPREHENSION

1. Who is this message from?

2. When was the message given?

3. What is the purpose of National Volunteer Week?

4. Why is Canada described as "a caring country"?

5. Why does the speaker say that we cannot be complacent? What is he implying?

6. What issues will the speaker be discussing with volunteers during National Volunteer Week?

7. Who will the recipients of the Caring Canadian Awards be?

DISCUSSION

Why do you think the speaker composed this message?

Listening

🔊 Track 01

CANADA'S TOP VOLUNTEERS: CHAMPIONS OF CHANGE

Listen to the audio. In this clip, you will hear an interview conducted by Mark Kelley with Bob Davisson and Bobby Hayes. Bob and Bobby were voted the top two volunteers in the Canada's Champions of Change contest. As you listen to the clip, take notes, and answer the following questions.

COMPREHENSION

1. Why were Bob Davisson and Bobby Hayes voted the two top volunteers?

   _____

2. What did they win? What are they going to do with it?

   _____

3. Based on the interview with the two men, decide whether the following statements are true (T) or false (F). If the statement is false, try to correct it.

Bob Davisson's Responses

   a. When Bob called the people from the schools he volunteers at in Haiti, they were quiet.

   b. That morning, from 9 till 10 o'clock, throughout the country of Haiti, the children in 56 schools were celebrating the great news.

   c. About 500–600 more kids are alive today because of Bob's volunteering.

   d. It's a good sign if the kids' hair is orange.

   e. It brings great joy to Bob's heart to see that so many kids are getting help.

   f. Bob is the only volunteer who helps those kids.

   g. Bob's advice to others is to start doing exactly what he is doing in Haiti.

Bobby Hayes's Responses

   h. As the kids were watching the program last night, they were in tears.

   i. Bobby wants to be recognized for what he does for the kids.

j. Bobby's advice to others is to never watch TV.

k. When Bobby goes back home, he is going to help a six-year-old boy whose mother just passed away.

Writing

Using all the verb tenses reviewed in this chapter, write a short autobiography (maximum 500 words). Follow the format below. Work on a separate sheet of paper.

Introduction
Introduce yourself and provide a little background information.

Body
Elaborate on highlights from your past: your childhood, family, primary- and secondary-school education, likes and dislikes, hobbies and interests, and so on.

Talk about your present: why you're studying English; if you live on your own, with your parents, or with roommates; what your interests outside of school are (part-time job, volunteer work, and so on).

Look into your future: What are your plans when you graduate? Will you continue your education? Will you work? Will you travel? Where will you live (in the city or in the country)? Will you start a family?

Conclusion
Try to tie all your points together.

CHAPTER REVIEW

Summary

- Verb tenses in English have three time frames: past, present, and future. Each time frame has simple, progressive, perfect, and perfect progressive tenses or aspects.

- The simple tenses are used to indicate simple or repeated actions.

  - The simple present indicates routine actions, facts, and characteristics and the immediate future.

  - The simple past indicates simple or repeated actions completed in the past.

  - The simple future tense, formed with *will* or *be going to*, indicates simple future actions.

- The progressive tenses are used to indicate temporary actions or continuing actions over a specific time. Progressive tenses create a link between two or more actions within a limited time frame.

  - The present progressive indicates temporary actions in the present or an expected immediate future action.

- The past progressive indicates temporary actions in the past. It also creates a link between two or more simultaneous temporary actions or a continuing action being interrupted by a simple action.

- The future progressive indicates temporary actions in the future and usually creates a link to other actions in a future or present time.

- Review the formation charts.

- We often use a progressive tense after *while* and use a simple tense after *when*.

- There are restrictions on the use of the progressive tenses. Review the chart of non-progressive (stative) verbs in Appendix A.

Denisse Reyes Betancourt.

EXERCISE 1

Combining tenses: Using the past, present, or future tenses, fill in the blanks with either the simple or the progressive form of the verbs in parentheses. The verbs that should be in negative form have been marked for you.

Anne is at home. There ₁ __will be__ (be) no one with her, and she ₂ __will be__ (be) in no hurry. She ₃ __will not have to__ (have to, negative) be anywhere. Her mother ₄ __is going__ (go) to work every morning, and Anne ₅ __stays__ (stay) home alone all day because she ₆ __has__ (have) a broken leg. Right now, she ₇ __is standing__ (stand) by the window, and she ₈ __is leaning__ (lean) on her crutches. It ₉ __is raining__ (rain) hard outside. She ₁₀ __looked__ (look) at the cars and the pedestrians, but she ₁₁ __is not seeing__ (see, negative) them because her mind is somewhere else. She ₁₂ __thought__ (think) about her recent accident.

Last week, a car ₁₃ __hit__ (hit) her while she ₁₄ __was riding__ (ride) her bike to school. The impact ₁₅ __threw__ (throw) her off her bike on the side of the road. As she ₁₆ __was trying__ (try) to pull herself to safety, the bike ₁₇ __landed__ (land) on her and ₁₈ __broke__ (break) her right leg in two places. And guess what the driver of the car ₁₉ __did__ (do) in the meantime? She ₂₀ __tried__ (try) to get away, but, fortunately, another driver ₂₁ __noticed__ (notice) just in time and ₂₂ __blocked__ (block) her way with

Denisse Reye Betancourt

his car. Someone 23 ___called___ (call) 911 and the rest, as they

24 ___Said___ (say), is history.

Tonight, when her mom 25 ___gets___ (get) back from work, she 26 ___will take___ (take) Anne for a checkup. Anne knows what her doctor 27 ___is going to do___ (do) and say. Her doctor, who 28 ___thinks___ (think) he is the funniest man on earth, 29 ___told___ (tell) her the same bad jokes again, and Anne 30 ___will pretend___ (pretend) not to have heard them and will laugh. At the end of the visit, the doctor 31 ___is going to prescribe___ (prescribe) some painkillers and 32 ___will tell___ (tell) her, "Don't worry Anne! I guarantee that next month, you 33 ___will ride___ (ride) your bike and you 34 ___will run___ (run) around like an athlete. A year from now, you 35 ___will not remember___ (remember, negative) which leg was broken."

Anne smiles at this thought. A sound 36 ___brought___ (bring) her back to the present. The phone 37 ___rings___ (ring). She 38 ___limps___ (limp) to the phone and 39 ___she picks up___ (pick) up the receiver. It 40 ___is___ (be) her mom.

EXERCISE 2

The sentences below are all written incorrectly. Based on what you have learned in this chapter, correct each sentence.

1. Every year, thousands of Canadians and immigrants are donating their time to charities and non-profit organizations.

2. Younger Canadians is more likely to volunteer than older Canadians.

3. When Eddy started volunteering at a local food bank, he wants to contribute to his community.

4. What some barriers are to volunteering?

5. Presently, Elie not working, but he helps out at the animal shelter.

6. My neighbour doesn't have a car, so next weekend, my dad take him grocery shopping.

7. I am understanding why you won't get involved.

8. They meet some nice people when they were travelling.

9. How do she spend her free time?

10. What will you doing at this time tomorrow?

Perfect Verb Tenses

OVERVIEW

- The perfect tenses link actions within and between time frames, clarify the sequence of events, and show the relationship between different actions.

- The perfect tenses have past, present, and future time frames.

- The perfect progressive tenses combine both the perfect and the progressive aspects.

Warm-up

Work in pairs. Using the following questions, interview your partner, and record his or her responses in complete sentences on a separate sheet of paper. Pay special attention to the underlined verb tenses. Your teacher will check your answers to see how well you already know these tenses.

1. <u>Had you learned</u> another foreign language before you started studying English?

2. How long <u>had you been studying</u> English when you started at this school?

3. How long <u>have you been studying</u> English now?

4. <u>Have you ever had</u> problems with verb tenses? What are your main problems in English?

5. How long <u>will you have been studying</u> English by the time we finish this program?

6. By the time we finish this program, do you think you <u>will have learned</u> enough English to study in an English-language university or college?

PERFECT TENSES

The perfect tenses are formed by using the auxiliary verb *have* and the past participle of the main verb.

Formation

	Positive	Negative	Question
Present Perfect	I **have lived** in Montreal for two years now.	I **have not** (haven't) **lived** in Montreal for two years.	**Have** you **lived** in Montreal for two years?
Past Perfect	I **had lived** in Montreal before I moved to Ottawa.	I **had not** (hadn't) **lived** in Montreal before I moved to Ottawa.	**Had** you **lived** in Montreal before you moved to Ottawa?
Future Perfect	I **will have lived** in Montreal for three years by the end of next year month.	I **will not** (won't) **have lived** in Montreal for three years by the end of next year.	**Will** you **have lived** in Montreal for three years by the end of next year?

- The present perfect is formed with the auxiliary verb *to have* (*have* or *has*) and the past participle of the main verb. (He has gone.)
- To make questions, invert the subject and the auxiliary *have*. (He has gone. → Has he gone?)
- To make negatives, place the negative marker (e.g., *not*, *n't*, *never*) immediately after *have* or *has*. (He has gone. → He hasn't gone.)
- The past perfect is formed with *had* and the past participle of the main verb. (He had gone.)
- To make questions, invert the subject and *had*. (He had gone. → Had he gone?)
- To make negatives, place the negative marker immediately after *had*. (He had gone. → He hadn't gone.)
- The future perfect is formed with *will have* and the past participle of the main verb. (He will have gone.)
- To create questions, invert the subject and *will*. (He will have gone. → Will he have gone?)
- To create negatives, place the negative marker immediately after *will*. (He will have gone. → He will not have gone.)

USE

The perfect tenses are used to create a link between time frames and to indicate the relationship between different actions within and between time frames. The perfect tenses also show the sequence of actions.

The **present perfect tense** creates a link between the time frames: past, present, and future.

The present perfect tense indicates an action that began in the past, is still in effect in the present, and will probably be (or has the possibility of being) in effect in the future.

I have lived in Calgary since 2010.

The present perfect tense also indicates a repeated action in the past that has a strong possibility of being repeated in the future.

We have already seen that movie twice.

The present perfect can also point to an action completed in the past without any mention of the time of completion.

I have seen that man before. (But I don't know—or it's not important—where or when.)

Some indicators of the present perfect are *so far*, *until now*, *since* (a date), *for* (an amount of time), *already*, *ever*, *never*, and *yet*.

The **past perfect tense** links actions that occurred in the past and clarifies the order in which they happened.

I had lived in Edmonton for two years before I moved to Saskatoon.

He had already left when she arrived. (He left first. She arrived later.)

Some indicators of the past perfect tense are *already, ever, never,* and *after*. *After* introduces the past perfect, and *before* introduces the simple past. For simultaneous actions in the past, use only the simple past or the past progressive tense.

The **future perfect tense** links actions that will occur in the future and clarifies the sequence of the actions.

It is used to show that one action will happen before a specific time or before another action in the future.

He <u>will have</u> already <u>left</u> by then.

He <u>will have left</u> by the time she arrives. (He will leave first. Then, she will arrive.)

Some indicators of the future perfect tense are *already*, *by the time*, *by then*, and *before*. Use the simple present to indicate the action is closer to the present. (In the example above, arriving happens after leaving, so *arrive* is in simple present tense and *leave* is in future perfect.)

EXERCISE 1

Fill in the blanks with the correct form of the perfect tense of the verbs in parentheses.

People tend to take everyday items for granted. They never stop to wonder who 1 _has come up_ (come up) with the original idea or why and when someone 2 _has invented_ (invent) something as common as a zipper, for example. Until 1913, when Canadian Gideon Sundback invented the zipper, the only clothing fasteners 3 _had been_ (be) buttons and hooks.

Over the years, many inventions 4 _had_ (have) a huge impact on our daily lives. Before 1940, the year that Norman Breakey invented the paint roller, people 5 _had painted_ (paint) walls, ceilings, and entire houses with paintbrushes. Can you imagine how long it used to take?

Green garbage bags 6 _____ (be) around since the early 1950s. Harry Wasylyk (from Winnipeg, Manitoba) and Larry Hansen (from Lindsay, Ontario) 7 _____ originally _____ (create) the polyethylene garbage bags in 1950 for commercial use, but the bags soon became popular for residential garbage as well. Although there are now many new varieties of garbage bags, including biodegradable ones, it's probably safe to say that all of us 8 _____ (use) the green ones at some time.

How many other daily items 9 _____ we _____ (benefit) from in the future without ever knowing that they are Canadian creations?

EXERCISE 2

Change each of the following positive sentences into a negative sentence. Then change each positive sentence into to a yes / no question. Review the formation charts if you need to.

Sentence: There have been many unusual Canadian inventions.

Negative: There haven't been many unusual Canadian inventions.

Question: Have there been many unusual Canadian inventions?

1. He had created many versions of the tool before he invented the best one.

    Negative: _____

    Question: _____

2. Scientists will have discovered new treatments for serious conditions before too long.

    Negative: _____

    Question: _____

3. That engineer has come up with a new method of replacing highway overpasses.

    Negative: _____

    Question: _____

4. Many parents have benefited from the invention of the Jolly Jumper.

    Negative: _____

    Question: _____

 # COMMUNICATIVE ACTIVITY 1

Truth or Lie

Work in pairs. Using the present perfect tense, write three sentences about yourself. One of those sentences has to be a lie. Show the sentences to your partner. Ask each other questions to determine which sentence is not true.

Student A: I <u>have travelled</u> to the moon.

Student B: It's a lie.

COMMUNICATIVE ACTIVITY 2

Find the Order

Work in pairs. You say two actions that you did yesterday by using the simple past tense. You partner has to make them into one sentence by using the past perfect tense to guess the correct order of the actions. Take turns. The student with the most correct guesses wins.

Student A: I did my homework. I watched TV.

Student B: When you <u>had done</u> your homework, you <u>watched</u> TV.

Student A: You're wrong. I did my homework after I had watched TV.

 COMMUNICATIVE ACTIVITY 3

I Predict

Work in small groups. Together, use the future perfect tense to discuss what you think the world will be like in 30 years. For example, predict what changes in education, technology, or the health-care system will happen in the next 30 years.

In 30 years, scientists <u>will have discovered</u> cures for all kinds of cancer.

PERFECT PROGRESSIVE TENSES

The perfect progressive tenses combine both the perfect and the progressive aspects. The perfect aspect provides the link between actions and between time frames. The progressive aspect emphasizes the continuing nature of those actions over a specific time. The perfect progressive tenses use the auxiliary verb *to have* and the past participle of the verb *to be* with the present participle (or the *-ing* form) of the main verb. The same rules for forming questions and negatives in the perfect tenses apply to the perfect progressive tenses.

Formation

	Positive	Negative	Question
Present Perfect Progressive	He **has been doing** homework for three hours.	He **has not** (hasn't) **been doing** homework for three hours.	**Has** he **been doing** homework for three hours?
Past Perfect Progressive	He **had been doing** homework for three hours when she arrived.	He **had not** (hadn't) **been doing** homework for three hours when she arrived.	**Had** he **been doing** homework for three hours when she arrived?
Future Perfect Progressive	By noon, he **will have been doing** homework for three hours.	By noon, he **will not** (won't) **have been doing** homework for three hours.	By noon, **will** he **have been doing** homework for three hours?

The present perfect progressive is formed with *has been / have been* and the *-ing* form of the main verb.

> I have been running since 4:00 PM.

The past perfect progressive is formed with *had been* and the *-ing* form of the main verb.

> I had been running for years before my accident.

The future perfect progressive is formed with *will have been* and the *-ing* form of the main verb.

> I will have been running for six years by next summer.

USE

The perfect progressive tenses are used to indicate temporary actions or to emphasize the continuing aspect of those actions over a limited time. They are also used to create a link between two or more actions within a limited time frame.

The **present perfect progressive** tense indicates and emphasizes the continuous and temporary nature of an action that began in the past, is still in effect in the present, and will probably continue in the future.

Some indicators for the present perfect progressive are *so far*, *until now*, *since* (a date), *for* (an amount of time), and *already*.

> I have been attending college for one-and-a-half years.

> He has already been working for that company for five years.

Note: You cannot usually use *ever*, *never*, or *yet* with the progressive tenses. When *never*, *ever*, and *yet* are used with the present perfect progressive, they present hypothetical situations.

> Have you never yet been walking down the street and seen a rainbow?

> Haven't you ever been looking for something and found something else that you had lost the day before?

The **past perfect progressive** tense shows and emphasizes the continuous and temporary nature of an action that occurred further in the past than another action.

Some indicators are *already* and *after*. *After* introduces the past perfect progressive and *before* introduces the simple past.

> They had been studying before they went out with their friends.

> He left the company after he had been working there for 10 years.

The **future perfect progressive** tense indicates and emphasizes the continuous and temporary nature of a future action.

Some indicators are *by the time*, *by then*, and *before*. Use the simple present to indicate the action is closer to the present.

> I will have been jogging for 40 minutes by the time I get home.

> We are going to have been doing housework all day before it's all finished.

Restrictions

1. The perfect progressive tenses **cannot** be used with repeated actions.

   > He has watched that movie seven times.

   NOT

   > He has been watching that movie seven times.

   The second sentence is not logical. It means that he has been watching the same movie from beginning to end without stopping for about 14 hours.

2. The progressive tenses are not usually used with non-action or stative verbs, verbs that describe a state, such as beliefs, knowledge, emotions, the senses, possession, or existence. Review the chart of stative verbs (non-action verbs) in Appendix A and the examples in the *Use* section of the progressive tenses in Chapter 1, pages 6–7. You cannot limit or apply a specific time frame to these kinds of actions without changing their meaning.

EXERCISE 3

Fill in the blanks with the correct form of the perfect progressive tenses of the verbs in parentheses.

Canadian innovations include many food items. People 1 _____ (enjoy) Canada Dry Ginger Ale since 1907 and chocolate bars since shortly after. Apparently, while Arthur Ganong and George Ensor 2 _____ (preparing) for a fishing trip, they invented the chocolate bar by forming chocolate and nuts into a log shape and wrapping it to make it easier to carry. Since 1931, parents 3 _____ (supplement) their babies' diets with Pablum cereal, which three doctors at Toronto's Hospital for Sick Children developed. Although we know that poutine is a Quebec creation, a few villages 4 _____ (claim) it as theirs since the late 1950s. It's hard to imagine what new food inventions we 5 _____ (consume) in the next 20 years.

EXERCISE 4

Change the following sentences to information questions. What you want to ask about is underlined. Review the formation charts if you need to.

Many Canadians have been using <u>Canadian inventions and innovations</u> for years without realizing they are Canadian.

What have many Canadians been using for years without realizing they are Canadian?

1. Many companies have been developing energy-efficient technology <u>for years</u>.

   _____?

2. <u>The researcher</u> had been trying to find a stronger alloy when he discovered an entirely new compound.

   _____?

3. He has been doing research on stem cells <u>to discover cures and treatments for many diseases</u>.

   _____?

4. They will have been seeking <u>a solution</u> for years before they find it.

   _____?

EXERCISE 5

In each set of sentences (A, B, and C), match each numbered sentence on the left to the correct lettered meaning on the right. This exercise measures your ability to understand smaller differences in meaning between tenses.

A	
_____ 1. He left the doors open.	a. The doors are still open.
_____ 2. He is leaving the doors open.	b. We don't know whether the doors are still open or not.
_____ 3. He has left the doors open.	c. He started leaving doors open a long time ago. It's a habit for him now.
_____ 4. He has been leaving the doors open.	d. Not all the doors are open yet.

B	
_____ 1. He wrote his masterpiece when he saw her.	a. He wrote his masterpiece during the time he saw her.
_____ 2. He had written his masterpiece when he saw her.	b. He started writing his masterpiece long before he saw her.
_____ 3. He was writing his masterpiece when he saw her.	c. He started writing his masterpiece after he saw her.
_____ 4. He had been writing his masterpiece when he saw her.	d. He completed his masterpiece right before he saw her.

c

_____ 1. I will find answers when you leave.

_____ 2. I will be finding answers when you leave.

_____ 3. I will have found answers when you leave.

_____ 4. I will have been finding answers when you leave.

a. I look for answers during the time you leave.

b. I start finding answers long before you leave.

c. I find the answers before you leave.

d. I find the answers after you leave.

EXERCISE 6

Circle the best tense based on the intended meaning of each sentence.

1. I'm sure I **heard / have heard** that song before.

2. Most of the students **studied / have studied** these tenses last semester.

3. I was late for the test. When I arrived the test **started / had started**.

4. I don't think I will finish my work any time soon. I'm pretty sure that when you arrive, I **will work / will be working**.

5. There's not much work left. I'm sure that when you arrive, I **will be painting / will have painted** the room.

6. That person looked familiar. For sure I **had seen / have seen** him somewhere.

7. Are you sure you **didn't see / haven't seen** my brother recently?

8. I can't sleep very well these days. I suppose I **have thought / have been thinking** too much about my problems.

9. There was no more food left. They **were / had been** eating when we arrived.

10. He was panting when he arrived. Obviously, he **had run / had been running**.

COMMUNICATIVE ACTIVITY 4

_Q&A_

Work in pairs. Write three questions for your partner by using three different perfect progressive verb tenses: a present, a past, and a future. Take turns asking and answering questions. Review the formation charts first if you need to.

Student A: How long have we been studying this chapter?

Student B: We've been studying this chapter for over an hour now.

BRINGING IT ALL TOGETHER

EXERCISE 7

Use the information from each pair of sentences to create one sentence in the indicated verb tense.

I first travelled to Japan. Then I went to Korea.

Past perfect: I had travelled to Japan before I went to Korea.

1. We live in Moncton. We moved there in 2011.

   Present perfect: _____

2. The kids will go to bed at 8:00 PM. We will come back home at 9:00 PM.

   Future perfect: _____

3. They were watching a movie from 5:00 PM till 6:00 PM. The power went off at 6:00 PM.

   Past perfect progressive: _____

4. She is cooking now. She started an hour ago.

   Present perfect progressive: _____

5. It was cold in the classroom. The custodian didn't turn the heater on.

   Past perfect: _____

6. Claudia and Mike are going to spend a year renovating their house. Then, all the renovations will be finished.

   Future perfect progressive: _____

COMMUNICATIVE ACTIVITY 5

Role-Plays

Work in pairs. Prepare a role-play for each situation below. Present your role-play to the rest of the class.

Situation A: You run into a friend of yours from high school. You haven't seen each other for many years now. Ask each other about what you have been doing since you finished high school. Try to use present perfect, present perfect progressive, past perfect, and past perfect progressive tenses.

Situation B: You're about to finish your post-secondary studies. Ask your partner about what his or her plans for the future are and what he or she will have done or will have been doing in the next 5 or 10 years. Try to use future perfect and future perfect progressive tenses.

Reading

Read the passage that follows.

CANADIAN INVENTIONS AND DISCOVERIES

Necessity is the mother of invention. Most inventions and discoveries have resulted from the need to solve problems or to find better ways of doing things.

Canadians are creative people. To date, Canadians have <u>patented</u> more than one million inventions. The list of Canadian inventions and discoveries is as varied as our landscape and our people. It includes such items as the paint roller, the snow blower, the Robertson screwdriver, the pacemaker, the chocolate bar, the Macintosh apple, Pablum, Canada Dry Ginger Ale, synchronized swimming, and the painted centre line on roadways. In fact, Canada has a long history of innovation. Among other creations attributed to the First Nations of Canada are the snowshoe, the birchbark canoe, the toboggan, and lacrosse, Canada's official national summer sport.

The need to find a better tool caused Peter Robertson to create his square-headed screw and screwdriver. He had been demonstrating a slot screwdriver when it slipped and injured his hand, so he invented the Robertson screwdriver.

It makes sense, given our climatic extremes, that the snow blower, the snowmobile, and insect repellent were invented by Canadians. Which one do you think came first? Before he sold his first snow blower to the town of Outremont, Quebec, Arthur Sicard had invented it in Montreal in 1925 because he had become tired of shovelling that white stuff. Although Joseph-Armand Bombardier had created his original snowmobile design in 1922, its patent did not become official until 1959. That was the same year Charles Coll created Muskol to help <u>repel</u> those <u>pesky</u> mosquitoes during the hot, humid Canadian springs and summers.

The medical field has also benefited from Canadian ingenuity. Dr. Frederick Banting and Dr. Charles Best discovered insulin as a treatment for diabetes in 1921. Wilfred Bigelow created the pacemaker in 1950, and George Klein invented the electric wheelchair in 1952. Although he had also introduced new surgical techniques and instruments, Dr. Norman Bethune is probably most famous for creating mobile blood <u>transfusions</u> during the Spanish Civil War in the late 1930s.

Technology is another area where Canadians have excelled for more than a century. Did you know that the first television camera was invented by a Canadian, François Henroteau, in 1933? Some well-known Canadian technological inventions from the late nineteenth century include

Thomas Ahearn's electric cooking range and the many machine and manufacturing inventions of Elijah McCoy. When you think about Canadians' passion for hockey, it's not surprising that in 1955, George Letzlaff, a *Hockey Night in Canada* employee, came up with the instant replay, an invention that revolutionized sports broadcasting. The IMAX film system has been wowing audiences since 1990.

In fact, modern communications would not be the same if such inventions as the telephone (Alexander Graham Bell in 1876), the Walkie-Talkie (Donald Hings in 1942), and more recently, the BlackBerry (Mike Lazaridis in 1999) and Java programming language (James Arthur Gosling in 1994) hadn't been created.

Sports, games, and other entertainment activities are also considered inventions, and many Canadians have made significant contributions. James Naismith of Almonte, Ontario, had been trying to find less boring training exercises for his students when he created the game of basketball in 1891 in Springfield, Massachusetts. Thomas Ryan came up with five-pin bowling in 1908. If Jacques Plante, a famous goaltender for the Montreal Canadiens hockey team, hadn't invented the goalie mask in 1960, the game of hockey would not be what it is today. Also, two board games rank high in the games category: Trivial Pursuit and Balderdash.

The list of Canadian inventions, innovations, and discoveries is long, and they have touched many aspects of our lives. What will Canadian and other inventors have come up with by the time we are halfway through this century?

ANALYZING THE READING

Read the passage again. <u>Underline</u> the verbs used in the perfect tenses. <u>Double underline</u> the verbs used in the perfect progressive tenses.

COMPREHENSION

Read the passage again and answer the following questions.

1. How many inventions have Canadians patented so far?

   _____

2. Which three inventions reflect the needs of people living in Canada? Why?

   _____

3. Name two medical advances and their creators mentioned in the text.

   _____

4. What invention from the late nineteenth century has improved everyday life for millions?

   _____

5. What invention has revolutionized sports broadcasting?

   _____

6. Where and when did Naismith invent basketball?

   _____

7. What had Naismith been trying to do when he invented basketball?

   _____

8. What does the author mean by saying that the game of hockey would not be what it is today without the goalie mask? How would the game be different?

   _____

DISCUSSION

1. Think about some of the inventions of the last 50 years. Which ones have had the most impact on your life personally and why?

2. Discuss the last question in the text: What inventions do you think inventors will have come up with by 2050?

Listening

🔊 Track 02

THE TECHNOLOGIES AND OTHER INNOVATIONS OF THE MIT MEDIA LAB

Listen to the audio. In this clip, you will hear a radio program conversation between the host, Anna Maria Tremonti, and her guest, Frank Moss. As you listen to the clip, take notes, and answer the following questions.

COMPREHENSION

1. Who is Nexie?

   _____

2. How long has Cynthia Breazeal been fascinated by robots? Why did she want to build robots?

   _____

3. What have Cynthia and her students been exploring at the MIT Media Lab for the past several years?

_____

4. What is the MIT Media Lab usually known for? When was it founded?

_____

5. For how many years was Frank Moss the director of the MIT Media Lab before he left his post?

_____

6. How does Frank Moss describe the MIT Media Lab? Who is usually at the lab? What are they doing there?

_____

7. What will the robots have been able to do by the time the students do more work on them?

_____

8. What's so special about the MIT Media Lab in terms of the approach to innovation? What's so special about the lab in terms of relationship between the students and the faculty?

_____

Writing

On a separate sheet of paper, write a two-paragraph composition in response to each of the following questions. Try to use the verb tenses reviewed in this chapter. If you are not familiar with the topic, do some research on it. Work on a separate sheet of paper.

1. What is the difference between innovation and invention?

2. What is creativity? How do great ideas start? What fosters and what hinders creativity?

3. Many inventors, scientists, great thinkers, musicians, and writers are often described as "geniuses." For decades, psychologists have tried to determine what defines "a genius," which, in turn, has led to a famous nature versus nurture debate. What is your opinion on the debate?

CHAPTER REVIEW

Summary

- The present perfect tense creates a link between the time frames: past, present, and future. It also indicates an action that began in the past, is still in effect in the present, and will probably be in effect in the future. It indicates a repeated action in the past that has a strong possibility of being repeated in the future.

- The past perfect links actions that occurred in the past and clarifies the order in which they happened.

- The future perfect links actions that will occur in the future and clarifies the sequence of the actions (which one will happen before the other).

- The perfect progressive tenses are used to indicate temporary actions or to emphasize the continuing aspect of those actions over a limited time. They are also used to create a link between two or more actions within a limited time frame.

- There are restrictions on the use of the progressive tenses. They cannot be used with repeated actions. They are not usually used with stative verbs. Review the chart of stative (non-action) verbs in Appendix A.

EXERCISE 1

Fill in the blanks with the correct tense of the verbs in parentheses. Consider all verb tenses you have learned in this and in the previous chapter as possible answers. There might be more than one correct tense for some blanks. The verbs that should be in negative form have been marked for you.

Although Uncle Cyrus is a very arrogant man, I have to admit he is a genius

when it ₁ _____ (come) to making money and innovating.

Cyrus's father, who ₂ _____ (run) his own business ever since

he dropped out of school at 15, always ₃ _____ (support) his

children in their business ventures.

   Little Cyrus ₄ _____ (start, already) making his

own pocket money before he was even 7. By the time he was out of primary school, he 5 _____ (learn) from his father how to operate a small business. He 6 _____ (experimented) with these types of businesses up until he graduated from high school, but he always 7 _____ (obsess) about that one innovation that would make him famous. One day, the idea he 8 _____ (search) for, for all those years, 9 _____ (strike) him suddenly when a mosquito 10 _____ (react) to the vibrations from his cellphone. He would make an inexpensive vibrating device that would repel mosquitoes!

He studied physics at university and tried several prototypes until finally, a decade after he originally 11 _____ (think) of the device, he 12 _____ (deliver) his product. To date, his company 13 _____ (produce) and 14 _____ (sell) more than 50 million units of the device called Stingone. Analysts predict by next year the company 15 _____ (sell) five times that number. For the past six months, shares of Stingone Inc. 16 _____ (trade) at record high prices, a trend that 17 _____ (continue) if the predictions come true.

This revolutionary device 18 _____ (eradicate, already) several insect-borne diseases in the world, and as Doctors Without Borders predict, by this time next year, it 19 _____ (remove, completely) several more threats. Awards and appreciation letters 20 _____ (pour) into Cyrus's office non-stop from all around the world. I sure 21 _____ (cheer) tomorrow night at the moment when my uncle 22 _____ (receive) the Nobel Prize.

Note: The story above is fiction. No such invention or company actually exists.

EXERCISE 2

The sentences below are all written incorrectly. Based on what you have learned in this chapter, correct each sentence.

1. Throughout history, many people with remarkable intellects have contribute to the human civilization.

2. By December, Zack will research on the role of the brain for four months.

3. Why has researchers been discussing the nature versus nature for so many years?

4. Mozart wrote 270 compositions before his 271st composition had become famous.

5. Elaine is a strong person who, despite her disability, has always been believing in herself and her potential.

6. The students will have understand Shakespeare's work by the time they finish their literature course.

7. Are you going to have thinking of new ideas for a week now?

8. I wanted to become an artist since the time I saw the paintings of the Group of Seven for the first time.

9. Even though Tom had been play the sonata for many hours, he still couldn't play it perfectly.

10. They are going to not have solved the problem by tomorrow morning.

Gerunds and Infinitives

OVERVIEW

Both gerunds (example: *reading*) and infinitives (example: *to read*) can appear in a variety of positions in a sentence. The most challenging position to language learners is usually the object position after the verb.

To determine whether you need a gerund or an infinitive after a verb, you have to look at the main verb in the sentence. Look at the following examples.

- Some verbs such as *enjoy* are always followed by gerunds.

    I enjoy reading novels.

- Some verbs such as *refuse* are always followed by infinitives.

    I refuse to read novels.

- Some verbs are followed by either a gerund or an infinitive with almost the same meaning.

    I love reading novels.
    I love to read novels.

- Some verbs are followed by gerunds and infinitives but with a significant change in meaning.

    I stopped to read a novel.
    I stopped reading novels.

Warm-up

Work with a partner. Interview each other about the things you like or dislike doing. Explain the reason for your answers. You may use the following list for question ideas.

ski	shovel snow
go to the gym	travel
take tests	eat exotic food
bike	wait in line

Student A: Do you like skiing?

Student B: Yes, I love skiing. I actually love all kinds of winter sports. I've been skiing since I was five.

Student A: Do you like going to the gym?

Student B: No, I hate going to the gym. I love participating in team sports. I find gym exercises boring and aimless.

GERUNDS AND INFINITIVES— COMMON PATTERNS

Formation

Sample Verb	Gerund Form	Negative Gerund Form	Infinitive Form	Negative Infinitive Form
swim	swimming	not swimming	to swim	not to swim

EXERCISE 1

Some common patterns for gerunds: Look at these common patterns for gerunds. Read the example for each pattern. Then, on the blank line provided, write a sentence of your own (using different verbs) for each pattern.

1. Subject of a verb

    Swimming is my favourite activity.

    Your sentence: _____

2. Subject complement (after the verb *be*)

    My favourite activity is swimming.

    Your sentence: _She I'm Swimming today_

3. Object (complement) of a verb

   She enjoys <u>swimming</u>.

   Your sentence: _____

4. Object (complement) of a preposition

   She insists on <u>swimming</u> every day.

   Your sentence: _____

5. Appositive (extra information), with commas before and after

   My favourite activity, <u>swimming</u>, keeps me in shape.

   Your sentence: _____

EXERCISE 2

Some common patterns for infinitives: Look at these common patterns for infinitives. Read the example for each pattern. Then, on the blank line provided, write a sentence of your own (using different verbs) for each pattern.

1. In a sentence beginning with "It"

   It is difficult <u>to swim</u>. (Instead of "To swim is difficult.")

   Your sentence: _____

2. Immediately after another verb (object of the verb)

   I want <u>to swim</u> more often.

   Your sentence: _____

3. After a verb + object

   I want you <u>to swim</u> more often.

   Your sentence: _____

4. After an adjective

   I find it easy <u>to swim</u> here.

   Your sentence: _____

5. After a noun

   I'm ashamed of my inability <u>to swim</u>.

   Your sentence: _____

COMMUNICATIVE ACTIVITY 1

Food Habits

Work in pairs. Take turns interviewing each other by using the questions below. Try to get your partner to explain as much as possible. On a separate sheet of paper, write down the answers your partner gives.

1. Is eating healthfully important to you?

2. Is there any food you particularly enjoy eating?

3. Is there any food you hesitate to eat?

4. Did anyone ever force you to eat this food?

5. Is there any food you are incapable of eating?

6. Is it difficult for you to digest certain foods?

7. Is there any food you find easy to cook?

8. Do you habitually go to restaurants on weekends?

GERUNDS AND INFINITIVES AS OBJECTS

Warm-up

Work in pairs. Use the words in each jumbled set to make a grammatically correct sentence. You may add words or change word forms if necessary. Share your responses with the rest of the class.

enjoy / read / the news / on the computer

I enjoy reading the news on the computer.

refuse / read / gossip magazines and tabloids

I refused to read/ I refuse to read

like / read / in bed / before /sleep

I like reading in bed before sleeping

always /stop / at the grocery store / on my way home / buy / groceries

I always stop at the grocery store on my way home to buy groceries

my doctor / ask me / stop / smoke / as soon as possible

to smoking

of

I am tired / listen / to you / all day

listening

_____

to   *surfing*

don't want / waste / my time /surf / the Internet all day

I do

_____

GERUNDS AND INFINITIVES AS OBJECTS OF VERBS

Both gerunds and infinitives can function as the object of a verb. Certain verbs in English always use gerunds (e.g., *enjoy*) as objects, and others always use infinitives (e.g., *refuse*) as objects. Numerous common verbs are regularly followed by either gerunds or infinitives. Sometimes there is little change in meaning (e.g., *start*), but in other cases the change in meaning is significant (e.g., *stop*).

Formation

Four groups of verbs take gerunds or infinitives as their object.

Verb Group	Description
1	verbs that are always followed by gerunds
2	verbs that are always followed by infinitives
3	verbs that are followed by either gerunds or infinitives with almost the same meaning
4	verbs that are followed by gerunds and infinitives but with a significant change in meaning

Verb Group 1—Common Verbs That Always Use Gerunds as Objects

I **admit to** *making* a mistake.
Do you **anticipate** *facing* more problems?
I **appreciate** *eating* exotic food.
I **avoid** *driving* during rush hour.
Would you **consider** *not putting* your personal information on the Internet?
He **delayed** *signing* the contract.
She **denied** *cheating* on the test.
We **discussed** *buying* a new car.
I **enjoy** *skiing*.
I **fear** *losing* my memory.
When I **finish** *writing* the letter, I'll mail it.
I **gave up** *smoking*.
His job **involves** *making* short trips to Nunavut.
He **keeps** *saying* no to me.

He **mentioned** *seeing* you at that party.

Do you **mind** *closing* the door?

Do you **miss** *playing* hockey?

They **postponed** *going* to school for another year.

You should **practise** *using* set phrases.

I **quit** *drinking* years ago.

I **recall** *attending* that meeting.

I don't **recollect** *meeting* her.

I **recommend** *studying* harder for your next test.

They **risk** *losing* their money.

He **suggested** *not leaving* too late.

Our society doesn't **tolerate** *drinking* and *driving*.

EXERCISE 3

Fill in the blanks with a gerund of your choice to make a meaningful sentence.

1. Many Canadians *enjoy* _____ hockey.

2. I'm all ready to head to the airport. I've *finished* _____ my suitcase.

3. I strongly *suggest* _____ your private and public lives separate.

4. He *delayed* _____ to my email.

5. Many people *avoid* _____ in bad weather.

Verb Group 2—Common Verbs That Always Use Infinitives as Objects

I cannot **afford** *to buy* this house.

He **agreed** *to pay* my tuition.

He **appeared** *to be* drunk.

They **arranged** *to talk* face to face.

They **asked** *to see* my passport.

Would you **care** *to dance* with me?

He **claims** *to be* innocent.

I **decided** not *to leave*.

I **demanded** *to know* their response.

She **deserves** *to get* a good mark.

When do you **expect** *to graduate*?

You **failed** *to tell* us the truth.

Don't **hesitate** *to call* me.

We **hope** *to see* you again soon.

I **intend** *to write* a novel.

I **learned** *to speak* Japanese when I was in high school.

I **managed** *to open* the door.

I **meant** *to call* you last night, but I fell asleep.

I **need** *to see* you soon.

They **offered** *to invite* all of us.

We **planned** *to review* the test together.

He is **prepared** *to leave* early.

She **pretends** *not to know* me.

We **promise** *not to call* you late at night.

He **refuses** *to leave*.

He **seems** *to know* the answer.

They **struggled** *to make* enough money to pay bills.

She **swears** *to tell* the truth.

I **want** *to finish* this list.

I do not **wish** *to continue* any longer.

EXERCISE 4

Fill in the blanks with infinitives of your choice to make meaningful sentences.

1. Children *want* _____ nice gifts for their birthday.

2. He *decided* _____ his money rather than spend it.

3. The teacher *needs* _____ the subject of your essay.

4. My friend *offered* _____ me 20 dollars.

5. He *hopes* _____ a good part-time job.

Verb Group 3—Common Verbs Followed by Gerunds or Infinitives *without* a Significant Change in Meaning

They **began** *to cry*.	They **began** *crying*.
She **started** *to read*.	She **started** *reading*.
He **continued** *to laugh*.	He **continued** *laughing*.
I **like** *to eat* chocolate.	I **like** *eating* chocolate.
I **love** *to read* poems.	I **love** *reading* poems.
I **hate** *to leave*.	I **hate** *leaving*.
I **prefer** *to listen* to pop music.	I **prefer** *listening* to pop music.

EXERCISE 5

Fill in the blanks with the gerunds or infinitives of your choice to make meaningful sentences. You can use both positive and negative forms.

1. They *like* _____ many different things on the weekend.

2. I *started* _____ more mistakes after the first one.

3. She *began* _____ dizzy and suddenly lost her balance.

4. The rain *continued* _____ all day.

5. When I am on vacation, I *prefer* _____ about my problems.

Verb Group 4—Common Verbs Followed by Gerunds or Infinitives *with* a Significant Change in Meaning

I will **remember** *to lock* the door. (I won't forget. I will certainly lock the door.)
I **remember** *locking* the door. (I have the memory of doing it. I'm sure I did it.)

I **forgot** *to lock* the door. (I didn't lock the door.)
I **forgot** *locking* the door. (I probably did it but I don't remember it. I don't have a memory of it.)

I **stopped** *locking* doors. (I don't lock doors any more.)
I **stopped** *to lock* the door. (I was going and I stopped because I wanted to lock the door.)

I **regret** *to leave* the party so early. (I'm sorry but I have to leave the party early.)
I **regret** *leaving* the party so early. (I left the party early and now I'm sorry.)

EXERCISE 6

Fill in the blanks with the correct gerund or infinitive form of the following verbs.

call   buy   do   make   tell   put   smoke

1. I *remembered* _____ a lottery ticket, and I *remember* _____ it in my wallet, but I cannot find it now.

2. He *stopped* _____ in his car, so he had to *stop* the car _____ a cigarette.

3. He has an awful memory. I asked him to lock the door. He never did it. He totally *forgot* _____ it. Then I asked him to make a shopping list. He made the list, but completely *forgot* _____ it and told me he had never made it.

4. I called the applicant and told her, "I *regret* _____ you that you did not get the job." She acted so hysterically that I *regretted* _____ her in the first place. I should have just emailed her, I think.

 # COMMUNICATIVE ACTIVITY 2

Picking Verbs out of a Hat

Your teacher will provide a mix of verbs from the boxes above, each written on a small piece of paper. Pick a piece of paper, and decide whether your verb is followed by a gerund, an infinitive, or both. Then make a sentence with your verb. If your sentence is not correct, you are eliminated from the game. The game continues until there is only one person left.

COMMON EXPRESSIONS THAT USE GERUNDS AS OBJECTS

English has numerous expressions that use gerunds as objects. It is important to learn them thoroughly for use in conversation and writing.

Have + fun / a good time / a hard time / trouble / difficulty + _____-ing
We **had fun** *watching* the game on TV last night.
We **had trouble** *finding* your house.
We **had a hard time** *choosing* a title for this book.

Spend / waste + time / money / energy + _____-ing
I **spent a lot of money** *travelling* all over Europe.
I **wasted my time** *trying* to find her.
I **spent all my energy** *shouting*.

Sit / stand / lie + adverb of place + _____-ing
She **lay on her bed** *daydreaming*.
He **stood at the door** *staring* at her.
He **sat there** *thinking* about his problems.

Cannot / can't + stand / help + _____-ing
I **cannot stand** *watching* those stupid reality shows.
I **cannot help** *laughing* at his jokes.

Go + recreational or sports activities in gerund form
Go *biking*, **go** *skiing*, **go** *shopping*, **go** *swimming*

Feel like + _____-ing
I **feel like** *flying*.
I do not **feel like** *talking* right now.

Be worth + _____-ing
This book **is worth** *reading* several times.

Be no use + _____-ing
It **is no use** *knocking*. He will not hear you.

EXERCISE 7

Fill in the blanks with the gerunds of your choice to make meaningful sentences.

1. I hate him. I cannot stand even _____ at him.

2. My stomach cannot digest this food. I feel like _____ up as soon as I eat it.

3. We interviewed only two people. Most of the other candidates were so unqualified that they were not worth _____.

4. It is no use _____. Your bus has already left. Wait for the next one.

5. I spent a lot of time _____ how to use the new computer software in the lab.

❖ COMMUNICATIVE ACTIVITY 3

Gerund Fun

Work with a partner. You each write 10 gerunds on a separate sheet of paper (e.g., *swimming*, *sleeping*, *doing*). Exchange your list with your partner. Try to use as many of your partner's gerunds as possible to fill in the blanks in the following sentences and form meaningful sentences. The person with the most meaningful sentences wins the game. Ask your teacher to judge if you and your partner disagree on correct sentences.

1. I had fun _____ last night.

2. I usually have trouble _____ in the mornings.

3. I feel like _____ right now.

4. Life is not worth _____ every day.

5. It's no use _____ like that.

6. I love to go _____ whenever I am in the countryside.

7. I cannot help _____ whenever I see him.

8. I can't stand _____ at parties.

9. I spend a lot of money _____ things.

10. When I was younger, I wasted my time _____.

GERUNDS AS OBJECTS OF PREPOSITIONS

Gerunds can functions as objects of prepositions. The challenge here is not only to remember to put the gerund form after the preposition but also to know which prepositions appear after which verbs, adjectives, or nouns.

Formation

Type	Example Sentence
adjective with preposition + gerund	I am **interested in** *learning* a new language.
verb with preposition + gerund	I **apologize for** *being* late.
noun with preposition + gerund	I am looking for an **alternative to** *driving* to work.

For a list of prepositions that usually appear after nouns, adjectives, and verbs, refer to Appendix C.

EXERCISE 8

Fill in the blanks with the gerunds of your choice to make meaningful sentences.

1. She insists on _____ to you in private.

2. I'm sick and tired of _____ to your complaints.

3. We are thinking about _____ him the truth.

4. I am looking forward to _____ you in person to discuss my resumé.

5. Our team is not playing very well. It is facing the possibility of _____ the game.

6. The mayor congratulated the organizers on _____ a record number of visitors to the festival.

7. I wanted to thank you for _____ such a good friend to me.

8. That country is in the middle of a revolution. We advise you against _____ it in the near future.

9. His wife never forgave him for _____ their retirement money in bad investments.

10. We tried to stop him from _____ after he had drunk so much, but he grabbed the keys and rushed out.

EXERCISE 9

Fill in the blanks with the correct prepositions.

1. I am accustomed _____ waking up early.

2. I am bored _____ sitting at the desk all day.

3. I am excited _____ joining the army.

4. He is proud _____ being a dad.

5. I made a mistake _____ spelling.

6. I have a talent _____ making jokes.

7. I have a good chance _____ passing this course.

8. We concentrated _____ improving our pronunciation.

9. His wife approves _____ selling the house.

10. I don't blame him _____ breaking the computer.

✥ COMMUNICATIVE ACTIVITY 4

How Well Do You Know Your Partner?

Work in pairs. Complete the following sentences about your partner by adding prepositions and gerunds. Make your guesses as specific as possible to make the game more interesting. Then switch your sentences with your partner to see who guessed more accurately about the other person. Work on a separate sheet of paper.

> You are interested in playing first-person shooter video games.

You are interested . . .
You are afraid . . .
You approve . . .
You are bored . . .
You are devoted . . .
You are familiar . . .
You are proud . . .
You have a talent . . .

PERFECT GERUNDS AND INFINITIVES

Perfect gerunds (*having* + past participle, e.g., *having been, having seen*) and perfect infinitives (*to have* + past participle, e.g., *to have been, to have seen*) are used to show that one action or situation happened or was completed before the other action or situation.

Formation

Look at the differences in meaning between the sentences in the formation chart.

Type	Example	Meaning
gerund	He doesn't mind **being** poor now.	(He is poor now and he doesn't mind it.)
perfect gerund	He doesn't mind **having been** poor before.	(He was poor before, but he doesn't mind it now.)
infinitive	He is pretending **not to hear** me now.	(I am calling him now, but he is pretending that he doesn't hear me.)
perfect infinitive	He is pretending **not to have heard** me yesterday.	(I am asking him now why he didn't answer when I called him yesterday, and he is pretending now that he didn't hear me then.)

EXERCISE 10

Fill in the blanks with the correct infinitive, perfect infinitive, gerund, or perfect gerund form of the verbs in parentheses.

1. The old man is thinking about _____ (travel) to Africa soon.

2. The old man always talks about _____ (travel) to Africa several times

   in his youth.

3. (I am chatting with a stranger online, and he is telling me that he lives in London now.) I think he is lying about _____ (live) in London.

4. (I am chatting with a stranger online, and he is telling me that he lived in London before.) I think he's lying about _____ (live) in London.

5. These are the things I wish _____ (experience) before I die.

6. These are the things I wish _____ (experience) before I grew up.

Note: It is sometimes possible to use a simple gerund or infinitive instead of the perfect forms because other elements in the sentence (such as adverbs of time) show the time difference clearly.

He remembered having been sick in those days.

He remembered being sick in those days.

❖ COMMUNICATIVE ACTIVITY 5

Q&A

Work in pairs. Together, fill in the blanks with simple or, where possible, with perfect gerunds and infinitives. Student A then poses the first set of questions for Student B to answer. Switch roles after each set of questions.

1. Think of a time when you failed at something in your life. How much do you mind now, _____ (fail) then? Based on your past experience, do you mind _____ (fail) in the future?

2. When did you learn _____ (write)? Is it important for you now _____ (learn) _____ (write) then?

3. Did you have a healthy lifestyle as a kid? Do you think you are going _____ (develop) health problems in the future as a result of not _____ (have) a healthy lifestyle as a child?

4. What's the stupidest thing that you remember _____ (do) in your life? Why do you think now that it was mistake _____ (do) such a thing then?

COMMUNICATIVE ACTIVITY 6

Travel Advice

Work in pairs and role-play the following situation.

Student A: You are planning a vacation, but you don't know where to go. Luckily, you can get some help from Joe, a travel expert on the radio. Call Joe and ask him which locations and hotel resorts offer the best vacations for the types of activities you'd like to do.

Student B: You are Joe and you reply to the questions, giving suggestions.

Below are some suggestions for verbs you can use. Pay attention to using gerunds and infinitives correctly.

enjoy skiing
can't afford to fly
encouraged to bike
practise snorkelling
afraid of scuba diving
love tasting exotic foods

 ## COMMUNICATIVE ACTIVITY 7

Comparing Two Celebrities

Work in pairs, with each student picking a favourite celebrity. Compare how the celebrities started their careers and their paths to fame and fortune.

> Jim Carrey started doing stand-up comedy acts when he was as young as 14. He always enjoyed making people laugh . . .

> Charlie Chaplin was very poor when he was a child. He made money by singing and acting on the streets of London. He couldn't afford to buy anything . . .

After discussing the two celebrities as a pair, share your findings about the similarities and differences in their careers with the rest of the class.

Reading

The passage below is a summary of one of the stories from Chaucer's *The Canterbury Tales*. Read the passage and answer the questions that follow.

THE WIFE OF BATH'S TALE

Once, long ago, a young and inexperienced knight was returning to Camelot to meet with King Arthur. He saw a fair <u>maiden</u> all alone in the woods and molested her. The angry commoners despised being insulted thus and asked King Arthur to bring the knight to justice. The King <u>sanctioned</u> killing the offender. The caring Queen, however, begged the king to permit her to pass a milder judgment on the knight.

When brought before her, the Queen informed the knight that he would live or die depending upon how successfully he answered this question: "What is the thing that women most desire?" The knight honestly admitted not having a ready answer, so the gracious queen postponed killing him and ordered him to return to the court within one year with the answer.

The knight started travelling from place to place in search of the answer. Some women said they wanted to have wealth and treasure; some said <u>jollity</u> and pleasure. Others said they expected to be <u>gratified</u> and flattered. And so it went. Days passed on, and he kept hearing different and confusing answers.

At the end of one year, the knight had almost given up searching and was riding back toward King Arthur's court in a <u>dejected</u> mood when suddenly, in a clearing in the wood, he saw twenty-four maidens dancing and singing. But as he approached them, they disappeared, as if by magic. There was not a living creature to be seen except an old woman, whose foul looks exceeded anything the knight had ever seen before.

The old woman approached the knight and insisted on knowing what he was seeking.

The knight explained his problem. The old woman said she could give him the answer, provided that he do whatever she would require for saving his life. The knight agreed, and they journeyed to the court.

Before the Queen once again, the knight said he had the answer to what women desired most, and the Queen ordered him to continue speaking. The knight responded that women most desire <u>sovereignty</u> over their husbands. None of the women of the court could deny the validity of this answer, so the knight was <u>acquitted</u>. Then the old woman told the court she had supplied the knight's answer. In exchange, the knight had, upon his honour, agreed to fulfill any request she made of him. She said that she would settle for nothing less than to be his very wife and love. The knight, in misery, agreed to marry her.

On their wedding night, the knight turned restlessly, paying no attention to the <u>foul</u> woman lying next to him in bed. She asked, "Is this how knights treat their wives?" The knight confessed that he resented having a wife who was so old, ugly, and vulgar. The old <u>hag</u> then gave the knight a long moral lecture and reminded him that her looks could be viewed as an asset. If she were beautiful, there would be many men who would desire her; so as long as she was old and ugly, he could be assured of having a virtuous wife. She offered him a choice: an old, ugly hag such as she, but still a loyal, true, and obliging wife, or a beautiful woman with whom he must take his chances with good-looking men who would visit their home because of her and not him.

The knight groaned and said the choice was hers. "And have I won the mastery," she asked, "since I'm to choose and rule as I think fit?" "Certainly, wife," the knight answered. "Kiss me," she said. "On my honour you shall find me both fair and faithful as a wife. Look at me." The knight turned, and she was indeed now a young and charming woman. And so, they lived happily ever after.

Adapted from Bruce Nicoll, *Canterbury Tales* Cliffs Notes Series.

COMPREHENSION

Answer the following questions in complete sentences.

1. What did the King decide to do with the knight?

   _____

2. What was the puzzle the Queen gave the knight?

   _____

3. How much time was the knight given to solve the puzzle?

   _____

4. Write some of the different answers he received from women.

   _____

5. What did the old woman in the woods look like?

   _____

6. What was the condition that the woman placed on the knight in return for her answer to the puzzle?

   _____

7. What was the answer to the puzzle?

   _____

8. What was the old woman's request in fulfillment of her condition?

_____

9. What two choices did she give the knight?

_____

10. Which choice did the knight pick?

_____

11. What happened at the end of the story?

_____

12. What do you like or dislike about this story? Why? Discuss your reasons with your classmates.

_____

Listening

◀)) Track 03

GERUNDS AND INFINITIVES

Read the questions below and see whether you can answer them without listening to the audio clip. Then listen to the interview "Gerunds vs. Infinitives" once and check your answers.

1. Two types of verbs are followed by both infinitives and gerunds. What are these two types? Give two examples for each type.

_____

_____

2. What was the old method of learning gerunds and infinitives?

_____

_____

3. What is the method that is recommended these days according to the clip?

_____

_____

4. Give two examples of gerund verbs that communicate something.

_____

_____

5. Give two examples of infinitive verbs of choice and intention.

_____

_____

COMPREHENSION

Listen to the audio again and answer the following questions.

1. What is the name of the program?

_____

2. Who is the guest on this program?

_____

3. What is her job?

_____

4. Where does she work?

_____

5. What is the nationality of the student who asked a question about gerunds?

_____

Writing

Choose one of the topics below and write a short essay (maximum 350 words) about the topic. Work on a separate sheet of paper.

- Write about the kind of expectations you would have of your children, the activities you'd enjoy with them, and the things you would want them to learn. Try to use some of the gerund and infinitive structures you learned in this chapter, such as *want to, expect to, intend to, enjoy doing, go hiking,* and so on.
- Some people remember their early childhood very well (as early as when they were three or four years old), and others do not remember anything before they were six or seven years old. What are some of your earliest childhood memories? Use verbs that are followed by gerunds, such as *remember, recall, imagine, hate, love, like, enjoy,* and so on.

CHAPTER REVIEW

Summary

Use	Gerund Example Sentence	Infinitive Example Sentence
as object of a verb	His job **involves** *making* short trips to Nunavut.	He **agreed** *to pay* my tuition.
verb + gerund; verb + infinitive (little meaning change)	She **started** *reading*.	She **started** *to read*.
verb + gerund; verb + infinitive (significant meaning change)	I **remember** *locking* the door.	I will **remember** *to lock* the door.
object of a preposition (adjective with preposition + gerund)	I am **interested in** *learning* a new language.	
object of a preposition (verb with preposition + gerund)	I **apologize for** *being* late.	
object of a preposition (noun with preposition + gerund)	I am looking for an **alternative to** *driving* to work.	
in common expressions and patterns	I **felt like** *throwing up* after eating too much.	

EXERCISE 1

take	demand	adjust	tell	become	give
confront	insert	track	pick	use	be
develop	publish	ask	get	see	do

Read the paragraph below, and fill in the blanks with the infinitive or gerund form of the verbs in the chart above or with verbs of your own choice. You may use some verbs more than once.

1 _____ pictures was one of Katy's favourite hobbies. When she was

a little girl, she spent lots of time 2 _____ pictures of everything: her

room, her toys, her friends, and even strangers.

In the old days, it used to be harder and more expensive ₃ _____ pictures. You would have ₄ _____ a sensitive roll of film into the camera properly and then take pictures. ₅ _____ the lighting and focusing was also manual. In time, and with lots of practice, a good photographer would learn ₆ _____ good locations, good lighting, and good positioning of the subjects for ideal pictures.

Katy grew up with her hobby. She never really cared ₇ _____ a professional photographer, but she managed ₈ _____ such excellent pictures that her friends kept ₉ _____ her ₁₀ _____ pictures at their parties. Later, when she visited her friends' homes, she would often find her work framed and on the walls, looking very professional. She enjoyed ₁₁ _____ that, but she still never wanted ₁₂ _____ a professional photographer. She loved ₁₃ _____ a hobbyist. For her, taking photos was a pleasure, a hobby, and nothing else.

One day, when she was trying ₁₄ _____ her friends on Facebook, she noticed that one of her friends had made a poster of a picture she had taken of him, and this poster had become famous and was on billboards and magazines in Italy! At first she felt proud of ₁₅ _____ the photographer, but then, as she looked closely, she realized that her friend had actually succeeded ₁₆ _____ a modelling contract because of this picture! He had never bothered ₁₇ _____ her. He had never even mentioned ₁₈ _____ her picture and had never offered ₁₉ _____ her any compensation or credit! She was shocked and disappointed.

Now she is pondering what ₂₀ _____. Is it a good thing ₂₁ _____ her friend and tell him the rights are hers? Will it tarnish the friendship ₂₂ _____ rights and credit for ₂₃ _____ the photo? Is it worth it ₂₄ _____ anything at all? What would you do if you were Katy?

EXERCISE 2

Puzzle

This puzzle contains 10 verbs that are always followed by the infinitive and 10 verbs that are always followed by the gerund. Find all 20 verbs and categorize them in the chart below. Then use each verb in a sentence. The first pair has been done for you. Try to use both simple and perfect gerunds and infinitives in your examples.

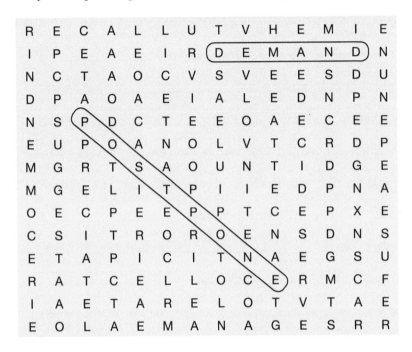

Verb Followed by Infinitive	Example Sentence	Verb Followed by Gerund	Example Sentence
demand	I demand to know my legal rights.	postpone	I postponed sending the receipt until I had received the money.

Modals

OVERVIEW

- Modal verbs are auxiliary verbs in the sense that they don't need another auxiliary in negative or question forms. They are different from other auxiliary verbs because they add meaning (modality) to the verbs that come after them.

- Modal verbs are used to talk about permission, possibility, ability, and necessity, among other things.

- Each modal verb can have more than one meaning (for example, *can* is used to show ability, possibility, and permission).

- The most common modal verbs in English are *can*, *could*, *will*, *would*, *shall*, *should*, *must*, *may*, *might*, and *ought to*.

Warm-up

Work in pairs. Carefully read each sentence in the chart below. Then, try to say the same thing with modal auxiliary verbs (*will, would, shall, should, can, could, may, might, must, ought to*). Consult the chart in the Formation section if you need to. The first one has been done for you.

Sentence without Modal Auxiliary	Sentence with Modal Auxiliary
Are you able to do the job?	Can you do the job?
Were you able to swim when you were five years old?	
You are not supposed to eat before washing your hands.	
It is required by law that you wear a seat belt.	
Pass me the salt please!	
Is it okay if I come in?	
I don't know where she is. It's possible she's at home. It's also possible she's at work.	
I'm pretty sure she is at home.	
I'm pretty sure she isn't at home.	

Formation

The following chart is a summary of the most common modal auxiliary verbs and their uses in English. You have studied most of these in previous levels. Cover the Example Sentences column with a piece of paper and try to come up with an example of your own before checking the example column.

Modal Auxiliary	Use	Example Sentences
will	• the future • friendly request	I will see you tomorrow. Will you close the door please?
would	• past habit • polite request • desire (usually with like) • hypothesis (conditional)	When I was younger, I would sleep more. Would you please close the door? I would like tea, please. He would if he could.

shall	• polite suggestion • legal obligation	Shall we dance? All dues shall be paid.
should	• advice • strong probability	You shouldn't drink and drive. He should be home by now.
ought to	• advice	You ought to listen to me.
can	• ability • casual request • typical possibility	Can you dance? Can you give me the pen please? Waves can reach high in this area.
could	• past ability • polite request • possibility (weaker than *may*)	I could dance when I was young. Could you listen to me? She could be your sister.
may	• polite request / permission • probability	May I leave? It may rain.
might	• possibility (weaker than *may*)	You might be able to do it.
must	• necessity • logical certainty	You must obey. This must be the right answer.

POLITE REQUEST AND PERMISSION: *will, can, could, would, may*

The modals *will, can, could, would,* and *may* are used for polite requests and permission. *Will* is the least formal, and *may* is the most formal form of polite request.

LEVELS OF POLITENESS

When requesting something or asking for permission, use the following modals, which have different levels of politeness. The chart on the following page lists the modals, with the most polite at the top.

Modal	Level of Politeness	Example Sentences
may	very refined, polite	May I leave the room? (request) You may leave the room.
would	very polite	Would you please do me a favour?
could	polite	Could you please close the door? (request)
can	casual, polite	Can you get the door, please? You can go now.
will	very casual	Will you pass the salt?

Notes

1. In polite requests (question form)

   May is most often used with *I*. We normally do not use it with other pronouns.

   May I open the window? (correct)

   ~~May you open the window?~~ (incorrect)

   Would is most often used with *you*. We normally do not use it with other pronouns.

   Would you please give me some money? (correct)

   ~~Would I please have some money?~~ (incorrect)

2. The expression *would like* is used to show desire.

   What would you like to have?

   I would like (I'd like) to have some chocolate ice cream.

EXERCISE 1

The following sentences are not polite or appropriate. Make them more polite by using the best modal auxiliary verb for each situation. Change the vocabulary, if necessary. There might be more than one correct answer.

1. Waiter to patron: What do you want to eat?

   What would you like to eat?

2. Student to teacher: I want to go to the washroom.

   May I go to the bathroom?

3. Father to teenage son: Turn down the music!

   Could you down the music?

4. Customer to cashier: Break this bill for me, please.

   Would you please break this bill for me.

5. Driver to bylaw officer: Is it okay if I park my car here overnight?

   Would it be ok if I park my car overnight here?

OTHER WAYS TO FORM POLITE REQUESTS

Besides using modal auxiliary verbs, several other structures can be used to form polite requests. Here are a couple of other structures:

Phrase	Polite Request	Positive Reply	Negative Reply
Do you mind if . . . ?	Do you mind if I turn up the music?	No, I don't mind. Please go ahead and turn up the music.	Yes, I do mind. The loud noise bothers me. Please keep it down.
Is it okay / all right if . . . ?	Is it okay if I open the window?	Yes, it's fine. Please go ahead and open it.	No, I'd rather you didn't open it. It is a bit cold in here. No, it's actually not okay. I feel cold.

Asking Your Boss

Imagine you are asking permission from your boss. Which type of structure is best for the following situations? Use structures from the two charts on pages 62 and 63. Discuss your answers with a partner.

- You want to ask for a day off.
- You want a longer lunch break.
- You would rather use the executive washroom and want to ask for the key.
- You want to know your boss's birthday so that you can send her a card.

ABILITY: *can, could, be able to*

Read the following passage carefully:

I <u>could</u> speak Arabic when I was a kid, but I forgot most of it. Now I <u>can't</u> speak much but I <u>can</u> still read and understand it. I'm sure, some day, with more practice, I <u>will be able to</u> speak Arabic again.

We use *could* for the past and *can* for present when we talk about **general ability** (things we can do any time, such as skills, talents, and so on). For future general ability, we use *will be able to*. *Could* is usually not possible when we talk about something we did only one time in the past but the negative (*couldn't*) is possible:

~~Finally, he could call her last night.~~ (incorrect)

Finally, he was able to call her last night. (correct)

He wasn't able to call her last night. (correct)

He couldn't call her last night. (correct)

We use *can* for the future only when the action depends on **present circumstances**:

I can send an invitation to you, if you want.

EXERCISE 2

Read the following email message to a mother from the assistant swim coach. Fill in the blanks with the correct positive or negative form of *can* and *could*, where possible. Use *be able to* only if *can* or *could* is not possible.

Hi, Marie.

In response to your question, normally, Pascal ₁ _____ hold his breath under water for five minutes. Last week during practice, he

₂ _____ hold it for five minutes and five seconds. But something happened during the contest yesterday. Pascal ₃ _____ concentrate

at all, and he lost. His coach still believes in him, though. He says, some day,

Pascal ₄ _____ break the world record.

    I ₅ _____ send you some pictures of Pascal's next practice

session if you want.

Take care,

Chantale

 ## COMMUNICATIVE ACTIVITY 2

Cellphone Power

Work in pairs. You and your partner will discuss advances in cellphone technology. What are some things that you couldn't do with your cellphone 10 years ago but you can today? What new things do you think you will be able to do with your phone 10 years from now?
    Write the results of your discussion in one paragraph and ask your teacher if you can present the results to class.

NECESSITY AND OBLIGATION: must / have to, shall / should, ought to / had better

Should, ought to, and *had better* are used to give advice, suggestions, or opinions about the right thing to do.

    Should and *ought to* are almost synonyms. However, *ought to* is used much less frequently than *should* and its negative (*oughtn't to*), and question forms (*Ought he to?*) are extremely rare in North American English.

    Had better is stronger than *should* and often stresses the consequences if the advice is not taken. Look at the following examples:

You should study harder for your next test. (It is advisable to do so.)

You ought to study harder for your next test. (It is advisable to do so.)

You had better study harder for your next test or you'll fail the course. (It is advisable to do so. Otherwise you suffer the consequences.)

Must is much stronger than *should* and *had better*. We use *must* mostly to give orders or specify rules that are necessary to follow.

    Compare the following:

You shouldn't stay in a parked car for a long time on hot summer days. (It is not a good idea to do so.)

You mustn't leave a baby in a parked car on hot summer days. (It is against the law.)

Must and *have to* (*have got to*) are almost synonyms and can be used interchangeably most of the time. *Have to / has to* is not as emphatic as *must*.

The negative forms (*mustn't* and *don't have to / doesn't have to*) are completely different, though. Compare the following:

You don't have to clean the table. (It's not necessary. You can do it if you want.)

You mustn't clean the table. (It is necessary that you don't clean it. It is forbidden.)

Note: In Canada and the UK, the word *shall* is commonly used in written contracts to show legal obligation.

The purchaser shall pay all dues to the vendor upon signing the contract.
(The purchaser is legally responsible to pay.)

Note: *Have to* is not an auxiliary verb. To make it negative, or to turn it into a question, we need to add another auxiliary.

He has to _____. → He **doesn't** have to _____.

→ **Does** he have to _____?

EXERCISE 3

Fill in the blanks with the correct negative modal form (*shall not, shouldn't, mustn't, don't have to, doesn't have to, had better not*). Use each once only.

1. He _____ work for a living like the rest of us because he is very rich.

2. It's supposed to be a secret so I _____ be telling you this. But since you are my best friend, I'll tell you.

3. They _____ cancel my favourite TV show or I'll cancel my cable TV subscription.

4. When travelling to the United States, you _____ take any Kinder Surprise eggs into the country. It's against the law.

5. When returning to Canada from abroad, you _____ declare goods under $200. The goods qualify under personal exemption rules.

6. The Client _____ remove, alter, disfigure, mark, or cover any numbering, lettering, or insignia displayed on the Equipment.

COMMUNICATIVE ACTIVITY 3

The Crazy Dictator

Work in pairs or small groups. Imagine you are a crazy dictator in control of a country called The Nonsensical Republic of Madness. Your goal is to write a charter that takes people's liberties away from them. Work on a separate sheet of paper, and write sentences reminding people of the laws of the land and their obligations as citizens of The Nonsensical Republic of Madness. Write what they should and should not do and what they must and must not do and what they don't have to do. You can even threaten them mildly by using *had better not . . . or . . .* structures. The crazier, the better!

> You must not smile or show any sign of happiness in public. You had better not do it in private either.

> You should not pronounce the name of the Leader Almighty without hailing him three times.

Share your work with the rest of the class.

CERTAINTY, PROBABILITY, AND POSSIBILITY: *will, must, can't, should, can, may, might, could*

Formation

Modal	Use	Example Sentences—Positive and Negative
will	certainty based on expectation	He will be asleep. He always sleeps at this time.
must	certainty based on deduction	He must be asleep. I can hear him snoring.
cannot (can't)	certainty based on deduction (negative of *must be*)	He cannot be asleep. I can hear him whispering.
should	strong probability	He should be asleep by now. He went to bed an hour ago.
can	typical possibility	Too much sleep can be harmful.
may	probability	Don't call him. He may be asleep.
might	possibility (weaker than *may*)	I have no clue. He might be asleep or awake.
could	possibility (much weaker than *may*)	He could be asleep, but I really doubt it.

We can use modal auxiliaries to specify the degree of certainty.

- We use *will* to talk about something we expect to be true based on previous knowledge or **experience**:

  He won't be home at this time of the day. He works full-time.

- We use *must* and *can't* to show we are pretty sure about something based on **evidence** or **logic**.

  It must be raining. (I can't see the rain myself but I'm pretty sure because I can hear raindrops on the roof.)

  That can't be your dad! (He looks way too young to be your dad.)

We often use the verb *be* after *must* and *can't* when we use them for deductive certainty at present time.

Compare:

We must be moving! (I'm pretty sure we are moving. I can feel it.)

We must move. (We have to move. It is necessary.)

- We use *should* to show that we are not 100 percent sure, but there's a **good chance** something is true.

  I've never done it myself but it shouldn't be too difficult to do. (There's no reason for it to be difficult.)

- *Can* is used to describe a **typically possible scenario**.

  We can get up to 300 centimetres of snow per winter here in Ottawa. (It doesn't mean that we get that much every year, but it is something that is normal.)

- *May, could,* and *might* are all used to talk about situations in which we are not sure what is true. *Could* and *might* are slightly less probable than *may*.

  Don't you cry! You still may be able to get that job. (The odds are not high but don't give up yet.)

  Although you might still get the job, the odds are not in your favour.

  A better opportunity could come your way. Who knows?

EXERCISE 4

Fill in the blanks for each conversation with the modal auxiliary verbs *will, must, can't, can, should, might, may,* and *could* to indicate the degree of possibility. There might be more than one possible answer for some blanks. Use each modal once only.

Are there any other towns or cities called London in the world, other than in England?

There <u>must</u> be one or two because I've heard of London, Ontario.

1. Does your chiropractor take appointments on weekends?

   He _____. We should call and find out.

2. Are the Ottawa Senators and Calgary Flames going to be in the playoffs this year?

They _____ if they both play as well as they have so far.

3. Is Parisa the young intern at the hospital that you told me about?

She _____ be. I forget her name, but she had brown hair and worked with Doctor Leblanc.

4. Do you think we will get that windstorm today? The meteorologists are pretty confident that it's heading this way.

No! They _____ be right. Look! It's so nice and calm!

5. I'm pretty sure it's your brother at the door. Don't you agree?

It _____ be him. Only his car screeches like that.

6. Do you know how long a dog lives?

On average 10 years, but some small dogs _____ live as long as 14 years.

7. What are the prizes for the contest?

You _____ win $10,000 cash or an all-expenses-paid trip to the Bahamas.

8. Someone's knocking!

Oh, that _____ be Nick. Tell him I'll be down in a minute.

COMMUNICATIVE ACTIVITY 4

Detective Work

Work in pairs. One partner chooses one of the following items, and the other forms sentences by using modals about the possibility of where the item could be. Then, switch roles until all items have been discussed.

- a pair of mittens
- a tote bag
- a pair of boots
- a coffee mug
- a wallet
- a cellphone
- a jacket

Student A: Where could my mittens be?

Student B: Well, they could be in your pocket. Maybe they're on the floor. They might be lost on the bus. Can you remember when you had them last?

BRINGING IT ALL TOGETHER

 COMMUNICATIVE ACTIVITY 5

In Other Words

Work in pairs. Each student creates a sentence by using a polite request modal auxiliary verb for each situation below. Then exchange your sentences with your partner and try to write the same request in different words without using any modal auxiliary, if possible.

Situation: The cashier at the drive-through asks the driver if she wants fries with her burger.

Student A: Would you like fries with your burger?

Student B: Is that with fries?

At the end of the activity, compare your sentences with your partner's and discuss how each alternative changes the effect of the sentence.

1. Children ask their teacher for permission to have a longer recess.

   _____

   _____

   _____

2. You want to find out where the nearest washroom is in the mall.

   _____

   _____

   _____

3. You want to drink water at your friend's house.

   _____

   _____

   _____

4. Your friends want to borrow your neighbour's barbecue.

   _____

   _____

   _____

5. Your children want to play with the neighbour's children in their backyard.

_____

_____

_____

 # COMMUNICATIVE ACTIVITY 6

Talent Time

Work in pairs. Think about some of your talents, skills, and abilities. Talk about how you acquired them, what you could do before, what you can do now, and what you think you will be able to do in the future. Take turns choosing a skill or ability to talk about.

English language skills:

Student A: I started learning English back in my country 10 years ago. In those days, I could read but I couldn't speak much. Pretty soon, I learned to talk about simple, everyday subjects. Now, I can discuss almost any subject, but I still make some mistakes and have minor issues with pronunciation. I hope that sometime in the near future, I will be able to have native-like fluency.

Student B: Were you able to practise speaking outside the classroom when you were in your country? I also learned English in my country, but I couldn't find anyone to practise it with.

 # COMMUNICATIVE ACTIVITY 7

Mind Your Ps and Qs!

Work in pairs. Discuss etiquette (manners) with your partner. You may focus on a specific area if you want, for example, dating etiquette. Discuss the things you should or would normally do or the things you shouldn't or mustn't do. Review modals of obligation and modals of necessity on pages 65–66, if needed. Remember to take notes about your partner's culture. You will be asked to write about it later in the Writing section of this chapter (on page 75).

 # COMMUNICATIVE ACTIVITY 8

In The News

Work in pairs or small groups. Your teacher will give you a newspaper or magazine. Read the articles and find and <u>underline</u> examples of modal auxiliary verbs that show different degrees of possibility (see page 67). Discuss the degree of possibility in each case, and decide why the writer has used that modal auxiliary, based on context.

If you finish sooner than other pairs, reread the articles and find examples of other types of modals (polite request, ability, obligation).

Reading

Read the passage and answer the questions that follow.

PLATONIC RELATIONSHIPS

Can men and women be friends? Of course, but there is a different set of rules for them than for other friendships. If you can make a <u>platonic</u> friendship work, you'll learn some valuable lessons about the opposite sex that will help you in your dating life or marriage. Here are some things to keep in mind when becoming friends with someone of the opposite sex.

Having Feelings of Attraction Doesn't Mean You Need to Act on Them

You might (initially at least) feel physically attracted to an opposite-sex friend when you first start hanging out with them. But just because you feel things doesn't mean you should act on them. What's more, you can't act on your feelings if you want to stay friends.

If either one of you is currently in a relationship already, you have even more reason not to proceed with your feelings. Your friend should just be a friend, and no more. If you focus on other things, your feelings of attraction will become less and less.

Understand Boundaries and Stick by Them

You don't necessarily have to spell out the boundaries in your friendship verbally, but do keep them in mind so you don't cross them yourself. If your friend expresses feelings of attraction, then you can <u>verbalize</u> what the appropriate boundaries should be so you both can stay on the same page.

Don't Fuel Gossip

There might be those that <u>coyly</u> ask you about your friendship, implying that the two of you might have something romantic going on in private. Some folks are very <u>skeptical</u> of platonic friendships, so don't fuel the gossip by saying:

> (With a smile or wink) "We're just friends."
> "Wouldn't you like to know?"
> "That's our business."

You [ought to] answer with "No, we really are just friends" and leave it at that.

Don't Flirt

A platonic friendship is not one where the people flirt but don't date. They're friends and friends only. If you try and change your relationship into a "friends with benefits" situation, you will ruin your friendship by pushing the boundaries. You mustn't <u>flirt</u>, hug, kiss, or do anything else that you would do with a date.

Watch for Feelings of Jealousy

Some opposite-sex friends get jealous when they see their pals in a happy romantic relationship. If you feel this way, it means you haven't come to terms yet with the fact that your relationship is platonic only. If you need to, take some time away from your friend so you can deal with the way you feel.

If you don't do this, you might be <u>sabotaging</u> your friend's happiness by making <u>subtle</u>, negative comments about the people he or she dates. You may try to talk friends out of people who could be good for them simply because you haven't accepted the platonic nature of your friendship yet.

Make Sure You're Open with Your Partner about the Friendship

[You should] be up-front with your partner about your platonic friendship. Tell your boyfriend or girlfriend (or spouse) about the times you talk to your friend or schedule time together. Be sure to include your partner when hanging out from time to time.

Learn From Your Opposite-Sex Friend

Having a platonic friendship that is not complicated by romantic feelings can actually teach you a lot about the opposite sex. The knowledge you gain can help you in your own romantic relationships. You'll see first-hand how the opposite sex reacts to getting dumped, what they find sweet and romantic, what things impress them, and more.

Opposite-sex friends, like all friends, will help you learn more about yourself so you can be better at all your relationships, platonic and otherwise. Make sure you understand the value of an opposite-sex friend so you don't cross a line that may end the friendship.

Source: Cherie Burbach, "How to Develop a Healthy Platonic Friendship," About.com

COMPREHENSION

1. According to the article, is it possible for men and women to be friends? Explain.

   _____

2. What advice does the writer give about having feelings of attraction toward your friend?

   _____

3. Name a couple of the boundaries mentioned in the article.

   _____

4. What particular feeling could sabotage (or work against) your platonic friendship?

   _____

5. What is one benefit of having a platonic friendship? How can this benefit help you with your future romantic relationships?

   _____

Listening

🔊 Track 04

ONLINE DATING TRENDS

Listen to the audio, a podcast from CBC Radio's show *Spark* called "Online Dating Data." Nora Young of CBC Radio One is interviewing Sam Yagan, co-founder of OKCupid, an online dating site.

Part 1

Listen to the audio, and decide which statements are true and which are false. Circle the correct answer.

1. The data haven't been updated in a while.   T / F

2. There is not a difference in what people want and what they say they want.   T / F

3. People's actions and statements always agree.   T / F

4. People intentionally exaggerate.   T / F

5. People "fudge" or fib a bit on their profiles.   T / F

Part 2

Listen to the audio again, and answer the following questions:

1. How does the interviewee answer the following question: "How likely is it that we'll meet our match if we're not being honest?"

_____

2. What was the article on Wall Street about?

_____

3. What is one piece of advice about looking younger in your profile photo?

_____

4. What advice is given to females as opposed to males?

_____

5. How does good grammar give a signal about your profile?

_____

6. How many people use this site?

_____

7. How is having more data to your advantage when going on a dating site?

_____

8. What mathematical system is used to gather the data?

_____

9. What analogy does the interviewee use to compare your profile?

_____

10. Which gender has it easier? What is said about the difference between males and females?

_____

DISCUSSION

Using modals, work in pairs to discuss the following questions:

1. Have you ever used a dating site?

2. Would you try it if you haven't yet? Explain.

3. If you ever register on a dating website, would you trust the website to have and use your personal information?

Writing

Write a 300- to 350-word essay on what you learned about etiquette in your partner's country / culture as he or she explained to you in Communicative Activity 7 (Mind Your Ps and Qs!). You may consult other sources, such as the Internet, if you run out of information or ideas.

CHAPTER REVIEW

Summary

Polite Requests

most formal ────────→ least formal

may → would → could → can → will

Ability

	Past	Present	Future
particular occasion	I was **able to** open the door.	I **can** open the door.	I **will be able to** open the door.
general ability	I **could** speak Spanish at age six.	I **can** speak English now.	I **will be able to** speak Urdu soon.

Necessity and Obligation

absolutely necessary ────────→ less necessary (but advisable)

must → shall → have to → had better → should / ought to

Certainty and Possibility

almost certain ────────────→ only probable or possible

will / must / can't → should → can → may → could / might

EXERCISE 1

Circle the best modal in the following sentences.

1. The plane (should, would) arrive any minute. They said there were no delays.

2. I'm very busy. (Mustn't, Couldn't) you drive her to school today?

3. The hotel receptionist says the computer is down and they (**shouldn't, can't**) check in anyone right now.

4. No one is answering her phone at home. She (**must, can't**) still be in the office.

5. He's on the other line. (**Will, Might**) you take that call now?

EXERCISE 2

Find and correct the errors in the use of modals in the following sentences. If the sentence is correct, write <u>C</u> next to it.

1. I don't know where she is. She can be at home.

2. I can try calling her if you want.

3. She couldn't finish her homework, but I could finish mine.

4. Would I open the door for you, please?

5. May you open the window, please?

6. In those days, you might smoke a cigarette in public buildings.

7. Carrie is not here. I believe she must stay home now.

8. I might tell you, but you have to promise to keep it to yourself.

9. I don't believe you. It mustn't be true.

10. You must study hard or you will fail the course.

EXERCISE 3

Below is a conversation between a groom and a best man, minutes before the wedding reception. Fill in the blanks with the correct modal. Sometimes there is more than one correct answer.

Best man: Hey, buddy! That was an awesome ceremony. Everything went well.

Groom: Thanks! I hope all goes well with the reception also.

Best man: Why ₁ _____ (negative) it? Everything is nicely organized.

Groom: Hey, you ₂ _____ (negative) embarrass me with your best man speech, ₃ _____ you?

Best man: No way! I 4 _____ (negative) do that to you! You're my

best buddy! But I 5 _____ ask you something.

Groom: Sure, what is it?

Best man: 6 _____ I share a story about us as roommates back in

university?

Groom: That depends on which story. I 7 _____ imagine which

stories you're thinking of.

Best man: Well . . . how about I share the one about when we were both late

with the rent and our funny encounter with the landlord.

Groom: If you're going to tell that one, you 8 _____ leave out all

the bad words the landlord said. Those words 9 _____

be inappropriate here.

Best man: You're right. I really 10 _____ be more careful. We

11 _____ (negative) to upset your bride or her family!

Ha ha ha!

Groom: Yes. Please, you 12 _____ be careful! Oh, you know

what you 13 _____ share? The story about you having

a flat tire and how it took us three hours to find a tire to replace it,

when you had a spare one in the trunk the whole time!

Best man: Wait a minute! That story 14 _____ make me look silly

and make you look like a hero!

Groom: That's the whole point! Go for it! You 15 _____ make

me look good! That's the best man's job! Ha ha ha!

Perfect Modals

OVERVIEW

- We use perfect modals to change simple modals of advisability (*should / ought to*), degrees of possibility or certainty (*must, can, could, may, might*), and willingness (*will, would*) into past forms (e.g., *should have, could have, would have*).

- We use perfect progressive modals to change present progressive modals (e.g., *should be going*) into past forms (e.g., *should have been going*).

- Perfect modals can be used for both possible and unreal situations.

- For extensive use of perfect modals in past unreal conditionals, see Chapter 12.

Warm-up

Work in pairs. All the sentences on the left are in the past tense. Read each sentence on the left and fill in the blanks on the right with the correct modal + verb combination to make a similar sentence in the present.

He **shouldn't have told** her the truth. → He **shouldn't tell** her the truth.

Past	Present
He **must have been** at home then, right?	He _____ at home now, right?
He **should have done** his homework last night.	He _____ his homework tonight.
He **can't have done** it.	He _____ it.
I'm pretty sure! He **must have been eating** then.	I'm pretty sure! He _____ now.
He **may have broken** the world record yesterday.	He _____ the world record tonight.
He was so hungry he **could have eaten** a cow.	He is so hungry he _____ a cow.

Now read the sentences on the left again, and decide if the action happened or not.

For example, when we say, "He shouldn't have told her the truth," did he tell her the truth or not?

Discuss your answers with the rest of the class.

PERFECT MODALS

Formation

Perfect modals are formed by adding *have* and the past participle of the verb to the modal as in *may have gone, should have talked, could have been,* and so on.

Positive	Negative	Question
I **should have sent** it.	I **shouldn't have sent** it.	**Should I have sent** it?
You **must have sent** it.	You **mustn't have sent** it.	**Must he have sent** it?
He **may have sent** it.	He **may not have sent** it.	**May he have sent** it?
She **might have sent** it.	She **might not have sent** it.	**Might she have sent** it?
We **could have sent** it.	We **couldn't have sent** it.	**Could we have sent** it?
They **would have sent** it.	They **wouldn't have sent** it.	**Would they have sent** it?

EXERCISE 1

Make perfect modals out of the simple modal sentences on the left.

She ought to go. → She ought to have gone.

Present	Past
1. He must be tired.	
2. Might she do it?	
3. He shouldn't speak.	
4. Couldn't we listen to them?	
5. They may leave.	
6. She wouldn't know.	

USE AND MEANING

As you might have noticed during the Warm-up and Exercise 1, perfect modals change the present tense simple modals into the **past tense**, usually with the same meaning that the modal had in the present tense (a present modal showing certainty changes to a past modal of certainty). The other modals that can be turned into perfect form are modals of advisability (*should / ought to*), possibility (*must, can, could, may, might*), and willingness (*will, would*).

He must be home. (certainty) → He must have been home. (certainty in the past)

He must go home. (necessity) → ~~He must have gone home.~~ (incorrect in the past with a perfect modal. Correct past tense: He had to go home.)

Perfect modals can be used to describe what happened (**possible** or **real** situations) or describe the opposite of what really happened (**unreal** situations).

Possible

Look at how these sentences change to the past tense:

He **must be home** <u>now</u>. (I'm pretty sure he **is** home now.)
He **must have been home** <u>last night</u>. (I'm pretty sure he **was** home last night.)

He **may be tired** <u>now</u>. (It is possible that he **is** tired now.)
He **may have been tired** <u>yesterday</u>. (It is possible that he **was** tired yesterday.)

He **could / couldn't be the killer**. (I'm pretty sure he **is / isn't** the killer.)
He **could / couldn't have been the killer**. (I'm pretty sure he **was / wasn't** the killer.)

You **might notice** the difference between simple and perfect modals. (It's possible that you **notice**.)
You **might have noticed** the difference between simple and perfect modals. (It's possible that you **noticed**.)

Unreal

All the examples above are possible (they could happen). We can also use some perfect modals to talk about **unreal situations**, situations in which **the opposite of what was expected** happened.

The perfect modals *should have / ought to have, might have, could have,* and *would have* can be used in this way. Look at these examples:

You **should study** harder. (It is a good idea that you do.)
You **should have studied** harder. (It was a good idea, but you didn't do it.)

You **might cut** yourself with that knife. (It's possible that you will cut yourself.)
You **might have cut** yourself with that knife. (It was possible for you to cut yourself, but fortunately you didn't.)

You **could tell** her the truth! (Telling her the truth is a good idea.)
You **could have told** her the truth! (It was possible for you to have told her the truth. Why didn't you tell her the truth?)

I **will lend** you my car. (I will do it.)
I **would have lent** you my car if you had asked. (You didn't ask me, so I didn't give you the car.)

Note: For more information on *would* and *would have,* as well as the other unreal perfect modals, refer to Chapter 12 (Adverb Clauses of Condition).

EXERCISE 2

Circle the sentence that best describes each situation, depending on whether the perfect modal refers to a possible or an unreal situation.

He ought to have gone home.

a. He went home.

b. He didn't go home. (B is correct.)

1. We should have closed the door.

    a. We closed the door.   b. We didn't close the door.

2. They must have gone there.

   a. They went there.   b. They didn't go there.

3. She shouldn't have done that.

   a. She did it.   b. She didn't do it.

4. I don't know whether he's guilty or not. He could have done it.

   a. It's possible he did it.   b. It's not possible he did it.

5. You're stupid. You could have told them the truth.

   a. You told them.   b. You didn't tell them.

6. He might have gone to school for all I know!

   a. It's possible he went to school.   b. It's not possible he went to school.

7. He is so reckless. He might have broken his neck.

   a. He broke his neck.   b. He didn't break his neck.

8. It couldn't have been better.

   a. It was very good.   b. It was very bad.

EXERCISE 3

Write a sentence to complete the situations below by using the modal given in parentheses. Use either a positive or a negative statement.

I did not graduate from university and get my degree. I started working instead. Now I have been refused a promotion because I do not have my degree.

(should) I should not have started working without my degree. OR I should have graduated from university.

1. I forgot to call my sister to wish her a happy birthday. Now she is upset.

   (ought to) _____

2. He drove the car without checking the oil. Now the engine has seized.

   (could) _____

3. Anna did not buy milk yesterday. Now she cannot have cereal for breakfast.

   (should) _____

4. I wanted to return your garden tools yesterday, but my roommate was using my car.

   (would) _____

5. André ate the entire bag of chips. Now he feels sick.

   (should) _____

6. Sue was late for class again today. Her car is broken.

   (ought to) _____

7. He ran five kilometres yesterday without stretching before and after. Today his legs are very sore.

   (should) _____

✦ COMMUNICATIVE ACTIVITY 1

Be the Detective

Work in pairs. Together, write four positive or negative deductions or conclusions about the following situations. Then discuss what the person should or should not have done differently.

> Celeste returned home from class yesterday. She went to her room, closed the door, and stayed there until this morning.
>
> She might have had a lot of homework.
>
> She could not have had a date.
>
> She may have been tired.
>
> Could she have had a headache?
>
> I think she should have talked to someone about her problem.

1. Brian and Sue are married. Sue lost her job. She found another job but it does not pay as well. They are having problems paying their bills. For the last month, Brian was not home on the weekends.

   _____

   _____

   _____

   _____

2. David always sits at the back of the class. For the last month, he has had headaches and his eyes feel tired.

   _____

   _____

   _____

   _____

3. Karen graduated in June. She has not found a job. Her resumé and her cover letter have not been updated. She has had four job interviews, and she was late for all of them.

_____

_____

_____

_____

4. Constable Gauthier arrived at the store. The front door had a broken lock. The cash register was empty. There was no one in the store.

_____

_____

_____

_____

PERFECT PROGRESSIVE MODALS

Perfect progressive modals are formed by adding *have been* and the *-ing* form of the verb to the modal, as in *may have been going, should have been talking, could have been sleeping,* and so on.

> The progressive tenses are not usually used with verbs describing beliefs, knowledge, emotions, the senses, possession, or existence. Review the chart of stative verbs in Appendix A.

Formation

Positive	Negative	Question
I **should have been doing** it.	I **shouldn't have been doing** it.	**Should** I **have been doing** it?
You **must have been doing** it.	You **mustn't have been doing** it.	**Must** you **have been doing** it?
He **may have been doing** it.	He **may not have been doing** it.	**May** he **have been doing** it?
She **might have been doing** it.	She **might not have been doing** it.	**Might** she **have been doing** it?
We **could have been doing** it.	We **couldn't have been doing** it.	**Could** we **have been doing** it?
They **would have been doing** it.	They **wouldn't have been doing** it.	**Would** they **have been doing** it?

EXERCISE 4

Change the following statements with modals into Wh- questions (information questions). Some sentences contain perfect modals, and others contain perfect progressive modals. The information you want to ask about is <u>underlined</u> and in **bold**.

The victims may have been exposed to <u>radiation</u>.

What may the victims have been exposed to?

1. She could have known about **the robbery at the bank**.

   _____

2. Slinger might have been working on a new story **right before he died**.

   _____

3. We must have been sleeping **upstairs** when you arrived last night.

   _____

4. **My sister** should have been finishing her project instead of spending time on Facebook.

   _____

5. He ought to have verified his facts **because he is now liable** for the expenses.

   _____

USE AND MEANING

Perfect progressive modals are the past tense equivalent of present progressive modals. Progressive modals talk about a situation that is in progress right now. The perfect progressive modals talk about a situation that was in progress at a specific time in the past or at the same time that something else was happening.

He must be sleeping now. (action in progress now)

He must have been sleeping at midnight. (action in progress at specific time in the past)

He must have been sleeping when you called him at midnight. (action in progress at the time of the second action: the call)

EXERCISE 5

Fill in the blanks on the right to finish the sentence. For each, make a perfect progressive modal sentence out of the simple progressive modal sentence on the left.

She ought to be going. → She ought to have been going.

Present	Past
1. He must be thinking right now.	He _____ right then.
2. Might she be doing it now?	_____ it last night?
3. You shouldn't be laughing when she is falling.	You _____ when she was falling.
4. Why couldn't we be doing something exciting at this party?	Why _____ something exciting at that party?
5. They may be leaving.	They _____ .
6. She wouldn't be singing.	She _____ .

EXERCISE 6

Read each group of words and phrases, and then rearrange them into a sentence. Do not add, change, or delete words.

the weather forecast / on vacation / they / before leaving / should have checked

They should have checked the weather forecast before leaving on vacation.

1. last night / might have been singing / rang / in the shower / she / when the phone

   _____

2. before / ought to have returned / the school / Sam / the books / he left / to the library

   _____

3. he / the clerk / the packing slip / sent the order / before / should have checked

   _____

4. the phone / James / when / must not have been sleeping / rang

_____

5. he / his tuition / because / Joe / has not paid / financial problems / might have
   been having

_____

COMMUNICATIVE ACTIVITY 2

Difficult Situations

Work in pairs. Discuss the situations below by using positive and negative sentences. Use both perfect modals and perfect progressive modals. Work on a separate sheet of paper, and write four sentences for each situation by using the modals provided.

> **Situation:** Mrs. Wilson was in the hospital. She had to get out of bed. She did not use the call button. She fell and broke her hip. **(must, should, could, would)**
>
> 1. Mrs. Wilson mustn't have wanted to use the call button.
>
> 2. She should have used the call button.
>
> 3. She couldn't have gotten out of bed without help.
>
> 4. She wouldn't have broken her hip if she had used the call button.

Situation 1: Robert got his learner's permit last week, but he needs to drive with a licensed driver. Yesterday, Joelle, Robert's girlfriend, called from the mall and wanted him to pick her up. She had spent all of her money and did not have money for the bus. He took his father's car and went to the mall to get her. He hit a parked car when he was leaving. **(should, might, could, would)**

Situation 2: Isabelle worked at the bank. Her mother was very sick and needed medication that she could not pay for. Isabelle took money from people's accounts to pay for the medication. After a month, Isabelle tried to put the money back but her supervisor asked her what she was doing. Isabelle was frightened and lied to her supervisor. The supervisor told the bank manager. The manager called the police. Isabelle was arrested. **(might, should, ought to, could)**

Situation 3: Danny and Sophie got married last year and moved from Toronto to Ottawa. Danny was transferred back to Toronto six months ago. Danny wanted Sophie to quit her job and come to Toronto with him but Sophie wanted to stay in Ottawa. She said she would see him once a month. Last month, Danny ran into an ex-girlfriend. They realized they were still in love with each other. Danny called Sophie and told her he wanted a divorce. **(ought to, could, should, would)**

BRINGING IT ALL TOGETHER

 ## COMMUNICATIVE ACTIVITY 3

Past Mistakes

Work in pairs. Listen to your partner talk about what mistakes he or she has made in life. As you are listening, try to formulate questions, suggestions, advice, and guesses by using perfect and perfect progressive modals. Discuss your thoughts, and see what she or he says. Switch roles and repeat the exercise.

Do you think you could have . . . ?

What would you have done if . . . ?

You should / shouldn't have . . .

I think you may have . . .

Couldn't you have . . .

Maybe you should have been doing . . . when . . .

I know how you must have . . .

COMMUNICATIVE ACTIVITY 4

World-Class Mistakes

Work in pairs. Read each anecdote below and discuss how the world would have been different without these mistakes. Guess what must have / might have / may have been going on in the minds of those involved when they made the bad decision.

What might have / could have / should have the people involved done differently?

What couldn't have been done differently? Do you think a similar incident might/could happen today?

1. Alexander of Macedon, perhaps the greatest general of ancient times, tried to be the greatest emperor of the largest empire ever seen. But you'll never find a record of the "Alexandrian Empire." This is because Alexander refused, even when suffering from an extended illness, to name an heir. The story is that when his general pressed the dying Alexander for a choice he answered, "to the strongest." More likely he said nothing, dooming his son and empire. After Alexander's death, the empire was divided, resulting in two centuries of war. What may have been the first and greatest opportunity to join the cultures of East and West into a peaceful whole was lost.

2. Christopher Columbus reached America in 1492. However, the profitable discovery that allowed Spain, England, and France to colonize the rich Americas was the result of a mathematical mistake. Columbus had been hoping to reach China and India, and he believed that those countries could be reached by sailing west across the Atlantic. Before leaving, he consulted the best scholars of his time who were mostly Muslims. They gave him the accurate distance to India in the Persian unit *farsang*, equal to three Hashemite miles, which happen to be much longer than the European mile. Columbus converted the numbers to European miles by mistake and concluded that India was much closer. This is why, of course, he called the Indigenous population of America *Indians*.

3. In the early twentieth century, Coca Cola's biggest rival, Pepsi, was close to bankruptcy. Coca Cola was given the chance to buy the company at least three times—but never did. Pepsi has since grown into a serious force in the cola market.

Adapted from Bill Fawcett, "10 of the Greatest Leadership Mistakes in History," *Huffington Post* article and "History's Great Mistakes," *The Telegraph*.

Reading

Read the passage and discuss the questions that follow.

NO MORE REGRETS

Got regrets?

Don't let your busy schedule run your life.

Most of us have regrets. But none of us want to have more of them. Think about how many times you've said (or thought to yourself): "I work way too much . . . ," "I should have followed my heart . . . ," "I really need to keep in better touch with my friends . . . ," "I wish I could take back what I said . . ."

While we can't erase our regrets from the past, we CAN learn how to <u>abolish</u> regret from our lives in the future. This doesn't mean that we won't make mistakes, but instead that we'll be better able to live with the decisions that we make. For instance, one morning last week before leaving for school my son asked me if I would play basketball with him when I got home from work. This couldn't have come at a worse time—I had two pressing deadlines, back-to-back conference calls that would go into the evening, and ten things on my to-do list that were still hanging over my head. Couldn't he see how busy I was? My first <u>inclination</u> was to tell him that we'd have to find another time. But when I looked into his eyes, what I saw was a little boy who just wanted to spend some quality time with his dad and now I was going to turn him away. What was I thinking? It wasn't his fault that I had so much on my plate.

With a little creativity, I worked my schedule around and had a basketball in hand when my son came down to greet me as I walked through the front door. His face lit up as we headed out to the driveway, which doubled as a <u>makeshift</u> half-court. We played "horse" and it was clear my son had been practicing. Although it was a little embarrassing to get beaten three times in a row by an 11-year-old, it was probably the most fun I've had in over a month.

To avoid the regret of not spending enough meaningful time with the people you care about most in your life, consider the following:

- <u>Strive</u> to balance the priorities that compete for your time.
- Get creative in how you schedule your day.
- Block out "quality time" and stick to those commitments.

While you can't always put life on hold, don't lose hold of what—and who—matters most to you.

Now it's your turn: think of a time when you've regretted not spending quality time with someone important in your life. What was the impact on your relationship with this individual? How did you work through this regret, if at all? What will you do differently or better to avoid this regret going forward?

Source: Marc Muchnick, PhD, "No More Regrets!" *Psychology Today*

DISCUSSION

Write down four things that you do to maintain balance in your life. In a group of four, discuss your ideas. How close do you come to maintaining a good balance in your life compared with the other three people in the group? Did anyone have ideas similar to yours? Did anyone have ideas that you would like to try? Take notes from your discussion.

 ## COMMUNICATIVE ACTIVITY 5

My Regrets

Reread the last paragraph of the reading passage. The author asks four questions. Think about them, and write a short composition (200 words) discussing your past regrets about how you handled a relationship. Refer to your notes from the group discussion. Use different perfect modals in your writing.

Tom Thomson 1877-1917 painter/peintre
CANADA ~~12~~

Listening

🔊 Track 05

THE DEATH OF TOM THOMSON—STILL A MYSTERY?

Listen to the audio. In this clip, you will hear an interview conducted by Steve Paikin with Roy MacGregor about the death of Canadian artist Tom Thomson. As you listen to the clip, take notes, and answer the following questions.

COMPREHENSION

1. How old was Tom Thomson when he died?

   _____

2. Was Thomson a member of the Group of Seven? (short answer)

   _____

3. Where was Thomson's body found?

   _____

4. What were the mysterious circumstances surrounding his death?

   _____

5. According to Roy MacGregor, how did Thomson get the mark on the left side of his head?

   _____

6. What does Roy MacGregor hope for regarding Tom Thomson and the mystery surrounding his death?

   _____

DISCUSSION

Work in pairs. Together, review the theories outlined in the audio for how Tom Thomson died. Then, one-by-one, take the theories and write them as complete sentences by using perfect modals, perfect progressive modals, or any of the alternative expressions for perfect modals. Exchange your work with your partner and edit the work for mistakes.

Writing

Write a short composition about something that you did in your life that you did not want to do. Were there options or alternatives from which you could choose? Why did you do it? What would you have done differently? What should you have done? Your composition should be 200–300 words long.

CHAPTER REVIEW

Summary

Modals used with the perfect and perfect progressive tenses can express possibility, certainty, advisability, or willingness.

- To form perfect modals, add *have* and the past participle of the verb to the modal.

    He could have talked.

- To form perfect progressive modals, add *have been* and the *-ing* form of the verb to the modal.

    He could have been talking.

- To change these forms into negative, just as with simple modals, add *not* right after the modal.

    He could not have talked

    He could not have been talking.

- To change these forms into questions, just as with simple modals, invert the subject and the verb.

    He could have talked. → Could he have talked?

    He could have been talking. → Could he have been talking?

- Perfect modal forms can refer to something that was possible (it could have happened), or they can refer to an unreal situation.

    He must have gone. (He most probably went.)

    He should have gone. (He certainly didn't go)

EXERCISE 1

Correct the formation errors in the following sentences. All sentences are wrong.

1. You should had included more information about your project.

2. The class would have been studied the assignment during the day.

3. They could be waiting for the train when you saw them.

4. She might have forgot about our lunch date today.

5. They might have been misunderstanding the instructions.

EXERCISE 2

Correct the usage errors (wrong modal verb used) in the following sentences. All sentences are logically wrong.

1. I told him to feed the dog, but he didn't. He must have listened to me.

2. I'm pretty sure she closed the door. She may have closed it.

3. This is impossible! An ordinary man might not have lifted such a weight.

4. I'm pretty sure she was at home yesterday. She should have been home.

5. If I had locked the door, the thief won't have taken my laptop.

EXERCISE 3

Complete each sentence with the appropriate modal and verb tense (simple, present progressive, perfect, or perfect progressive). There might be more than one correct answer for some blanks.

1. You _____ (work) hard if you want to succeed.

2. Honey! _____ you _____ (study) for the test now instead of playing games?

3. Sandra _____ (take) the bus to the airport last night. I'm not really sure.

4. We _____ (give) you a call when we get back. Who knows?

5. At least you _____ (mention) that you were bringing friends home!

6. He _____ (drive, negative) the getaway car at the time of the robbery because he was giving me driving lessons then.

7. I'm sorry! I _____ (write) to you sooner.

8. Look! Everywhere is wet. It _____ (rain).

9. What's that awful smell coming from the kitchen? Something _____ (burn).

10. I'm not sure but he _____ (drink) when I called him. He was babbling nonsense and he didn't make sense at all.

Active and Passive 1

OVERVIEW

- There are two voices in English sentence structure: the active and the passive.

- The active is used most often. In the active voice, the subject is in control of the action, so the active verb has more impact.

- The passive is used in certain circumstances:

  - to emphasize the object or the recipient of the action

  - to avoid stating who or what is doing the action

  - to maintain objectivity

- The passive is found most often in news, legal, and scientific reports.

Warm-up

Work in small groups. You have four minutes to answer as many of the following questions as you can. If you have a smartphone or computer, you can use it to search for answers on the Internet. The group with the most correct answers wins.

1. How many *Star Trek* movies **have been released** to date?

2. Which chess piece **was originally called** "the elephant"?

3. Which acid **can be found** in vinegar?

4. What religious book **is divided** into 114 chapters called *suras*?

5. Which actor **was accidentally killed** on the set while his movie *The Crow* **was being filmed**?

6. There are bumps on the tongue that carry the taste buds. What **are they called**?

7. What is the word we use in English to describe what **is being done** to the food in the top picture?

8. What **was** the brontosaurus **renamed** in 1903, when it **was discovered** that the original fossils of that dinosaur **had been given** an earlier name?

9. Which famous novel by Mark Twain begins with this notice: "Persons attempting to find a motive in this narrative **will be prosecuted**; persons attempting to find a moral in it **will be banished**; persons attempting to find a plot in it **will be shot**."

10. Why **are** some verbs **marked** in bold in this quiz?

Some questions were based on *Ken Jennings's Trivia Almanac*.

SWITCHING ROLES: AGENTS AND TARGETS, SUBJECTS AND OBJECTS

In the active voice, the agent (or the doer of the action) is more important than the target (the receiver of the action), so the agent comes at the beginning of the sentence (subject position). Look at the following examples. The agents (*the ladder* and *the dog*) are in subject position. The objects, *the pedestrian* and *the man*, receive or are affected by the action.

subject	+	verb	+	object
The falling ladder		hit		the pedestrian.
AGENT				TARGET

subject	+	verb	+	object
The dog		bit		the man.
AGENT				TARGET

In the passive voice, the target (the receiver) becomes the subject because it is more important. The targets (*the pedestrian* and *the man*) are now in the subject position, but they are still receiving the action. The passive verb is formed with the appropriate tense of the verb *be* + **the past participle** of the original verb.

Formation

SIMPLE TENSES

	Active	Passive
present	He **fixes** the windows.	The windows **are fixed** (by him).
past	He **fixed** the windows.	The windows **were fixed** (by him).
future (*will*)	He **will fix** the windows.	The windows **will be fixed** (by him).
future (*be going to*)	He **is going to fix** the windows.	The windows **are going to be fixed** (by him).

- Only transitive verbs, that is, verbs with direct objects, can be used in the passive voice.

    The cat **chased** the mouse.

    The verb *chase* is transitive. *The mouse* is its direct object. → The mouse was chased by the cat.

    They **went** to school.

(The verb *go* is intransitive and cannot have a direct object and, therefore, cannot be changed to the passive.)

- The verb *be* must be in the same tense as the active verb.
- The new passive subject must agree with the verb.
- To form the passive structure, change an object pronoun to a subject pronoun.

    They warned **him.** → **He** was warned (by them).

- To create a question, since the main verb has more than one word, invert the order of the subject and the verb.

    Regulations **are governed** by the provinces.

    Are regulations **governed** by the provinces?

- To create a negative statement in the passive, the word *not* is placed after the first *word of the passive verb group*.

  The provinces do not govern regulations.

  Regulations are not governed by the provinces.

- If the agent is needed to form the passive, use *by* to introduce it. Note that in the charts, parentheses ( ) are used to indicate that the agent is not necessary or is not desirable.

PROGRESSIVE AND PERFECT TENSES

	Active	Passive
present	He **is fixing** the windows.	The windows **are being fixed** (by him).
past	He **was fixing** the windows.	The windows **were being fixed** (by him).
present	He **has fixed** the windows.	The windows **have been fixed** (by him).
past	The workers **had rejected** the offer.	The offer **had been rejected** (by the workers).
future (*will*)	He **will have fixed** the windows.	The windows **will have been fixed** (by him).

The perfect progressive form is rarely used in the passive voice since it is too awkward.

MODALS

	Active	Passive
simple	**He should fix** the windows.	The windows **should be fixed** (by him).
perfect	He **should have fixed** the windows.	The windows **should have been fixed** (by him).

All the modals follow the same pattern as in the chart above. Review the modals in Chapters 4 and 5 if necessary.

Remember that we must use the auxiliary verb *do*, *does*, or *did* to form questions and negatives with *have to*.

He doesn't have to fix windows. → Windows don't have to be fixed.

Does he have to fix the window? → Does the window have to be fixed?

When changing an active sentence to the passive voice, the target of the verb becomes the new subject.

Step 1: Identify the target. Ask yourself who or what received the action.

The dog bit **the man.** → *The man* is the new subject.

Step 2: Identify the tense of the active verb.

The dog **bit** the man. → *Bit* is in the simple past.

Step 3: Use the same tense of the verb *be* + the past participle of the active verb.

The man **was bitten** by the dog. (simple past + the past participle)

Step 4: Check that the new subject and verb have the correct agreement. For example, if the target is plural and the agent was singular, check the agreement in the affected tenses.

He has delivered the packages. → The packages have been delivered.

EXERCISE 1

Change all the sentences in the following passage from the active to the passive. Work on a separate sheet of paper.

The paramedics <u>rushed</u> <u>the injured worker</u> to the hospital.

<u>The injured worker</u> <u>was rushed</u> to the hospital (by the paramedics).

The police found the body in the wooded area near the park. The police have identified the victim as John Smith. His family had reported him missing a week ago. The authorities suspect foul play. A spokesperson for the police will provide more details at a news conference later today.

When changing a passive sentence to the active voice, the doer or agent in control of the action becomes the new subject.

Step 1: Identify the new subject. Ask yourself who or what is in control of the action. If there is a phrase with *by* + a noun, that noun is the subject. If no agent is stated, create a logical one.

The man was bitten **by the dog.** → *The dog* is the active subject.

The victim was taken to the hospital. What is a logical subject?

→ **The paramedics** took the victim to the hospital.

Step 2: Identify the tense of the verb *be*.

The man **was** bitten by the dog. → *Was* is in the simple past.

Step 3: Change the past participle of the active verb to the same tense as the verb *be*.

The dog **bit** the man. (simple past of the verb *bite*)

Step 4: Check that the new subject and verb have the correct agreement.

EXERCISE 2

Change all the sentences in the following passage from the passive to the active. Create a doer or agent if necessary.

The instructions should have been followed.

They should have followed the instructions.

Although the samples of the concrete had been sent for testing, the results would not be known for three days. To maintain workplace safety, the construction site has been shut down until then. The perimeter excavation could be continued, but the interior construction had to be stopped.

EXERCISE 3

Fill in the blanks with the passive voice of the verb in parentheses. Use the correct form and tense of the verb.

The investigation _____ (conduct) by the Food Inspection Agency last year.

The investigation **was conducted** by the Food Inspection Agency last year.

The hearing into the alleged criminal negligence case against the water treatment plant manager 1 _____ (postpone) until next month. The defence team had asked the judge for a longer postponement. The attorneys claimed that they 2 _____ (give, not) sufficient time to prepare their client's defence before the hearing was to begin. However, their request 3 _____ (deny). The manager 4 _____ (charge) on September 15 with criminal negligence causing death after the authorities had concluded their investigation into how the contaminated water got into the town's water system. The new start date for the hearing 5 _____ (announce) soon.

✳ COMMUNICATIVE ACTIVITY 1

Dictionary Definitions

Work in pairs. Choose three to five words or expressions from the list on the next page. Come up with definitions for them. Try to use both the active and the passive voice. The first one is done for you.

fire safety: Precautions that **are taken** to prevent or reduce the likelihood of a fire.

- ~~fire safety~~
- traffic / road signs
- air conditioners
- safety shoes
- legislations
- helmet
- blood glucose meter
- vaccines
- pliers
- Taser
- hair dyes
- pesticides

USE

The passive voice has three main uses. It can be used to

- emphasize the target
- avoid stating who or what is doing the action
- maintain an objective view

1. Sometimes we want to emphasize the target or emphasize the action itself more than the agent:

    The accident victim was taken to the hospital. (emphasis on the receiver or target)

    Sometimes we want to emphasize the result:

    At least 20 homes were destroyed by the wildfire. (emphasis on the result)

2. Sometimes we want or need to avoid identifying the agent

    - because the agent is not known or is not important, or it is not appropriate or desirable to do so
    - to avoid either placing blame or taking responsibility for an action

        The equipment was stolen during the blackout. (unknown agent)

        The mail was delivered at 12:00 noon. (not important)

        John was held responsible for the accident. (not desirable to say by whom)

        An accounting error was made in the last statement. (no blame or responsibility)

3. Sometimes we want to create an objective or authoritative tone.

    Safety guidelines must be followed. (authority)

    The soil samples will be tested for contamination. (objectivity)

RESTRICTIONS

- Certain transitive verbs cannot be changed to the passive voice even though they have a direct object. They become awkward and illogical.

  I have two friends. (correct)
  ~~Two friends are had by me.~~ (incorrect)

  Sarah resembles her mother. (correct)
  ~~Her mother is resembled by Sarah.~~ (incorrect)

- Other verbs that cannot be used in the passive include the following:

  become   cost   equal   fit   lack   look   like   mean   suit

- For some other verbs, the context determines whether they can be used in the passive or not.

  hold:

  She held her nose. (correct)

  ~~Her nose was held.~~ (incorrect)

  but

  Frank Burns holds the world record for that event. (correct)

  The world record for that event is held by Frank Burns. (correct)

  contains:

  The pitcher contains water. (correct)

  ~~Water is contained by the pitcher.~~ (incorrect)

  but

  The dam contained the flood water. (correct)

  The flood water was contained by the dam. (correct)

- Do not use the passive voice with the imperative. The passive voice makes commands seem unclear and archaic.

  Be gone from here. (sounds Shakespearian)

  Go away from here. (sounds more normal and direct)

EXERCISE 4   *Home work.*

Change the following sentences from the active to the passive or from the passive to the active. If it is not possible to change the verb from the active to the passive, briefly explain why. Review the steps listed on page 99.

All accidents **must be reported** to the manager.

Workers **must report** all accidents to the manager.

Even limited exposure to asbestos can become a serious health issue. (cannot be passive)

1. Safety regulations must be followed at all times on a construction site.

   cannot to be active, to long)

2. His supervisor approved his request for sick leave. *Act*

Supervisor approved his sick leave request.

3. The inspector had four recommendations for improving the plant's security.

4 recommendations where made to improve plan security.

4. Had the safety of the crowd been put at risk by the actions of the security officers?

the Security officers put the crowd surety ut risk.

5. The cause of the train derailment is being investigated.

train derailments cause is being investigated.

6. The approaching hurricane will probably cause a lot of damage.

A lot of damage will probably be caused by the approaching hurricane.

7. The hospital allows visitors from 11:00 AM to 8:00 PM every day. → visitors are allows from 11:00 am to 8:00 by the hospital.

8. Should safety procedures be reviewed every year?

Safety procedures should be reviewed every year

9. The new machinery comes with an extensive instruction manual.

A extensive instruction manual comes with a new machine

10. Some people did not use the emergency exits during the fire drill.

the emerging exists during the fire

EXERCISE 5

Fill in the blanks with either the active or the passive voice, whichever works. Use the correct form and tense of the verb to emphasize the result.

While the boys _____ (play) ball hockey, they _____
(almost, hit) by a speeding car.

While the boys **were playing** ball hockey, they **were almost hit** by a speeding car.

I have to buy a new handlebar for my bicycle. It $_1$ _is change_ (damage)
by the accident I had yesterday. While I $_2$ _was riding_ (ride) home
from school yesterday, I $_3$ _was nearly run over_ (nearly, run) over by a bus.
As I was trying to avoid being hit, I $_4$ _lost_ (lose) control and
ended up in the ditch. The bus driver $_5$ _did not stop_ (not, stop) to see

if I was all right. I went to the emergency room at the hospital near my place. I
was examine ₆ _____ (examine) by the doctor on duty. I ₇ _____ *was told*
(tell) that nothing ₈ _____ *was broken* (break), fortunately. When I got home,
I phoned the bus company. The person in charge said an investigator would take
my statement and that my bike ₉ _____ *will be repair* (repair). However, I think
the bus driver ₁₀ _____ *will be charge* (charge) by the police.

EXERCISE 6

There is an error involving the passive structure or its use in each of the following
sentences. Correct the mistakes.

Ten dollars is cost by that hamburger. (Incorrect. Cost cannot be used in the passive.)

That hamburger costs ten dollars.

1. The package has be shipped by courier.

    _____

2. The health and safety responsibilities are going to be enforce by the manager.

    _____

3. Two complaints have the manager.

    two complaints have been giving
    to the manager

4. A thorough assessment must be did by the inspector.

    A thorough _____

5. A structural engineer was become by my sister.

    _____

✾ COMMUNICATIVE ACTIVITY 2

Trivia Game

Work in two teams. Based on what you have learned in this grammar section, use the
active or the passive voice to write 10 definitions that will describe 10 different objects or
places. The sentences will be used as quiz questions for the other team. Take turns giving
the definitions. The team with the most correct answers wins.

This gem resembles a diamond.   Answer: zirconium

**It is a continent that was discovered by Christopher Columbus.
Answer: North America**

USING *BY* AND THE DOER OR AGENT

The doer or agent in the *by* phrase in a passive sentence is the active subject in the active sentence. In most cases, 80 percent of the time, the doer is not stated in the passive structure.

In passive sentences, use *by* and the agent if it adds important or necessary information or if the sentence is illogical or does not make sense without it. Use it to place the same emphasis on the receiver of the action as on the agent in control of the action.

Frank Burns holds the world record for that event.
The world record for that event is held by Frank Burns. (important and necessary)

His own carelessness caused his injury.
His injury was caused by his own carelessness. (both equally important)

Do not use *by* and the agent if

- it doesn't add any necessary information or clarification
- the agent is unknown, doesn't want to be known, or is already understood through the context

The medical examiner will conduct an autopsy to determine the cause of death.
An autopsy will be conducted to determine the cause of death. (understood)

Someone broke into the lab last night.
The lab was broken into last night. (unknown agent)

EXERCISE 7

Change the following sentences from the active to the passive. Eliminate the *by* + agent when possible.

Francisco prepared detailed instructions for installing the transformer.

Detailed instructions for installing the transformer were prepared.

1. Someone should have reported the chemical spill to the authorities.

_____

2. The supervisor's lack of action caused the incident.

_____

3. The workers will have completed all the work by the end of next week.

_____

4. How should we write the safety manual?

_____

5. Careful planning could have prevented the accident.

_____

6. The inspectors have assessed all the damage.

_____

7. We have established clear safety procedures for the workplace.

_____

8. The company must remove all the contaminated material from the building.

_____

9. Before they found the source of the poor air quality, several employees had reported unusual health problems.

_____

10. The municipal building inspector will do the hazard assessment tomorrow.

_____

COMMUNICATIVE ACTIVITY 3

Is the Agent Necessary?

Work in pairs. Use the following words to make sentences in the passive voice. Determine whether or not the *by* and agent is necessary. Briefly discuss why.

this shirt / make

This shirt was made in Canada. (The *by* + agent part is not necessary, as it is already understood through context.)

the light bulb / invent

The light bulb was invented by Henry Woodward and Mathew Evans. (Here, the *by* + agent part is necessary because it contains important information.)

1. Poland / surround

_____

2. my bike / steal / yesterday

_____

3. my neighbour's cat / chase / now

_____

4. Volkswagens / produce

_____

5. *Romeo and Juliet* / write

_____

BRINGING IT ALL TOGETHER

 ## COMMUNICATIVE ACTIVITY 4

Scrambled Parts

Work in pairs. You will be given two sets of jumbled words, one for you and one for your partner. One set consists of positive or negative sentences, and the second consists of questions asking for additional information.

   Student A forms the sentence from his or her jumbles. Student B finds the appropriate question from among his or her jumbles. Finally, together they think of a possible answer.

Student A: to / the / submitted / essays / be / have

The essays have to be submitted.

Student B: the / have / essays/ when / to / do / submitted / be

When do the essays have to be submitted?

Student A and B: The essays have to be submitted by Friday.

Jumbled Sentences

1. must / the / be / bills / paid

2. of / students / tested / usually / the / the / are / end / at / semester

3. sent / letter / was / the / yesterday

4. job / has / for / been / Hyan / hired / the

5. informed / Paulina / been / had not

6. now / renovated / the / is / house / being

7. until / be / the / later / dinner / not /served / will

Jumbled Questions

1. being / house / renovated / why / the / is

2. the / why / end / semester / students / tested / at / usually / are / of / the

3. Paulina / what / about / had not / informed / been

4. has / what / he / job / hired / for / been

5. yesterday / was / whom / letter / to / sent / the

6. bills / paid / what / be / what

7. served / when / the / will / dinner / be

✵ COMMUNICATIVE ACTIVITY 5

What Are the Steps?

Work in pairs. First, using the active voice, write down two or three steps that you should or must take for the following tasks. Then, rewrite the same steps by using the passive voice. The hints for the possible steps are in the parentheses.

writing a research essay (research, organization, references)

Active voice	Passive voice
1. You should research the topic.	1. The topic should be researched.
2. You have to organize your points well.	2. The points have to be well organized.
3. You must reference the sources.	3. The sources must be referenced.

- making a cup of tea (water, a tea bag)
- planting vegetables (soil, weeds, seeds, water)
- changing a tire (a jack, a spare tire, a safety cone, a wrench)
- sending an email with an attachment (a message, a document / file, an attachment)
- setting up a table at a restaurant (a tablecloth, dishes, silverware, napkins)
- colouring hair (hair product, protective gloves, dye, timer)
- arresting a person (identification, search, person's rights, handcuffs)
- extinguishing a fire (water, a fire extinguisher)

Reading

Read the passage and answer the questions that follow.

HARD TIMES

In 1839, Charles Dickens, whose popular novel *Oliver Twist* had just been published, took a trip to Manchester, a city in northwest England. It was a trip that was to change his life and result in one of his most bitter and <u>controversial</u> novels, *Hard Times*.

In Manchester, Dickens was taken to see cotton mills typical of those that had <u>sprung up</u> in northern England as a result of the Industrial Revolution. The invention of the steam engine in the late eighteenth century was a major force behind this "revolution." Power became accessible and inexpensive, and factories boomed with production.

There was a darker side to this productivity, however. The methods of organizing the workers for maximum efficiency often led to miserable working conditions: long hours, hard work, dangerous machinery. Young children were often put to work, despite laws that were meant to prevent the abuse of minors. Workers were housed in <u>slums</u> with <u>filthy</u> conditions. Factories poured poisonous smoke into the atmosphere, darkening the skies and threatening the health of anyone who lived in the town.

Laws were passed that offered some protection to these workers, but factory owners often disregarded them, and the laws were difficult to enforce. So the dangerous machinery and poor <u>sanitation</u> continued, and many owners felt they had no responsibility to their employees except to pay them wages that were established by the laws of supply and demand. <u>Prosperity</u>, so said many in charge, depended on high profits and inexpensive labor.

The basis for much of this abuse, according to writers such as Dickens and the essayist and historian Thomas Carlyle (to whom *Hard Times* is dedicated), was the political philosophy of Utilitarianism. Utilitarianism had its roots in the laissez-faire doctrine of the economist Adam Smith, expressed in his book *The Wealth of Nations* (1776). Laissez-faire means, in the original French, "leave alone," and Smith's book detailed his opposition to governmental <u>interference</u> in the economy of a nation.

Smith's ideas were elaborated by the philosopher Jeremy Bentham, the founder of Utilitarianism, and then further developed by the economist and philosopher John Stuart Mill. In simple terms, the Utilitarians sought "the greatest happiness for the greatest number"—in other words, whatever was correct for the majority, particularly in regard to economic profit, was thought to be correct for everyone. The Utilitarians brought about important social reforms.

Yet, as Dickens and others pointed out, Utilitarianism was subject to abuse, particularly where the poor minority were concerned. In <u>striving</u> for greater profits that would benefit the nation, management often <u>exploited</u> the workers, and politicians <u>winked at</u> their exploitation. In *Hard Times*, Gradgrind Sr. is portrayed as a strict Utilitarian, who practices his philosophy at home and in the school he governs. Like others of his kind, he sees little reality beyond profit and loss.

After visiting Manchester, Dickens wrote to a friend: "I went to Manchester and saw the worst cotton mill. And then I saw the best . . . There was no great difference between them." The workers made a lasting impression on Dickens. He wrote: ". . . what I have seen has disgusted me and astonished me beyond all measure. I mean to strike the heaviest blow in my power for these unfortunate creatures."

For Dickens, striking the "heaviest blow" meant using his pen. Few writers have ever been so popular in their lifetimes. His work combines elements of hilarious and thrilling entertainment with sharp condemnations of society, and many readers believe he blended these elements more skillfully than any other novelist in the English language—before or since.

Adapted from Michael Adams, *Charles Dickens's Hard Times*.

COMPREHENSION

1. What had just happened in 1839 right before Dickens was taken to see cotton mills in Manchester?

_____

2. Why did so many cotton mills appear at this period in history?

_____

3. What were the working conditions and living conditions like for mill workers?

_____

4. Were there any new laws to protect workers? Were any laws enforced?

_____

5. How were the workers' wages determined?

_____

6. Define *Utilitarianism*. Explain the role of Adam Smith, Jeremy Bentham, and John Stuart Mill in the development of the philosophy of Utilitarianism.

_____

7. According to Dickens, what was the problem with Utilitarianism?

_____

8. What did Dickens decide to do after visiting the factories in Manchester? How?

_____

9. Who is Gradgrind Sr.? What does he symbolize?

_____

10. According to many readers, what has Dickens done more skillfully than any other novelist in the English language?

_____

ANALYZING THE READING PASSAGE

Reread the passage. This time, <u>underline</u> all passive structures in the text. Why do you think the author has used the passive so frequently? Refer to page 101 for uses of the passive.

Listening

🔊 Track 06

PUTTING THE SPOTLIGHT ON WORK-RELATED ASTHMA

In this clip, Dr. Michael Pysklywec, an Occupational Health Physician, explains in an interview what work-related asthma is, who's most at risk and how this condition is diagnosed. Listen to the audio once or twice, and answer the following questions.

COMPREHENSION

Part 1

1. Who is the guest on this program? Where does he work?

   _____

2. How common is asthma in Canada?

   _____

3. Name three characteristics of asthma.

   _____

4. What percentage of adult asthma is work-related?

   _____

5. Which of the following industries was not mentioned as a high-risk environment for asthma?

   a. baking
   b. office work
   c. hairdressing
   d. agriculture
   e. health care

6. What are some of the symptoms of asthma?

_____

7. What are the three steps involved in diagnosing work-related asthma?

_____

8. Can asthma be cured? Explain.

_____

9. Listen to Dr. Mike's advice about prevention and fill in the chart below:

	Definition	Actions to Be Taken
Primary Prevention		
Secondary Prevention		

10. What four steps can be taken by employers to ensure workplace safety regarding asthma? Which step is the most important one?

_____

Part 2

Listen to the audio one more time. Several passive structures are used during this interview. List 10 sentences in the clip that contain the passive voice.

Writing

Walk around your classroom and check the items on the following **Classroom Safety Audit** checklist. If the rule has been observed, put a check mark next to it. If not, mark it with an X.

Also look for any other workplace health and safety hazards that you have learned about in this chapter or that you can think of. If you do not know the answers to some questions, ask your teacher or other school authorities.

Once you have finished, write a short audit report (300–350 words) by using the passive voice to report what has been done and what needs to be done. Also, make recommendations as to what can, may, should, and must be done to make your school and classroom safer and healthier places.

Regular Classroom Safety Checklist

General

1. Do windows open easily and stay open according to their design? ☐

2. Is air quality, temperature, and ventilation acceptable to meet applicable standards? ☐

3. Are ventilation and heating ducts kept unobstructed by books, paper, and so on? ☐

4. Are ceiling tiles in place, unbroken, and with no sign of mould? ☐

5. Are the ceiling, walls, and floor free from water leaks? ☐

6. Are floor tiles or carpeting securely fastened to reduce trip hazards? ☐

7. Are floors free from slip, trip, and fall hazards? ☐

8. Are audiovisual screens and maps securely suspended by using fittings designed for that purpose? ☐

9. Are shelves or shelving units firmly anchored to the wall? ☐

10. Storage of all items should follow these guidelines: heavy objects on low shelves, light objects on high shelves, and breakable objects, such as glass items, on low shelves. ☐

11. Are step stools or small ladders available for reaching stored items from high shelves? ☐

12. Is storage on top of wall-mounted cupboards limited to lightweight objects, such as empty boxes? ☐

13. Do paper cutters have guards in place, and is the torsion spring adjusted to hold the blade up when it is released? ☐

14. Are there first aid stations and trained first aiders available? ☐

15. Do all staff members know where the stations are located, and are the trained staff locations identified? ☐

16. Is there an asbestos management program, and do all staff members know where the asbestos log is kept in the school? ☐

Fire Safety

1. Are legible fire exit and route signs in appropriate locations? ☐

2. Is there a fire safety plan, and is the teacher aware of the content and location of the plan? ☐

3. Are ceilings or exit doors free of combustible material, such as artwork, posters, paper, and so on? As a guideline, no more than 20 percent of the total wall surface (including boards, cupboards, windows, and so on) are to be covered with combustible materials. ☐

4. Where there is an exit door, is there a clear path through the classroom furniture? As a rule of thumb, the width of the clear path should be the same as the width of the door(s). ☐

Electrical

1. Are CSA or Electrical Safety Authority approval labels on all electrical equipment? ☐

2. Are there ground pins on three wire electrical plugs? ☐

3. Are electrical outlets, cover plates, and wall switches secure and undamaged? ☐

4. Are multi-use extension cords equipped with power bars? ☐

Source: Education Safety Association of Ontario, 2001

CHAPTER REVIEW

Summary

- Although the active voice is used most often, the passive, found frequently in news, legal, and scientific reports, is used in certain circumstances: to emphasize the target or the recipient of the action, to avoid stating who or what is doing the action, or to maintain objectivity.

- Only transitive verbs, verbs with direct objects, can be used in the passive voice. However, certain verbs cannot be used in the passive even though they have a direct object.

- Review the steps to take when changing sentences from the active to the passive or the passive to the active.

- Use by + the agent only if the phrase adds important or necessary information or if the sentence is illogical or does not make sense without it. The by + agent is also used to place the same emphasis on the receiver of the action as on the agent in control of the action.

EXERCISE 1

Fill in the blanks with the correct tense of the verbs in parentheses. Both the active and the passive will be needed for this task.

The chemicals _____ (mix) together an hour ago.

The chemicals **were mixed** together an hour ago.

Recently, when the pipes in the kitchen started to leak, my roommate 1 _____ (decide) it was a great opportunity to practise his plumbing repair skills. Unfortunately, we realized too late that we should have called a plumber. The drainpipe seemed to be the source of the leak. Indeed, the pipe 2 _____ (crack) somehow.

The necessary parts and tools 3 _____ (purchase) from a local hardware store. A couple of hours later, the leaky part of the drain 4 _____ (replace). My roommate was satisfied that the job had been done well, and some money 5 _____ (save). When I turned on the tap so he could see if the drain was sealed, he 6 _____ (lie) on his back with his head under the sink. In a matter of seconds, he yelled at me to shut it off, fast. He quickly 7 _____ (get) himself out from under the sink. He was shocked and completely soaked. There was another leak, this time in the hot water pipe. The water was so hot he 8 _____ (scald). To add to the problem, the next section of the drain 9 _____ (install) properly either. Since it 10 _____ (be) already nine in the evening, we decided to call a pro to fix it the next day.

EXERCISE 2

Change the following sentences from the active to the passive or from the passive to the active. If it is not possible to change the verb from the active to the passive, briefly explain why. If possible, eliminate the *by* + agent phrase in the passive sentences. Review the steps in the Formation section before you begin, if necessary.

Any environmental issues **should be reported** to the manager.

Workers **should report** any environmental issues to the manager.

Exposure to strong chemicals **can become** a serious health issue. (The verb *become* cannot be passive.)

1. The emergency procedures were established in case of a fire.

   _____

2. In the event of a spill, you should use the biohazard spill kit installed beside the door of each lab.

   _____

3. Safety training has been provided for all the workers.

   _____

4. Emergency crews must follow the HAZMAT protocols.

   _____

5. The report contains five recommendations for improving our safety procedures.

   _____

EXERCISE 3

There are five errors involving the passive structure in the following passage. Based on what you have learned in this chapter, correct each error.

The following safety rules must been observed at all times in the science lab.

1. Protective glasses and clothing must be worn.

2. Food and beverages is not permitted.

3. Personal items should be leave on the counter beside the door.

4. All equipment should be turned off at the end of the session.

5. Each station has to cleaned and disinfected at the end of the session.

6. Safety procedures are find in the Safety and Hazards Manual and must be followed in the event of an accident.

Active and Passive 2— Complex Structures

OVERVIEW

This chapter goes beyond the regular passive verb forms that you learned in Chapter 6 and focuses on complex passive structures, such as grammatical structures that follow passive verbs, infinitive and gerund passive forms, passive participles, passive with *get*, and causative passive.

Warm-up

Work in pairs. Ask and answer the following questions. Discuss your responses. It is ideal if the two partners are not from the same culture or region.

- What are some of the gestures that are considered rude in your culture?
- Tell me about one thing that is done in other cultures but would make you feel embarrassed if you were to do it.
- What kind of a person is normally regarded as a role model in your culture?
- What are some of the things that you think women are not supposed to do?
- In your culture, is it generally believed that men and women are equal?
- Are there any foods or beverages that are consumed in other countries but are not to be consumed in your culture?
- How do you feel about being kissed on the cheek by a person of your gender?
- Is there anything that is accepted as normal behaviour in other cultures but if you did it in your culture you would get arrested?

GRAMMATICAL STRUCTURES THAT FOLLOW PASSIVE VERBS

Formation

Structure	Example Sentences
passive verbs + nouns	Dan **was considered** <u>a loser</u> by his own family.
passive verbs + adjectives	Last week, Dan **was found** <u>drunk</u> at a local casino.
passive verbs followed by infinitives	Dan **is known** <u>to be</u> very irresponsible with money.
passive verbs followed by *that* clauses	I **was told** <u>that</u> Dan is not very good with loans.

PASSIVE VERBS + NOUNS/ADJECTIVES

Look at the following sentences:

They consider <u>him</u>   <u>a loser.</u>   → He is considered a loser.

        object   noun complement

They consider   <u>him</u>   <u>crazy.</u>   → He is considered crazy.
            object   adjective complement

Transitive verbs that take an object + a noun or an adjective complement can be used in the passive verb + noun / adjective pattern. These verbs are labelled as [VN-ADJ] and [VN-N] in Oxford Learner Dictionaries.

EXERCISE 1

Change the following sentences into the passive voice.

Manufacturers **make** products much more durable. → Products **are made** much more durable.

1. He **found** Mary unconscious on the floor.

   _____

2. Ancient Greeks did not **regard** women **as** citizens.

   _____

3. Banting and Best **called** the newly discovered hormone insulin.

   _____

4. Today, people **see** Terry Fox **as** a great Canadian hero.

   _____

5. The court **presumes** all people innocent until it **proves** them guilty of crime.

   _____

COMMUNICATIVE ACTIVITY 1

Canadian Trivia

Work in pairs. Take the following Canadian trivia quiz. Then compare your answers with those of other pairs.

1. He is **considered** the father of the Canadian health-care system.

2. This Canadian island is **regarded** as the fifth largest in the world.

3. This female short-story writer is **called** the Canadian Chekhov.

4. She was the first woman **appointed** as Canada's Governor General.

5. She was **elected** as Ontario's first female premier.

PASSIVE VERBS FOLLOWED BY INFINITIVES

Verbs that are followed by an object and an infinitive can often be turned into passive verbs followed by infinitives.

Look at the following example:

subject + verb + object + infinitive	→ subject + passive verb + infinitive
He told me to leave.	→ I was told to leave.

Note: Verbs such as *see*, *hear*, and *make* that are not followed by infinitives in active mode can also be used in passive + infinitive structures. Look at the following example:

I **have** often **heard** them **yell** at their son. → They **have** often **been heard to yell** at their son.

EXERCISE 2

Change the following sentences to the passive voice.

1. They **asked** the prime minister to step down.

   _____

2. We **expect** leaders to be courageous.

   _____

3. My people **have chosen** me to speak for them.

   _____

4. They **made** him do stupid things.

   _____

5. I **saw** the suspects leave together.

   _____

COMMUNICATIVE ACTIVITY 2

Q&A

Work in pairs. First, work separately without showing your work to your partner. Student A makes six half-questions in the passive, using the verbs in the box on the next page. Student B makes six funny or unusual infinitive structures of his or her choice. When done, combine your work to form six complete questions. The result will sometimes be very funny. Exchange the questions with another pair to answer.

| tell | expect | choose | make | hear | see |

Verb: ask

Student A: Have you ever been asked . . . / Student B: to kiss a frog

Result: Have you ever been **asked to kiss** a frog?

PASSIVE VERBS FOLLOWED BY *THAT* CLAUSES

Look at the following examples:

They say that Canadians love to complain about the weather. → It is said that Canadians love to complain about the weather.

Historians believe that Montreal took its name from Mount Royal. → It is believed that Montreal took its name from Mount Royal.

If the source of the report is not important, it is possible to introduce a report with a passive structure instead of an active one, using the structure *it* + passive + *that* + clause.
Refer to Chapters 9 and 10 for more information about *that* clauses.

EXERCISE 3

Add the word *it* to the words in *italics*, changing the verb into passive. Use the preceding examples as guidelines.

1. *I understand that* there will be no tax increase this year.

   _____

2. *The police think that* the money was stolen some time after the bank closed.

   _____

3. *Some experts suggest that* exercise is an antidepressant.

   _____

4. *Economists expect that* the price of oil will increase in the near future.

   _____

5. *The journal CPJ reports that* 2012 was the worst year ever for journalists.

   _____

It is sometimes possible and even preferable to use infinitives instead of *it* + passive + *that*. Reserve the *it* + passive structure for *that* clauses that are longer. With shorter clauses, use infinitives if possible.
Look at the following example. Which sentence do you prefer?

It is rumoured <u>that she is very rich</u>. → <u>She</u> is rumoured <u>to be very rich</u>.

EXERCISE 4

Change the following sentences into infinitive or perfect infinitive structures. Start your sentences with the underlined words.

It is not expected that <u>you</u> work overtime. → <u>You</u> are not **expected to work** overtime.

1. It's known that <u>he</u> is a very modest man.

   _____

2. It was believed that <u>the earth</u> is flat.

   _____

3. It's thought that <u>she</u> is the NDP's star candidate.

   _____

4. It's reported that <u>several people</u> lost their jobs during the recession. (perfect infinitive)

   _____

5. It's said that <u>they</u> divided the responsibilities among themselves. (perfect infinitive)

   _____

INFINITIVE AND GERUND PASSIVE FORMS

Formation

Structure	Example Sentences
passive infinitives	I did not expect **to be taken** seriously when I offered to help Dan.
perfect passive infinitives	Dan was known **to have been rejected** by his family before.
passive gerunds	I honestly did not like **being asked** for a loan.
perfect passive gerunds	I now blame myself for **having been approached** for money.

PASSIVE AND PERFECT PASSIVE INFINITIVES

Use the verb *be* + the past participle of the verb to form passive infinitives:

Take the pills with plenty of water. → **To be taken** with plenty of water.

Keep your visitor pass visible at all times. → **To be kept** visible at all times.

Do not consume the product after the expiry date. → **Not to be consumed** after the expiry date.

Use *to have been* + the past participle of the verb to form perfect passive infinitives:

We believe he **was interviewed** by the press. → He is believed **to have been interviewed** by the press.

It seems **they left** the suitcases behind on purpose. → The suitcases seem **to have been left** behind on purpose.

We think **he was framed** by his partner. → He is thought **to have been framed** by his partner.

To review perfect infinitives, see Chapter 3, pages 48–50.

 ## COMMUNICATIVE ACTIVITY 3

Quotations

Work in pairs. Fill in the blanks with past participles and any other words you need to make memorable and wise quotations. When finished, share your quotations with other pairs and vote for your favourite quotations.

It's better to have been honoured and then despised than never to have been

_____ at all.

It's better to have been honoured and then despised than never to have been honoured at all.

Those who mistreat others are often the ones to have been _____ themselves.

It's always good to be _____.

It's better to be _____ than _____.

It's hard to be _____.

It's sadder to have been _____ than _____.

EXERCISE 5

Change the following sentences into the passive by using passive infinitives and, where possible, perfect passive infinitives. The beginning of each sentence has been given as a clue.

> I need you to take me seriously. → I need to be taken seriously.

1. There are exact measures that we need to take to avoid such problems.

   There are exact measures that need _____

2. Is it better for governments to provide health care and education?

   Is it better for health care _____

3. They were supposed to have provided him with the necessary equipment a long time ago.

   He was supposed to _____

4. They thought the abandoned car had been stolen.

   The abandoned car _____

5. It seems he was born to be a leader.

   He seemed _____

PASSIVE AND PERFECT PASSIVE GERUNDS

Use *being* + the past participle of the verb to form passive gerunds.

> Passive gerunds usually appear in the same structures as gerunds appear (e.g., after prepositions and after gerund verbs). Refer to Chapter 3, pages 37–47, to review gerund structures.

> I will join the room after they invite me. → I will join the room after **being invited**.
>
> I enjoy it when they treat me like royalty. → I enjoy **being treated** like royalty.
>
> He anticipates that he won't be elected. → He anticipates **not being elected**.

Use *having been* + the past participle of the verb to form perfect passive gerunds.

> He went to court after he had been ticketed for speeding. → He went to court after **having been ticketed** for speeding.
>
> He didn't mention that he had been arrested before. → He didn't mention **having been arrested** before.
>
> They divorced after they had been married for 20 years. → They divorced **after having been married** for 20 years.

> To review perfect gerunds, see Chapter 3, pages 48–50.

EXERCISE 6

Make the following sentences more concise by replacing the underscored parts with passive gerunds or perfect passive gerunds.

> Cynthia didn't mention <u>that she had been fired before.</u> → Cynthia didn't mention having been fired before.

1. Each piece of software is tested repeatedly before <u>it is released</u> to the market.

   _____

2. He was handed over to the police after <u>he had been interrogated</u> by border agents.

   _____

3. I hate <u>it when I'm told what to do.</u>

   _____

4. He was angry about <u>the fact that he had not been consulted</u> earlier.

   _____

5. We pride ourselves on <u>the fact that we are not rude.</u>

   _____

 COMMUNICATIVE ACTIVITY 4

Getting to Know You

Work in pairs. Take turns posing and answering questions by using passive infinitives and gerunds. Use the hints below to form your questions. You may write down your questions individually before posing them.

Do you enjoy being . . . ?
Do you expect to be . . . by your . . . ?
Did you . . . after having been . . . ?
Are you excited to have been . . . ?
Have you ever refused to be . . . by . . . ?
Is it normal not to be . . . ?
Do you anticipate being . . . ?
Do you resent not having been . . . ?
Do you appreciate being . . . ?
Have you ever . . . after having been . . . ?
Will you ever stop being ...?
Do you feel lucky not to have been . . . ?

PARTICIPLE ADJECTIVES

Formation

Structure	Example Sentences
active participle	This is a seriously **embarrassing** situation. It was an extremely **frightening** experience.
passive participle	I feel **embarrassed** when I say no. He looks like a **frightened** kid.

- Participle adjectives are adjectives formed from a verb.
  - An **active participle** is formed by adding *-ing* to the verb.

    amaze → amazing   confuse → confusing

    embarrass → embarrassing   break → breaking

  - The **passive participle** has the same form as the past participle of the verb.

    amaze → amazed   confuse → confused

    embarrass → embarrassed   break → broken

- Active participles have an active meaning. In other words, the noun that follows these adjectives is the doer of an action.

  An **amazing** story amazes us and a **confusing** story confuses us.

  The audience was captivated by the **amazing** show. (the show amazes the audience)

- Passive participles have a passive meaning. The noun that follows these adjectives is the receiver of an action.

  An amazed audience is amazed by someone or something else. A confused person is in confusion because of someone or something else.

  The teacher looked **confused.** I think my answers were confusing.
  (The answers confuse the teacher.)

  The **disgusted** look on Zahra's face told me that she hated the food.
  (The food disgusted Zahra.)

In short, if you are interesting, you interest others. If you are interested, others interest you.

EXERCISE 7

Fill in the blanks with the correct participle form of the verbs in parentheses.

Last night, I listened to a 1 _____ (fascinate) program on the radio

about a 2 _____ (bore) young man who decided to bring more colour

to his 3 _____ (bore) life by embarking on an 4 _____

(excite) journey to the Amazon. In general, it was a very 5 _____

(inspire) story, but the narrator's voice was 6 _____ (irritate), and

one part of the story in particular was so 7 _____ (complicate) that it

proved to be a bit too 8 _____ (confuse). The story also had a very 9

_____ (disappoint) ending. It is 10 _____ (amaze) how

many potentially good stories are ruined by bad endings.

✦ COMMUNICATIVE ACTIVITY 5

Collocations

Work in pairs. Fill in the blanks with as many words as you can, using the part of speech cue in parentheses. When you are done, compare your results with those of another pair.

(adverb) _____ interested

very interested

deeply interested

especially interested

extremely interested

keenly interested

particularly interested

1. **interesting** _____ (noun)

2. (verb) _____ **exhausted**

3. (adverb) _____ **exhausting**

4. **disappointed** _____ (preposition)

5. a very **isolated** _____ (noun)

PASSIVE WITH *GET*

Formation

Structure	Example Sentences	Explanation
passive with *get* and passive with *be* (no significant change in meaning)	We don't know why he **was arrested**. We don't know why he **got arrested**.	The two sentences are almost synonyms. The second sentence (with *get*) is more common in speaking than in writing.
passive with *get* and passive with *be* (significant change in meaning)	What is it like to **be married**? What is it like to **get married**?	The first sentence is about married life. The second sentence (with *get*) is about the process of marrying (e.g., engagement, wedding, costs).

In spoken or informal situations, the verb *get* can replace *be* in passive structures. The passive with *get* is not common in written English.

> I **was never paid**. → I never **got paid**.

> **Were** you **invited** to the party? → **Did** you **get invited** to the party?

In the examples above, there's not much change in meaning. Sometimes, however, the meaning changes when we switch *be* with *get*. In the following examples, *get* implies the idea of change, whereas *be* describes a state.

> We are engaged. (It is already done.) → We are getting engaged. (It's not done yet, but it will be soon.)

> I am married (already). → I am getting married (soon).

We can also use the passive with *get* to talk about negative experiences, or difficulties and unexpected results, as in the following:

> get arrested, get caught, get killed, get injured, get lost, get bored, get depressed, get fired, get divorced

EXERCISE 8

Fill in the blanks with the correct form of the verb *get* and the past participle of the appropriate verb from the following list.

kill	throw	leave	start	stop

1. It's easy to set up a Wi-Fi connection. Here's a router and some cables. We have

   everything we need to _____.

2. Last week, she _____ by the police for talking on her cellphone while driving.

3. Every year in North America, a lot of food _____ away.

4. Several Canadian soldiers have _____ by friendly fire in the past couple of years in Afghanistan.

5. The minister of education promised that no child _____ behind after the new act is put into practice.

 COMMUNICATIVE ACTIVITY 6

Q&A

Work in pairs. Take turns asking and answering questions by using the passive with *get*.
    You may use the preceding expressions or come up with your own structures. Avoid short answers. Explain the answer in detail. Try to maintain a conversation.

Student A: Why do you think some people **get fired**?

Student B: Poor performance is the number one issue that can **get you fired**. You can also get into trouble if you bring your personal problems to work.

CAUSATIVE VERBS

Note the difference between these two sentences:

I fixed the TV. (I myself fixed it.)

I had the TV fixed. (I arranged for it to be fixed.)

We use the causative form when the subject is the cause of the action, not the actual doer.
    If you make your sister apologize, you cause her do the action. Your sister is the doer (the agent), and you are the cause (the subject).
    The verbs *make*, *have*, and *get* are used in causative sentences.

Formation

Causative Verb	Active	Meaning	Passive
make	I made him <u>do</u> it.	to force	N/A
have	I had him <u>do</u> it.	to request	I had it done.
get	I got him <u>to do</u> it.	to persuade	I got it done.

ACTIVE CAUSATIVE

Causative sentences can be active (we know the agent).

We use *make* when there is the idea of **force** involved. When you make people do something, you are pushing them to do something that they probably do not want to do.

> They made the engineer leave. (They forced the engineer to leave.)

We use *have* when we **request** something (with or without pay).

> They had the engineer design the system. (They paid him to design it.)

We use *get* often to show that we had to **persuade** someone to do something.

> They finally got the engineer to approve the plans. (They convinced him to approve it.)

Note that in active causatives, *make* and *have* are followed by the simple form of the verb.

> I **made** him **leave.**

Get, however, is followed by the infinitive form.

> I **got** him **to leave.**

PASSIVE CAUSATIVE

Causative sentences (with *have* and *get*) can also be passive (when we do not know the agent).

> *to have / to get* + something + the past participle of the verb

> They had the engineer design the system. (active) → They had the system designed. (passive)

> They got the engineer to approve the plans. (active) → They got the plans approved. (passive)

- It is not possible to use *make* in passive causatives.
- There is not much difference in meaning between *have* and *get* in passive causatives.

EXERCISE 9

Rewrite the following sentences as active causatives. Then change each active causative into the passive.

> Sentence: They requested that the agent list their property.

> Active causative: They had the agent list their property.

> Passive: They had their property listed.

1. The owners persuaded the contractor to reinstall the windows.

   Active causitive: _____

   Passive: _____

2. He asked his sister to deliver his message to her.

   Active causitive: _____

   Passive: _____

3. The editor convinced the author to change the last chapter.

   Active causitive: _____

   Passive: _____

4. The blind student requested that an assistant read her exam to her.

   Active causitive: _____

   Passive: _____

5. The director encouraged the coordinators to write a new policy.

   Active causitive: _____

   Passive: _____

COMMUNICATIVE ACTIVITY 7

Getting It Done

Work in pairs. Choose any five of the ten jobs listed below, and use them to write five active causative sentences. Then exchange your sentences with your partner, and take turns changing the active sentences to the passive. Try to use both *have* and *get*.

Job: carpenter

Student A: I had the carpenter build two tables for my cottage.

Student B (orally): I had two tables built for my cottage.

| plumber | gardener | butcher | taxi driver | soldier |
| dentist | cashier | hairdresser | midwife | lawyer |

BRINGING IT ALL TOGETHER

✷ COMMUNICATIVE ACTIVITY 8

It's in the News!

Work in pairs. Your teacher will give you a newspaper. Read the newspaper, and look for the structures you learned in this chapter. Try to find at least one example for each type. Write the examples in the chart below.

Structure	Example	Page Reference
passive verb + noun		
passive verb + adjective		
passive verb followed by infinitives		
passive verbs followed by *that* clauses		
passive infinitive		
perfect passive infinitive		
passive gerund		
perfect passive gerund		
active participle adjective		
passive participle adjective		
passive with *get*		
active causative with *make*		
active causative with *get*		
active causative with *have*		
passive causative with *get*		
passive causative with *have*		

Reading

Read the passage below.

SAMUEL CUNARD, THE CANADIAN TYCOON

Samuel Cunard was born in Halifax in 1787. From early on, he was taught to earn his own pocket money. He bought and sold items at auctions, grew and sold vegetables, and even knit stockings for sale. At 17, he ran his own general store. Samuel's father, who had noticed his son's <u>entrepreneurial</u> spirit, got Cunard Jr. to join his new shipping company as a partner, where he became the brains behind the business and came to be recognized as a <u>shrewd</u> but honest, devoted, and hard-working businessman.

Samuel's business <u>acumen</u>, combined with opportunities created by the war being waged against Napoleon in Europe, brought the company considerable profits, which enabled him to have more advanced sailing ships built and added to his fleet. However, Samuel considered sailing ships unreliable and decided to invest in steamships. At the time, it was believed that there was no future in steamships, but the tide turned in 1833 when *Royal William*, a Quebec-built steamship accomplished what had been considered <u>insane</u> and crossed the Atlantic entirely by steam. Five years later, after having been awarded a British government contract to run regular mail service across the Atlantic, Cunard had four steamships built, including a paddle steamer named *Britannia* that left Liverpool for Halifax and Boston on July 4, 1840. In 1845, Cunard moved his business to Boston, and in 1848, he moved to London, England, where he built the *Andes*, a ship made of iron and driven by propellers rather than paddlewheels.

During the Crimean War, in 1854, eight of Cunard's ships got chosen to help the British Army carry troops and supplies to Crimea. In 1856, Cunard launched *Persia*, the largest ship in the world at the time of her launch. *Persia* won a medal for the fastest westbound transatlantic voyage. Samuel Cunard was made a <u>baronet</u> in 1859 by Queen Victoria for his services during the war. He died in London in 1865, leaving behind several records and a <u>legacy</u> that lives on to this day.

Here are some more interesting facts about Cunard:

- Cunard used a system of sailing lights that reduced the danger of collision. The system was later adopted by the entire maritime industry.
- Unlike other shipping companies of the time, thanks to its safety protocols, no passenger died on the Cunard Line for more than six decades of operation, until 1915 when *Lusitania* was <u>torpedoed</u> by a German submarine.
- Cunard ships were the first in the world to offer electric lights and wireless communication.

- A huge part of the second floor of the Maritime Museum of the Atlantic in Halifax is dedicated to Samuel Cunard's life.
- Founded in 1840, Cunard Line is still operational today out of Southampton, England.

Principal source: Stephen Franklin, *The Heroes: A Saga of Canadian Inspiration*

COMPREHENSION

Fill in the timeline below based on information from the passage. The first one has been done for you.

1787 → Samuel Cunard was born in Halifax

1804 → _____

1833 → _____

1838 → _____

1840 → _____

1845 → _____

1848 → _____

1854 → _____

1856 → _____

1859 → _____

1865 → _____

1915 → _____

Today → _____

Read the passage a second time, and answer the following questions.

1. How did Samuel make money as a kid?

_____

2. How did most people describe young Samuel after he joined his father's company?

_____

3. Which two elements enabled young Samuel to have more sailing ships added to his fleet?

_____

4. Why did Samuel decide to switch from sailing ships to steamships?

_____

5. What was the common belief about steamships at the time?

_____

6. What was special about *Andes*?

_____

7. Why did *Persia* win a medal?

_____

8. Why was Cunard's system of sailing lights adopted by the entire industry?

_____

9. Which two innovative services were offered on Cunard ships for the first time in the world?

_____

10. Where in Halifax can you find more information about Cunard?

_____

ANALYZING THE READING PASSAGE

The passage above contains several instances of the complex active and passive structures you learned in this chapter. Read the passage again and <u>underline</u> as many of them as you can.

Listening

🔊 Track 07

THE HALIFAX EXPLOSION

Listen to audio, a podcast called "Today in Canadian History," once or twice.

COMPREHENSION

Part 1

Based on the audio, decide whether the following statements are true (T) or false (F). If a statement is false, try to correct it.

1. The Halifax Explosion happened on December 6, 1917, after two ships collided in Halifax Harbour.

2. The Halifax Explosion was the world's largest explosion.

3. The harbour was protected against enemy submarines by two sets of nets that were closed during the day to stop submarines from entering the harbour.

4. The ship that exploded was a large French munitions ship called *Mont Blanc*.

5. The second ship was a Belgian ship called *Imo* that was planning to carry supplies from New York to Norway.

6. When the two ships collided, metal scraping against metal created sparks that ignited the benzol on board *Mont Blanc*.

7. Many people stopped work or school and came to watch the ship on fire.

8. The explosion shattered all the glass windows within a 10-kilometre radius.

9. One quarter of the city's population was left without shelter.

10. Dead bodies were still being discovered several months after the explosion.

Part 2

Listen to the clip one more time, and answer the following questions.

1. Why was Halifax Harbour so busy in that particular year?

   _____

2. How much of each of the following substances was *Mont Blanc* carrying?

   a. wet and dry picric acid: _____

   b. TNT: _____

   c. guncotton: _____

   d. benzol: _____

3. Provide the following statistics:

   a. number of homes damaged: _____

   b. number of homes completely destroyed: _____

   c. number of people left without shelter: _____

   d. number of people killed: _____

   e. number of people blinded by flying glass: _____

4. In your own words, write the story of the Patterson family.

   _____

   _____

   _____

5. Who was Vincent Coleman, and why is he called a hero?

   _____

6. At the end of the program, the host talks about other important events from Canada's past that happened on December 6. What happened on December 6 in each of the following years?

   a. 1803: _____

   b. 1900: _____

   c. 1921: _____

Part 3

Listen to the clip one last time to find and write 10 passive structures that you learned in Chapters 6 or 7. Work on a separate sheet of paper.

Writing

What have you learned from your parents? Work in pairs to explore this topic. Discuss what your parents made you do and what they let you do when you were a kid. Later on, when you grew up, what did they get you to do? What has this taught you about life? Consequently, what would you, as a parent, let or make your children do? What would you get them to learn or get them to do?

   After the discussion, individually, write a short composition of about 250 words about your experience as a kid and the effect it has had on you as an adult or a parent. Use a variety of causative patterns (both active and passive), and, if possible, use the active and passive participles (e.g., interesting / interested, boring / bored).

CHAPTER REVIEW

Summary

- Passive verbs can be followed by
    - nouns → Cunard **was regarded** as <u>a business genius.</u>
    - adjectives → His ships **were considered** extremely <u>safe.</u>
    - infinitives → He **was believed** <u>to be</u> hard working and honest.
    - *that* clauses → At the time, **it was believed** <u>that</u> there was no future in steamships.
- Passive verbs can appear as simple or perfect gerunds and infinitives:
    - gerund → Cunard benefited from the war **being waged** in Europe.
    - infinitive → He came **to be recognized** by all as an honest man.
    - perfect gerund→ He started a steam line after **having been awarded** a contract.
    - perfect infinitive → He was proud **to have been recognized** by the Queen.
- The verb *be* can sometimes be replaced by *get* in informal English, mostly in these cases:
    - when the plan is in progress (he is getting engaged versus he is engaged already)
    - when we are talking about unexpected and negative experiences (getting divorced, getting killed, getting lost)
- The present participle of a verb can act as an active adjective (boring person); and the past participle of the verb can act as a passive adjective (bored person).
- Passive causatives are formed by deleting the agent and changing the verb to past participle: He had his son send the letter. → He had the letter sent.

EXERCISE 1

Fill in each blank with the correct form of the verb in parentheses. Use either an active form or a passive form, depending on what will make sense in the sentence.

I had my sister <u>help</u> (help) me with my chores.

1. I know many people find exams ＿＿＿＿＿＿＿＿＿ (frighten), but I did not see

   many ＿＿＿＿＿＿＿＿＿ (frighten) faces at the exam session yesterday.

2. Joe got his parents ＿＿＿＿＿＿＿＿＿ (buy) him a new bicycle.

3. I made my friend ＿＿＿＿＿＿＿＿＿ (promise) not to reveal my secret.

4. Joe got his bicycle ＿＿＿＿＿＿＿＿＿ (repair) yesterday.

5. The authorities had the spam messages _____ (trace) and they all seem to have come from infected computers in Europe.

6. She _____ (tell) that her application had been rejected.

7. Spreading hate messages _____ (consider) a crime in several countries in the world.

8. The old man _____ (find) unconscious on his bedroom floor.

9. It is important for the assignments _____ (to hand) in on time.

10. Allison fell in love again despite _____ (leave) broken-hearted several times before.

11. Can you get arrested without _____ (charge)?

12. I am afraid your file seems _____ (misplace).

13. He _____ (suppose) to follow the orange signs so that he would

not _____ (lose) inside the garden maze.

EXERCISE 2

The sentences below are all written incorrectly. Based on what you learned in this chapter, correct each sentence by deleting, adding, or changing words. There might be more than one way to correct some sentences.

1. Can you give me an example of people who are claimed being immortal?

2. It was generally believing that he was a caring and giving soul who got his friends to be better people.

3. The organizers made the cheering spectators to keep quiet before the amazing show could get started.

4. The tycoon was rumoured to be bankrupted because of his gambling addiction, as well as some bad investments.

5. It is easy to have been confused in such an embarrassing situation.

6. I got the distracted driver stop searching his pockets for his misplaced cellphone before getting all of us killed.

7. It was recommended that they get rid of that irritated noise before getting started with any other repairs.

8. The supposedly frightening man, who was considering armed and dangerous, turned out to be a harmless, frightened tourist.

9. I will never forget the experience of given so much loving care by total strangers. Thank you!

10. He started teaching at the well-known university after been invited as a visiting professor.

Part 1 Review

Self-Study

OVERVIEW

The self-assessments in this unit give you a chance to review and reinforce the grammar points from Part 1 (Chapters 1–7).

Check your knowledge, and if you find areas that need more attention, go back to the appropriate chapter and review the material.

EXERCISE 1

Fill in the blanks with the appropriate or best tense of the verbs in parentheses. Both active and passive verbs are used. Review the verb charts in Chapters 1, 2, and 6, if necessary.

Canadian inventors _____ (make) significant contributions to the aerospace industry.

Canadian inventors **have made** significant contributions to the aerospace industry.

In 1958, Canada's aerospace industry $_1$ _____ (be) on the leading edge of research and development. The Avro Arrow, the CF-105, was the shining light. It $_2$ _____ (develop) to be used in the Cold War defence systems. It was a marvel, an innovation well ahead of its time and its competitors, and it $_3$ _____ (surpass) all expectations in test flights. The Arrow was a supersonic jet interceptor designed to fly in all weather conditions and in particular over the Arctic.

Then suddenly, in 1959, its program $_4$ _____ (shut) down, the prototypes $_5$ _____ (destroy), and the industry was decimated. Politics and economics $_6$ _____ (seem) to be at the root of the decision by the Diefenbaker government. $_7$ _____ they $_8$ _____ (cower) at the demands of the United States? The United States $_9$ _____ (put) a lot of pressure on the Canadian government to buy American Bomarc missiles. They had also decided not to purchase the Arrow for their own armed forces. Or was it also bad timing? The Russians $_{10}$ _____ (just, launch) the first satellite, *Sputnik*. On the other hand, had the Canadian government simply chosen to ignore the potential value of such innovation because of its political policy of economic austerity? Diefenbaker $_{11}$ _____ (win) the election on his platform of curbing the overspending of the previous government. After all, the Arrow $_{12}$ _____ (cost) taxpayers a lot of money. The decision was—and still is—truly controversial.

However, the consequences of the cancellation of the Arrow are well known. The aerospace industry lost all its impetus. More than 14,000 people ₁₃ _____ (let go) from their jobs at Avro. Repercussions ₁₄ _____ (feel) in related and supply industries as well. Many of the scientists and engineers ₁₅ _____ (end) up working for British and American aviation and research companies. Canada lost more than just the Arrow; it lost many innovators. That loss is a prime example of what ₁₆ _____ (often, refer) to as the "brain drain"—Canada's best and brightest people going to other countries to be able to pursue their careers. There ₁₇ _____ (be) political fallout as well; Prime Minister Diefenbaker lost the confidence of the Canadian population and the next election.

What if the Arrow had not been cancelled? Can you imagine the possibilities? Canada ₁₈ _____ (be) at the forefront of the aeronautic and space industry today. Before the Arrow's demise, the designers at Avro ₁₉ _____ (develop) prototypes and plans for lunar search robotics and even a kind of flying saucer. Of course, Canadian researchers ₂₀ _____ (continue) to innovate and create. Today, Canada is well known for the Canadarm, an essential robotic tool on the International Space Station. The Beaver is still the aircraft of choice of bush pilots. However, ₂₁ _____ our scientists ever _____ (be able) to come up with another invention, creation, or innovation such as the Arrow?

EXERCISE 2

Fill in the blanks with the infinitive or gerund form of the verbs in the parentheses.

_____ (design) furniture and space at work so it's more comfortable and safe is called ergonomics.

Designing furniture and space at work so it's more comfortable and safe is called ergonomics.

Ergonomists intend _____ (optimize) overall work performance by

_____ (maximize) workers' productivity and _____ (minimize) their fatigue and discomfort.

Ergonomists intend **to optimize** overall work performance by **maximizing** workers' productivity and **minimizing** their fatigue and discomfort.

1. I like _____ (use) visual aids when teaching English.

2. Last semester, I wanted _____ (learn) how to use Prezi.

3. I spent a lot of time _____ (create) Prezi presentations for my students.

4. However, I had a really hard time _____ (be) productive at work because of the discomfort I was feeling while sitting at my desk.

5. I found it hard _____ (work) in my office for a long time.

6. When I told my friend about it, she seemed _____ (know) the source of the problem. It was my computer chair.

7. I regret _____ (not, find) out about it earlier.

8. Presently, I avoid _____ (sit) at my desk for long periods.

9. I have already brought this to my director's attention, and he promised

    _____ (take) care of it.

10. I hadn't heard back from him in the last two weeks, so I reminded him about it.

    He apologized for _____ (not, follow) it through.

EXERCISE 3

Complete each of the following sentences by using the modals from the list below. Use each modal only once.

should	must have	would have	couldn't have
shouldn't	might	can	have to
should have	may	can't	don't have to
must	may have	could	will
mustn't	would	could have	had better

1. They never called me for the job. They _____ hired someone else.

2. I _____ definitely discuss it with my boss. That's a promise.

3. Now that I finished my cooking course, I _____ finally cook well.

4. He's not sure yet what he'll do for his holidays. He _____ travel to PEI or just go camping close to home.

5. The movie we saw yesterday was very violent. We _____ seen something else.

6. Why didn't you call us to help you move last weekend? We _____ helped you.

7. They _____ liked to live in the countryside.

8. They _____ been studying all evening long. The hockey game was on, and I know they love hockey.

9. If you have a concussion, you _____ ignore it. Go to a hospital right away.

10. Based on the safety rules, all work accidents _____ be reported to the supervisor.

11. _____ you please bring me some water?

12. I asked Mia what had happened, but she _____ tell me nothing.

13. Since we haven't saved enough money, we _____ buy a house this year.

14. Kids _____ spend a lot of time playing computer games. That's just my opinion.

15. _____ I call you back in an hour?

16. I am off today. I _____ go to work.

17. I have a driving test next month. I _____ prepare for it or otherwise I will fail it.

18. In their last year of high school, students _____ decide whether or not they want to continue their studies at a college or university level.

19. I have a dilemma. What _____ I do?

20. I can't remember when I left you a message. It _____ been yesterday or two days ago.

EXERCISE 4

Read each sentence carefully to come up with the best verb to complete each sentence. Then put the correct **passive form** of the verb in the blanks. Each blank stands for one missing word. More than one correct answer is possible for some of the sentences.

Prizes _____ _____ _____ at the ceremony tomorrow.

(Tips: Because of the words *prize* and *ceremony*, we understand that the missing verb is *award* or *give*. Because of the word *tomorrow*, we have to use the future passive.)

Prizes **will be awarded / will be given** at the ceremony tomorrow.

1. Travel arrangements can _____ _____ through any licensed agency.

2. On July 17, 1812, American troops _____ badly _____ by the British on Lake Huron.

3. The soldiers _____ either killed or _____ prisoners.

4. When you _____ _____ to somebody's house for supper, you are expected to bring a gift.

5. As we are reporting here, investigations _____ _____ _____ out by the police as to what caused the explosion.

6. I wonder how many prizes _____ _____ _____ by Canadian athletes at the Olympics since the beginning of the games?

7. A lot of money is going _____ _____ _____ in the building project.

8. This problem _____ not yet _____ _____ to my attention when I signed the papers.

9. Dishes need _____ _____ _____ as soon as supper is over.

10. Your parcel _____ _____ _____ tomorrow morning by courier.

EXERCISE 5

Determine which of the following is incorrect or is the most awkward sentence. (Circle) its letter.

1. a. The door opened.

   b. The door was opened.

   c. The door was open.

   d. The door got open.

2. a. I worried about you.

   b. I was worried about you.

   c. You worried me.

   d. You were worried me.

3. a. They divorced last year.

   b. They were divorced last year.

   c. They got divorced last year.

   d. They made divorced last year.

4. a. They got the door fixed.

   b. They had the door fixed.

   c. They got me to fix the door.

   d. They had me to fix the door.

5. a. He published all his books anonymously.

   b. All his books were published anonymously.

   c. All his books published anonymously.

   d. All his published books were anonymous.

6. a. He is believed to be honest.

   b. I believe him to be honest.

   c. It is believed that he is honest.

   d. He believes to be honest.

7. a. All applications must be submitted by applicants before midnight.

   b. Applicants must submit their applications before midnight.

   c. All applications must be submitted by midnight.

   d. Please have your application submitted before midnight.

8. a. She was sent flowers by mail.

   b. Flowers were sent to her by mail.

   c. She was received some flowers by mail.

   d. Flowers were received by mail.

9. a. It is a confusing problem.

   b. The problem is confused.

   c. I am confused by the problem.

   d. This problem is confusing me.

10. a. He was likely to have been drunk at the time of the accident.

    b. He must be drunk at the time of the accident.

    c. He admitted having been drunk at the time of the accident.

    d. He admitted being drunk at the time of the accident.

EXERCISE 6

Some of the underlined words are used incorrectly. Circle the grammatically incorrect forms. Then, correct the mistake.

1. He refused <u>accepting</u> that all his friends <u>had been admitted</u> to university while he <u>might not</u> even be able <u>to get</u> his high school diploma.

2. He <u>was believed to be</u> the <u>last surviving</u> person <u>to have experience</u> life in the nineteenth century.

3. I appreciate <u>having been given</u> the opportunity <u>to participate</u> actively <u>at</u> such a significant event.

4. You <u>will be given</u> a list of the things you <u>must</u> to do before <u>opening</u> the <u>sealed</u> envelope.

5. I <u>had been studying</u> hard since last week because I <u>am expected to get</u> good marks.

6. A <u>little known</u> fact about Michael Ondaatje is that <u>after leaving</u> Sri Lanka he decided <u>to live</u> in England before <u>him coming</u> to Canada.

7. <u>Was not</u> his family plan <u>to move</u> to Canada after <u>having lost</u> property that they <u>owned</u>?

8. He <u>must not be blamed</u> for something that other people <u>must have done</u> and that they <u>did not</u>.

9. Before <u>casting our votes</u> at the poll, we <u>were advised reading</u> all the information <u>printed</u> on the back of the ballot sheets.

10. My <u>having failed</u> the exam does not mean that I <u>can be given</u> advice by anyone who <u>happens to had passed</u> the test.

8 Clause Introduction— Adjective Clauses

OVERVIEW

- Sentences are made of principal structures called clauses. A sentence may consist of one or more clauses.

- A clause that can stand alone as a sentence is called a **main** (or an independent) clause. A clause that cannot stand alone as a sentence is called a **subordinate** (or a dependent) clause.

- A **simple sentence** is composed of one main clause.

- A **compound sentence** is composed of two or more main clauses connected by coordinating conjunctions (such as *and*, *or*, *but*, or *so*).

- A **complex sentence** is composed of a main clause and one or more subordinate clauses joined together by a subordinating conjunction (such as *when*, *where*, *which*).

- A **complex-compound** sentence is composed of at least three clauses, joined together by both coordinating and subordinating conjunctions.

- Subordinate (dependent) clauses are normally categorized based on their function as **adjective**, **adverb**, and **noun** clauses.

- An **adjective (or a relative) clause** is a subordinate clause that modifies a noun in the main clause.

Clause or Sentence Type	Example Sentences	Explanation
main clause	Jack entered the room.	The meaning is complete. The clause can stand by itself.
subordinate clause	1. When Jack entered the room, . . . 2. . . . who was late.	The meaning is not complete and the clause cannot stand alone.
simple sentence	1. Jack entered the room. 2. The teacher didn't see Jack. 3. Jack was late.	Each example consists of only one main clause, so each one is considered one simple sentence.
compound sentence	Jack entered the room, **but** the teacher didn't see him.	The coordinating conjunction (*but*) is connecting two main clauses (or two simple sentences).
complex sentence with adjective clause	Jack, **who was late**, entered the room.	The subordinate clause (*who was late*) is added to the main clause (Jack entered the room). *Who was late* is an adjective that describes Jack.
complex-compound sentence	Jack, **who was late**, entered the room, <u>but</u> the teacher didn't see him.	The complex sentence (Jack, who was late, entered the room.) is connected by a coordinating conjunction (*but*) to the next sentence (The teacher didn't see him.).

Warm-up

Work in pairs. The chart below has two sets of four clauses. Combine each set of four clauses to make one complex-compound sentence. Use the spaces provided after the chart to write your answers.

	Main Clauses	Subordinate Clauses
1	He finds the process challenging.	who is trying to learn English
	Khalid is a student.	because English is very different from his first language
2	Jill loves Jack.	whenever there's a good opportunity
	She wants to make friends with him.	who lives across the street

1. _____, but _____.

2. _____, and _____.

COORDINATION

Coordination is the process of joining two or more words, phrases, or clauses to give them equal importance. We can join two main (independent) clauses to make a compound sentence. Main clauses (or sentences) can be combined by punctuation (usually a semicolon) alone, by coordinating conjunctions (*for, and, nor, but, or, yet, so*), or by conjunctive adverbs (such as *moreover, however, otherwise, therefore*).

Formation

Sentence Combination Method	Punctuation	Example Sentence
1. joined by punctuation alone (used in writing)	A semicolon (;) comes between the two sentences.	I reviewed the lesson; I didn't understand much.
2. joined by a coordinating conjunction (mostly used in informal and less formal situations)	A comma comes after the first sentence followed by a coordinating conjunction.	I reviewed the lesson, **but** I didn't understand much.
3. joined by a conjunctive adverb (mostly used in formal writing or formal conversation)	A semicolon comes after the first sentence followed by a conjunctive adverb and a comma.	I reviewed the lesson; **however,** I didn't understand much.

1. JOINING MAIN CLAUSES BY PUNCTUATION ALONE

A semicolon is used to join two **closely related** main clauses. Do not use it to join unrelated clauses.

EXERCISE 1

Work in pairs. Each quotation below is missing a semicolon. Put a semicolon (;) in the appropriate place. Then, choose your favourite quotation from the list, and discuss it with your partner.

1. An insincere and evil friend is more to be feared than a wild beast a wild beast may wound your body, but an evil friend will wound your mind.
   —Buddha

2. Alone we can do so little together we can do so much.
   —Helen Keller

3. Unquestionably, it is possible to do without happiness it is done involuntarily by nineteen-twentieths of mankind.
   —John Stuart Mill

4. The hero created himself the celebrity is created by the media.
   —Daniel J. Boorstin

5. The world could get along very well without literature it could get along even better without man.
   —Jean-Paul Sartre

6. Selfishness is not living as one wishes to live it is asking others to live as one wishes to live.
   —Oscar Wilde

2. JOINING MAIN CLAUSES WITH COORDINATING CONJUNCTIONS

Coordinating conjunctions (such as *and, but, so, nor, for, yet, or*) are used to connect two related main clauses and to clarify their relationship. Study the chart below for the function and an example of each conjunction.

Conjunction	Function	Example Sentence
and	linking ideas	Mary went into the department store to buy shoes, **and** I waited for her outside.
but	contrasting ideas	I went in, **but** I couldn't find her.
so	expressing a result	I couldn't find her, **so** I called her cellphone.
nor	expressing a negative idea	With all the noise, I couldn't hear her, **nor** could she hear me.
for	expressing a reason	I went to the front desk, **for** I thought I could get some help there.
yet	expressing an unexpected idea	The lady there looked very busy, **yet** she proved very helpful.
or	expressing an alternative	She said I could go to the second floor and find Mary there, **or** she could call the shoe department and let Mary know I was waiting at the front desk.

EXERCISE 2

Work in pairs. Fill in the blanks with the most appropriate conjunction from the chart above. Then, choose your favourite quotation or proverb from the list, and discuss it with your partner.

1. The absent are never without fault, _____ the present without excuse.
   —Benjamin Franklin

2. Do not blame God for having created the tiger, _____ thank him for not giving it wings.
   —Proverb

3. As you sow, _____ shall you reap.
   —Galatians 6

4. Though this be madness, _____ there is method in it.
   —*Hamlet*

5. Get busy living, _____ get busy dying.
   —*The Shawshank Redemption*

6. Give me the benefit of your convictions, if you have any; _____ keep

   your doubts to yourself, _____ I have enough of my own.
   —Johann Wolfgang von Goethe

7. Give a man a fish, _____ you feed him for a day; show him how to

   fish, _____ you feed him for a lifetime.
   —Proverb

8. Ask advice, _____ use your own common sense.
   —Proverb

9. Agree, _____ the law is costly.
   —William Camden

10. Tell not all you know, _____ do all you can.
    —Proverb

11. Blessed is he who expects nothing, _____ he shall never be disappointed.
    —Alexander Pope

12. Beauty is only skin-deep, _____ ugly goes to the bone.
    —Proverb

3. JOINING MAIN CLAUSES WITH CONJUNCTIVE ADVERBS

Conjunctive adverbs (or transitional expressions) are mostly found in formal writing and formal conversation. These adverbs join two complete ideas and show their relationship. The most common conjunctive adverbs are shown in the chart.

Adverb	Function	Example Sentence
moreover, in addition, besides, furthermore	indicates addition	I don't like the style of this blouse; in addition, it is one size too small for me.
otherwise	indicates condition	Put on warm clothing; otherwise, you'll catch a cold.
however, nevertheless, still, nonetheless	indicates contrast	She read the book five times; still, she didn't understand it.
therefore, consequently, thus, hence	indicates result	I am able to think; therefore, I exist.

EXERCISE 3

Join pairs of the sentences below to make four meaningful sentences, connecting each pair with a suitable adverb from the conjunctive adverbs chart above. Make sure you use appropriate punctuation and capitalization if necessary.

> Aunt Marie came to Sherbrooke to take care of her nieces; <u>otherwise,</u> she would have stayed in Montreal.

she would have stayed in Montreal ✓
their babies are born with problems, such as neurological disorders
his fiancée's parents have promised to help with the costs
I later discovered that his wife was an obsessive shopper
some women suffer from malnutrition during their pregnancy
the nuns from a nearby convent took care of the injured knight
Aunt Marie came to Sherbrooke to take care of her nieces ✓
his employer has agreed to give him a loan for the wedding
he would have died of his battle wounds
I attributed his habit of controlling his wife's purse strings to his male chauvinism

_____

_____

_____

_____

SUBORDINATION

Subordination is the process of joining two or more clauses to give one clause (the main clause) more importance than the other ones (the subordinate clauses). The result of subordination is a complex sentence. There are three types of subordinate clauses: adjective (relative), adverb, and noun clauses.

Formation

Type of Clause	Example Sentence	Analysis
1. adjective clause	This is the student **who arrived late.**	The clause (*who arrived late*) modifies the noun (*student*). Therefore, it is an adjective.
2. adverb clause	He came in **although he arrived late.**	The clause (*although he arrived late*) modifies the verb (*came in*). Therefore, it is an adverb.
3. noun clause	I don't know **who arrived late.**	The clause (*who arrived late*) replaces the noun in the sentence (I don't know something.). Therefore, it is a noun.

EXERCISE 4

Complete the following clauses in your own words to make complex sentences. Then, decide which type of clause each one is: adjective (adj.), adverb (adv.), or noun (n.). Circle your choice.

Canadarm was a mechanical arm that **was used on the Space Shuttle to move payloads. (adj.)**

1. The year 1945 is the year when _____ adj. adv. n.

2. I don't know when _____ adj. adv. n.

3. I wake up when _____ adj. adv. n.

4. Justin Bieber is the Canadian singer who _____ adj. adv. n.

5. Do you know who _____ adj. adv. n.

6. I was born in a country where _____ adj. adv. n.

7. I know what maple syrup is, but I don't know where _____ adj. adv. n.

8. I parked my car where _____ adj. adv. n.

ADJECTIVE (RELATIVE) CLAUSES

An adjective clause, just like an adjective, modifies a noun or pronoun. Adjectives usually come before nouns, whereas adjective clauses come after the nouns (antecedents) they modify.

<u>Canadian</u> traditions (adjective for the noun *traditions*)

Traditions **that are so typically Canadian** (adjective clause for the noun *traditions*)

The words that introduce adjective clauses are called relative pronouns (*that, who, whom, whose, which*) or relative adverbs (*when, where, why*).

Formation

Antecedent	Introductory Word	Example Sentences
a person	who (subject / object) whom (object) that* (subject / object)	This is the <u>man</u> **who** bought my car. These are the <u>executives</u>, one of **whom** will be the next CEO. She is the <u>woman</u> **that** I want to marry.
a thing	which (subject / object) that* (subject / object)	This is the <u>car</u>, **which** I bought myself. This is the <u>car</u> **that** I bought.
a time	when	There was a <u>time</u> **when** everybody was happy.
a place	where	This is the <u>country</u> **where** I was born.
a reason	why	This is the <u>reason</u> **why** I cannot go there.
a possessor (person or thing)	whose	This is the <u>man</u> **whose** son is in the race. This is the <u>company</u> **whose** logo won an award.

That is more common in conversation. *Who* and *which* are more common in writing or formal language.

   That cannot be used after a comma (,). Always use *who* or *which* after commas.

   That cannot be used immediately after a preposition. Always use *whom* or *which* after prepositions:

That is the <u>book</u> to **which** I refer all the time.

COMMUNICATIVE ACTIVITY 1

Guess What?

Work in pairs. Partner A thinks of a person, a place, a time, or an object. He or she then uses one of the patterns listed to give clues to Partner B. Partner B has to use the clue to guess the answer. Partner B has only two guesses for each statement. When Partner B guesses correctly three times, partners change roles.

Partner A: This is the year when the Second World War ended.

Partner B: 1943?

Partner A: No! Make a second guess.

Partner B: 1945!

Partner A: Yes! Next one.

Patterns:
This is the place / city / country where . . .
This is the time / day / year when . . .
This is the person / man / woman / singer / actor who / whom / whose . . .
This is the invention / tool / object which / that . . .

EXERCISE 5

Check your knowledge of Canada and adjective clauses. Fill in the blanks with the correct words from the list below. You can use each word once only.

Vancouver	Terry Fox	that
Ottawa	Michael Ondaatje	when
Toronto	James Naismith	where
Alberta	who	why
Nunavut	whom	whose
	which	

1. _____, a Canadian who was teaching in the United States, invented a

    game _____ later became known as basketball.

2. _____ was a Canadian _____ lost his leg to cancer and

    decided to raise money for the Canadian Cancer Society by running across Canada.

3. _____ is a Canadian author _____ novel *The English Patient*

    was turned into an award-winning Hollywood movie.

4. _____ is a city _____ you can ski in the mountains and swim

    in the ocean at the same time of the year.

5. The year 1905 was the year _____ the province of _____

    officially joined the Canadian confederation.

6. The _____ International Film Festival, _____ was founded

back in 1976, is now one of the most prestigious film festivals in the world.

7. _____'s strategic location was the main reason _____ it was

chosen as Canada's capital.

8. _____ makes up one-fifth of Canada's land mass and has 23,000

inhabitants, most of _____ are Inuit.

EXERCISE 6

Use adjective clauses to combine the pairs of sentences. Make sure to delete repeated
elements.

I saw <u>the accident</u>. <s>The accident</s> happened on March Road yesterday.

I saw the accident *that* happened on March Road yesterday.

1. Ralph Steinman was a Canadian scientist. He received the 2011 Nobel Prize in
   Medicine after his death.

   _____

2. The tennis player is sad. He lost the game.

   _____

3. We are making complex sentences. The sentences contain adjective clauses.

   _____

4. The film was good. We saw it together last week.

   _____

5. He enjoyed the film. They saw the film together last week.

   _____

6. I love the actor. We saw him in *Bon Cop, Bad Cop*.

   _____

7. She saw a cat. The cat's head was stuck in a box.

   _____

8. I talked to Ben Mulroney, the Canadian television host. Ben's father was a prime minister.

   _____

9. Vancouver is one of the most beautiful cities in the world. We spent our honeymoon there.

   _____

10. I was born in the year 1969. The first human stepped on the moon then.

    _____

✣ COMMUNICATIVE ACTIVITY 2

This Is the House That Jack Built

Work in pairs. Combine all the sentences below into one long sentence by using only the relative pronoun *that*. When your sentence is complete, time yourselves reading the sentence as fast as you can without making any mistakes. The person who reads the sentence faster is the winner.

This is the farmer.
The farmer kept the cock.
The cock woke the priest.
The priest married the man.
The man kissed the maiden.
The maiden milked the cow.
The cow tossed the dog.
The dog worried the cat.
The cat killed the rat.
The rat ate the malt.
The malt lay in the house.
Jack built the house.

PUNCTUATION OF ADJECTIVE CLAUSES

Do not use commas if the clause gives essential information about the noun. In this case, if you delete the clause, the sentence will be incomplete.

Use commas if the clause gives extra information about the noun. In this case, if you delete the clause, the sentence is still complete.

The author who wrote *The English Patient* is Canadian.

(Without "who wrote *The English Patient*," we do not know which author is Canadian.)

Michael Ondaatje, who wrote *The English Patient*, is Canadian.

(Even without "who wrote *The English Patient*," we know who is Canadian: Michael Ondaatje.)

Sometimes, when the same sentence is written with or without commas, there is a change in meaning.

The students who were angry about tuition hikes went on strike. (Only those students who were angry went on strike.)

The students, who were angry about tuition hikes, went on strike. (All the students were angry and went on strike.)

EXERCISE 7

Add a comma (,) where necessary in the sentences below.

1. Nunavut which makes up one-fifth of Canada's land mass has only 23,000 inhabitants.

2. I went to Toronto which is Canada's largest city.

3. As soon as I entered I went to an agent who was talking on the phone.

4. I went to my car which was parked near the restaurant.

5. We went to the Hi-Fi Club where we danced all night.

6. I went to a large city which was near the sea.

7. I went to a car which was parked near the restaurant.

8. We went to a club where we danced all night.

9. As soon as I entered I went to an agent. The agent who was talking on the phone did not even hear me.

PREPOSITIONS AND ADJECTIVE CLAUSES

Most prepositions can be used either at the beginning (formal) or at the end (conversational) of adjective clauses.

Formal: A wallet is a small case in *which* you carry your money.

Conversational: A wallet is something (that) you put your money in.

The following prepositions can appear only at the beginning of the adjective clause:

after	below	besides	before	because of	during

These are the hours during which I check my email. (correct)

~~These are the hours which I check my email during.~~ (incorrect)

If the preposition is part of a fixed expression or phrasal verb, it cannot be separated from its parts and does not come at the beginning of the adjective clause.

These are the incidents **which** they have <u>come across</u>. (correct)

~~These are the incidents across which they have come.~~ (incorrect)

When prepositions come at the beginning of the adjective clause, *that* and *who* change to *which* and *whom*. It is not normal to use prepositions and *that* or *who* together in an adjective clause.

This is the man **that** I talked to you <u>about</u>. (correct)

This is the car **that** I talked to you <u>about</u>. (correct)

This is the man <u>about</u> **whom** I talked to you. (correct)

This is the car <u>about</u> **which** I talked to you. (correct)

~~This is the man <u>about</u> who I talked to you.~~ (incorrect)

~~This is the car <u>about</u> that I talked to you.~~ (incorrect)

EXERCISE 8

Combine the following sentences by using adjective clauses. If possible, write two versions: one formal and another conversational.

A mother's love is something. Nothing can compete with a mother's love.

A mother's love is something (that) nothing can compete with.

A mother's love is something with which nothing can compete.

1. A friend is a person. I can be sincere with a friend.

   _____

   _____

2. Ramadan is a month. Muslims fast during Ramadan.

   _____

   _____

3. A landlord is a person. You rent an apartment from a landlord.

   _____

   _____

4. A gorge is a deep, narrow valley. A river sometimes runs through a gorge.

   _____

   _____

5. French Canadians are people. Most of the French Canadians live in Quebec.

   _____

   _____

6. A first name is a word or words. A person is identified by a first name.

_____

_____

7. Gandhi was the leader. Because of Gandhi's efforts, India gained independence from Britain.

_____

_____

DELETING RELATIVE PRONOUNS

Who, *which*, and *that* can be deleted without any change in meaning if they are the objects of the verb that follows.

Note: Do not delete the relative pronoun if it is the subject of the verb.

I like the actor. We saw ~~him~~ in *Bon Cop, Bad Cop*. (The repeated part is the object)

I like the actor that we saw in *Bon Cop, Bad Cop*. (correct)

I like the actor we saw in *Bon Cop, Bad Cop*. (correct)

I like the actor. ~~He~~ appears in *Bon Cop, Bad Cop*. (The repeated part is the subject)

I like the actor that appears in *Bon Cop, Bad Cop*. (correct)

~~I like the actor appears in *Bon Cop, Bad Cop*.~~ (incorrect)

EXERCISE 9

In each sentence below, remove the relative pronoun, if possible. If it is not possible to remove the relative pronoun, write N/A (not applicable) beside the sentence.

I bought the wallet that I saw at the store yesterday. → I bought the wallet ~~that~~ I saw at the store yesterday.

This is the necktie that makes me look older. → <u>N/A</u>

1. Dr. Roberta Bondar, who was the first Canadian woman in space, is also a

   neurologist. _____

2. Today I gave a lecture about Alice Munro, the woman that I consider to be the

   greatest Canadian short-story writer of all time. _____

3. The Canada Post stamp which you see here on the left commemorates the famous

   Inuit artist Pitseolak Ashoona. _____

4. The stamp which commemorates Pitseolak was issued in 1993. _____

REDUCING ADJECTIVE CLAUSES

Short sentences are not always better than long sentences. Sometimes we need longer sentences to avoid ambiguity, to create variety, or to give more emphasis. In general, however, if you can say the same thing with fewer words, the shorter version might be more effective.

Here are some techniques for replacing relative clauses with shorter alternatives.

1. Removing the Relative Pronoun and the Verb Be before a Participle

When relative pronouns *who*, *that*, and *which* are used before the verb *be* (*am* / *is* / *are* / *was* / *were*) and are followed by participles (e.g., *-ing* and *-ed* forms), we can delete both the relative pronoun and the verb *be*.

who / that / which	am / is / are / was / were	-ing / -ed	I saw a man who was running. I saw a man running. He came from a country that was ruined by war. He came from a country ruined by war.

2. Using Appositives instead of Adjective Clauses

In these cases, there is no subject and verb after the comma.

Paul, **who is the president of the company,** is retiring this year. → Paul, **the president of the company,** is retiring this year.

I went to Montreal to visit Eve, **who is my second cousin.** → I went to Montreal to visit Eve, **my second cousin.**

3. Prepositional Phrases

These phrases replace the relative pronoun and verb with a preposition.

I admire people **who have integrity.** → I admire people **with integrity.**

I live in an apartment **that doesn't have air conditioning.** → I live in a house **without air conditioning.**

4. Adjectives instead of Relative Clauses

If you can use an adjective, why use a whole clause?

I looked at **the sky that was blue.** → I looked at **the blue sky.**

This product contains **components that are made of plastic.** → This product contains **plastic components.**

This city has **neighbourhoods that are dangerous.** → This city has **dangerous neighbourhoods.**

EXERCISE 10

Reduce the following sentences to shorter alternatives. The numbers in parentheses are clues to the techniques you learned in the section "Reducing Adjective Clauses."

1. A room that has no books is a body that has no soul. (3)

   _____

2. Wear the coat that is old and buy a book that is new. (4)

   _____

3. Money which is spent on the brain is never spent in vain. (1)

   _____

4. The dog which is scalded fears the water that is cold. (4)

   _____

5. A penny that is saved is a penny that is gained. (1)

   _____

6. The man who has a big nose thinks everyone talks of it. (3)

   _____

Work in pairs to choose your favourite proverb from the list above. Discuss why you like it.

BRINGING IT ALL TOGETHER

 ## COMMUNICATIVE ACTIVITY 4

Comparing Sentences

There are sometimes different ways to convey the same message. A good writer or speaker knows which version is the best for his or her purposes. In small groups, read the following sentences and discuss how the meaning changes in each sentence. What is each sentence emphasizing? Take notes based on your discussions and share your thoughts with the other groups.

1. Mavis Gallant is a Canadian author, but she lives in Paris.

2. Mavis Gallant lives in Paris, but she is a Canadian author.

3. Mavis Gallant is a Canadian author, yet she lives in Paris.

4. Mavis Gallant lives in Paris, yet she is a Canadian author.

5. Mavis Gallant, who is a Canadian author, lives in Paris.

6. Mavis Gallant, who lives in Paris, is a Canadian author.

7. Mavis Gallant, the Canadian author, lives in Paris.

8. Canadian author Mavis Gallant lives in Paris.

✻ COMMUNICATIVE ACTIVITY 5

Combining Sentences

Combine each of the following pairs of sentences in as many ways as you can. Be ready to explain how the meaning changes in each version.

1. Mike lives in Victoria. Mike works in Vancouver.

    _____

    _____

    _____

2. I admire people. People have passion.

    _____

    _____

    _____

Reading

Read the passage and answer the questions that follow.

CANADIAN HEROINES

1 Who is your favourite Canadian heroine? . . . Perhaps pilot Helen Harrison who <u>ferried</u> Spitfires and other military planes during World War II, mountaineer Phyllis Munday, the first woman to climb the highest peak in the Canadian Rockies, or maybe Gudridur the Viking, the adventurous Icelandic explorer who visited North America five hundred years before Columbus. What about singing sensation La Bolduc or Helen McNicoll [the accomplished impressionist painter]? Maybe the best-selling author Mazo de la Roche or explorer Agnes Deans Cameron?

2 If you've never heard of these people it's not surprising. Women are practically invisible on the pages of Canadian history textbooks, too often overshadowed by the <u>feats</u> of famous men. The faces of politicians such as Sir John A. Macdonald and Sir Wilfrid Laurier stare at us from <u>crumpled</u> bills in our wallets, but there is never a female face to greet us—aside from the Queen of England. At least more and more Canadian women are showing up on commemorative stamps, reminding us of some of the notable women who have helped develop Canada.

3 Are there really few heroines in Canadian history that we would be interested in knowing about and remembering? Perhaps the word *heroine* <u>conjures up</u> visions of women in Greek mythology, or the legendary Joan of Arc. But are there heroines in Canadian history?

4 Dictionaries define a heroine as a woman noted for courage and daring action, or a woman noted for special achievement in a particular field. Every country has its heroines, and Canada is no exception. Our history is coloured with amazing women who have done fascinating things.

5 Many Canadian heroines should be recognized for their brave deeds or heroic actions. Countless other heroines made notable achievements in many fields. Heroines in sport, science and medicine, business, arts and entertainment, exploration, literature, politics, social reform, and many other fields. Some faced incredible obstacles to fight for their beliefs and to improve the quality of life for others. They battled prejudice, <u>discrimination</u>, <u>repression</u>, and worse to follow their dreams and excel in their chosen paths . . .

6 Each of these heroines in Canadian history, being neither a mythological character nor a super-heroine from a comic book, is a human being: an imperfect person with strengths and weaknesses. A woman who reflects social behaviours and attitudes of her time—some of which are objectionable by modern standards. Were her achievements any less? Can we still celebrate the achievements of the heroines while acknowledging their <u>flaws</u>?

7 There are so many amazing women in the history of Canada. Their faces should not be forgotten but recognized and celebrated as Canadian heroines.

Abridged from Merna Foster, *100 Canadian Heroines: Famous and Forgotten Faces.*

COMPREHENSION

1. What is the main idea of this passage? Where in the passage can you find the main idea?

   _____

2. Who are the following people?

   a. Helen Harrison: _____

   b. Phyllis Munday: _____

   c. Gudridur the Viking: _____

d. La Bolduc: _____

e. Helen McNicoll: _____

f. Mazo de la Roche: _____

g. Agnes Deans Cameron: _____

h. Sir Wilfrid Laurier: _____

i. Sir John A. Macdonald: _____

3. Why does the author mention the Queen of England?

_____

4. What is the dictionary definition of *heroine*?

_____

5. Name some of the obstacles Canadian heroines had to overcome.

_____

_____

ANALYZING THE READING PASSAGE

Variety is the key to good writing. The writer of "Canadian Heroines" has used a variety of structures to avoid repeating adjective clauses.

Read the passage again. Find the structures listed in the chart below, and copy the clause containing each structure beside its name. The first one has been done for you.

Structure	Paragraph	Clause
infinitive instead of relative clause	1	the first woman **to climb** the highest peak in the Canadian Rockies (instead of: The first woman who climbed . . .)
adjective clause with *who*	1, 2, 6	
adjective clause with *that*	3	
adjective clause with *which*	6	
appositive	1	

continued on next page

ructure	Paragraph	Clause
simple adjective instead of adjective clause	1	
preposition *with* instead of adjective clause	6	
reduced adjective clause (*who* and the verb deleted before participle)	4	

Listening

🔊 Track 08

ROOM FOR ALL OF US

Listen to the audio once or twice, and answer the questions that follow.

COMPREHENSION

Part 1

1. What is the subject of Adrienne Clarkson's book?

   _____

2. Why did she write this book?

   _____

3. What is the Cultural Access Pass (CAP) program?

   _____

4. Who created the program?

   _____

5. Why was it created?

   _____

6. Answer the questions in the chart below about some of the immigrant groups that have come to Canada.

Immigrant Group	How many came to Canada?	Why did they immigrate?	When did they immigrate?	What was their contribution to Canada?
Americans (draft resisters)				
Vietnamese (boat people)				
Africans (Ismailis)				

7. Who are the following people? What do we learn about them in this interview? Write as much as you can. Use a separate piece of paper if necessary.

   a. Andy Barrie: _____

   b. John Tran: _____

   c. Rathika Sitsabaiesan: _____

   d. Nadir Mohamed: _____

Part 2

Listen to the interview one more time; this time, listen for the adjective clause structures you learned about in this chapter. Try to find at least one example for each of the following structures:

   a. *who* clause: _____

   b. *which* clause: _____

   c. *that* clause: _____

   d. *where* clause: _____

e. *of whom* clause: _____

f. *at which* clause: _____

g. *when* clause: _____

h. *to whom* clause: _____

i. reduced clause: _____

j. deleted relative pronoun: _____

Writing

Research the life story of a famous Canadian woman. Write a short biography (maximum 400 words) citing her achievements and her background. Remember to use structures that you learned in this chapter. Use a variety of structures, especially adjective clauses (refer to "Reducing Adjective Clauses" on page 163) to make your writing both more effective and more natural.

CHAPTER REVIEW

Summary

- Coordination gives ideas equal importance. Coordination is used to connect main clauses.

- Subordination makes one idea (the subordinate clause) less important than another (the main clause). Subordination is used to connect ideas logically, concisely, and effectively.

- Subordinate clauses can be categorized as adjective, adverb, or noun clauses.

- Adjective clauses modify nouns (people, things, possession, time, places, and reason) by using relative adjectives (*that, who, whom, which, whose*) or relative adverbs (*when, where,* and *why*).

- *Who, which,* and *that* can be deleted when they are not the subject of the clause.

- Adjective clauses can be replaced by other structures to create variety, conciseness, or a change in emphasis.

EXERCISE 1

The sentences below are all written incorrectly. Based on what you have learned in this chapter, correct each sentence by making only one type of change. You may add or remove words or punctuation marks, or replace one word with another. There might be more than one way to correct some of the sentences.

1. They live in a city which it is very crowded.

2. He lives in Montreal, that is the largest city in Quebec.

3. The heroine of the story was a woman who was trying to rescue a country was filled with corruption.

4. She talked to people some of who disapproved of the system.

5. Iraq which is in the Middle East, is an oil-rich country.

6. He would love to visit Calgary and Edmonton, so he doesn't have time to visit both places.

7. He would love to visit both Calgary and Edmonton; moreover, he doesn't have enough time.

8. He would love to visit Calgary and Edmonton, he doesn't have time to visit both places though.

9. I read about a scientist who's inventions changed the world.

10. These are the dates during when you may file your tax return.

EXERCISE 2

Fill in the blanks with the correct word from the list below. Each word can be used once only.

that	who	whom	whose	but	or	yet	therefore	otherwise	still

1. See first, think later, then test. But always see first. _____ you will only see what you were expecting. Most scientists forget that.
   —Douglas Noel Adams

2. In science, credit goes to the man _____ convinces the world, not to the man to _____ the idea first occurs.

3. We can have democracy in this country, ＿＿＿＿＿＿ we can have great wealth

   concentrated in the hands of a few, ＿＿＿＿＿＿ we can't have both.
   —Louis D. Brandeis

4. God could not be everywhere; ＿＿＿＿＿＿, he created mothers.
   —Jewish proverb

5. Nothing is more powerful than an idea ＿＿＿＿＿＿ time has come.
   —Victor Hugo

6. We know very little, and ＿＿＿＿＿＿ it is astonishing that we know so much.
   —Bertrand Russell

7. Every civilization ＿＿＿＿＿＿ has ever existed has ultimately collapsed.

8. I do not know everything; ＿＿＿＿＿＿ I understand many things.
   —Goethe

Noun Clauses

OVERVIEW

- Noun clauses are dependent clauses; they contain a subject and a verb but cannot stand alone.

- Noun clauses function as nouns; they often appear in the same sentence positions as nouns (such as subject, object, or complement positions).

- Noun clauses begin with *that*, *if*, *whether*, or wh- question words (such as *when*, *where*, and *why*).

Warm-up

Work in pairs. Each partner picks one of the boxes below and completes the questions in his or her own words, writing the sentences down. Then, the partners take turns posing the questions for their partners to answer. Avoid short answers. Try to explain as much as you can in response to each question so that you have a real conversation. The first pair has been done for you.

Partner A	Partner B
Have you decided if . . .	Do you agree that . . .
Do you believe that . . .	Do you know whether . . .
Do you know when . . .	Can you teach me how . . .
Can you guess how much . . .	Do you understand if . . .
Do you have any idea whether . . .	Aren't you surprised that . . .

Partner A: Have you decided if you want to continue studying at this school next year?

Partner B: Yes, I have decided to stay here, but I'm not sure which courses I want to pick.

Partner B: Do you agree that learning a second language is hard and time-consuming?

Partner A: Certainly! The toughest part for me is the pronunciation of words that I have never heard before. I can never be sure if I am saying them right.

NOUN CLAUSE PATTERNS

Formation

We use the term *noun clause* to refer to clauses that behave like nouns. They have the same functions in the sentence as a noun. Study the comparisons below.

Function	Example with Noun	Example with Noun Clause
subject of verb	The reason is not important	Why you did it is not important.
object	I see the problem.	I see that the handle is broken.
object of preposition	I am worried about the money.	I am worried about whether I can get the money.
complement	Our infrastructure is the target.	Our infrastructure is what the enemy will target first.

Noun clauses can also appear in the following patterns.

After an adjective: It is **clear** <u>that light travels faster than sound</u>.

After a noun: It is a **fact** <u>that light travels faster than sound</u>.

EXERCISE 1

Complete the following sentences in your own words.

1. How you say something is sometimes more important than what _____.

2. I believe that Canadians _____.

3. I don't know why some people _____.

4. I want to talk about how _____.

5. We are who _____.

6. It is unbelievable that _____.

7. It is a truth that my country _____.

COMMUNICATIVE ACTIVITY 1

Q&A

Work in pairs. First, work individually to complete the questions in column A on a separate sheet of paper. Then, exchange the questions with your partner. Write the answers to your partner's questions by using the patterns in column B. After you are both comfortable with the patterns, repeat the exercise orally, without pen and paper. The first one has been done for you.

Column A	Column B
Why do you . . .?	Why I . . . is . . .
Do you believe that . . .?	I think that . . .
Are you interested in why . . .?	No, but I am interested in how . . .
What matters most to you in your . . .?	. . . is what matters most to me in my . . .
Did you know that . . .?	Wow! I had no idea that . . .
Is it true that . . .?	No, it is not true that . . . / Yes, it is true that . . .

Partner A: Why do you always come to class late?

Partner B: Why I come to class late is a secret. I won't tell you why.

Partner B: Why do you scratch your head when someone asks you a question?

Partner A: Why I scratch my head is a mystery to me. I really don't know why.

SUBORDINATING CONJUNCTIONS IN NOUN CLAUSES

Noun clauses begin with *that* or (in the case of embedded questions) with *if, whether,* or wh- question words (such as *when, where,* and *why*).

Formation

NOUN CLAUSES WITH *THAT*

Noun clauses with *that* often follow verbs that express **opinions, thoughts,** and **feelings**. We can also use *that* clauses after **adjectives** and **nouns**.

> I **believe** that he is retiring. (opinion)
>
> I **feel** that I should be retired. (feeling)
>
> I am **happy** that he is retiring. (after an adjective)
>
> I heard a **rumour** that he is retiring. (after a noun)

See Chapter 10, pages 197–198, for the use of *that* in reported speech.

In informal English, *that* is often omitted:

> I believe that he is retiring. → I believe he is retiring.

EMBEDDED QUESTIONS

One of the most common uses of noun clauses is in embedded questions. Adding an introductory sentence to a question changes the question into a statement and results in a noun clause.

There are two very common types of questions in English:

1. Yes / no questions (questions that begin with an auxiliary)

2. Information questions or wh- questions (questions that start with question words, such as *why, when, where*)

The following chart summarizes the process for embedding each of the two question types.

1. Yes / No Questions

Introductory Sentence or Phrase	Yes / No Question	Change Question to Statement	Add *If* or *Whether*	Combine
I don't know.	Will the plane arrive on time?	The plane will arrive on time.	if / whether the plane will arrive on time	I don't know if / whether the plane will arrive on time.

2. Information Questions (Wh- questions)

Introductory Sentence or Phrase	Information Question	Change Question to Statement	Combine
I don't know	Why are you tired?	Why you are tired	I don't know why you are tired.

ADDING -*EVER* TO WH- WORDS

We can add the suffix -*ever* to some wh- words to mean "no matter" or "any."
Read the following sentences with wh + *ever* noun clauses:

You can go **wherever** you want. (no matter where, anywhere)

You can call **whenever** you want. (no matter when, any time)

You can talk to **whomever** you want. (anyone)

You can do **whatever** you want. (anything)

You can choose **whichever** you like. (no matter which one)

You can do it **however** you like. (any way)

REDUCING NOUN CLAUSES TO INFINITIVES

Sometimes it is possible to change a noun clause to an infinitive and create more concise sentences.

Often, we can change a wh- noun clause containing *should*, *can*, or *could* to an infinitive.

I know <u>what</u> I <u>should</u> do. → I know <u>what to do</u>.

Do you know <u>where</u> I <u>can</u> find him? → Do you know <u>where to find</u> him?

We can also change noun clauses with some expressions of necessity and advice to infinitive phrases.

He asked <u>that we take</u> the test. → He asked <u>us to take</u> the test.

He advised <u>that we take</u> the test. → He advised <u>us to take</u> the test.

EXERCISE 2

Combine each pair of sentences below with *that*.

Hockey and lacrosse are Canada's national sports. Did you know?

Did you know that hockey and lacrosse are Canada's national sports?

1. Canadians consume more macaroni and cheese than any other nation on earth. Can you believe it?

   _____

2. Canadian economy is slowing down. Experts agree.

   _____

3. On average, women live longer than men. It is a fact.

   _____

4. Canada has the largest number of lakes worldwide. It is interesting to know.

   _____

EXERCISE 3

Fill in each blank with the correct word from the list. Each word is used once.

whichever	however	wherever
whomever	whenever	whatever

You can eat <u>whatever</u> you want. I don't care anymore.

1. There are three packages. You can pick _____ matches your needs.

2. Immigrants to Canada can settle _____ they want.

3. We will do _____ it takes to succeed.

4. Give this package to _____ opens the door.

5. He is on the phone _____ I see him.

6. You can travel to Vancouver _____ you want. I will go there by plane.

EXERCISE 4

For each pair of sentences below, make a new sentence two ways. First, use the second sentence as a noun clause. Second, reduce the noun clause to an infinitive.

Please tell me. How can I send money overseas?
→ Please tell me how I can send money overseas.
→ Please tell me how to send money overseas.

1. Please tell me. How can I submit my homework online?

   _____

   _____

   _____

2. I have forgotten. Where should I go after the exam?

   _____

   _____

   _____

3. I can't decide. Should I go to university or should I join the army?

   _____

   _____

   _____

4. Her mother begged. She should go to university.

   _____

   _____

   _____

5. Our teacher requires this. We should hand in homework on time.

   _____

   _____

   _____

 COMMUNICATIVE ACTIVITY 2

True or False?

Some of the eight sentences below are scientifically proven to be true and some are false. Work in pairs. Partner A uses the patterns in Column A to ask a question or make a statement about each sentence. Partner B responds by using the patterns in Column B. The partners then discuss why they think the sentences are correct or wrong.

A	B
Do you think (that) . . .?	I don't believe (that) . . .
Do you agree (that) . . .?	I don't think (that) . . .
Did you know (that) . . .?	I suppose (that) . . .
Have you heard (that) . . .?	I assume (that) . . .
I have learned (that) . . .	I know (that) . . .
I suspect (that) . . .	I've read somewhere (that) . . .

Bats are blind and they use echolocation to find their way around.

Partner A: Did you know that bats are blind and use echolocation to find their way around?

Partner B: I know that some bats use echolocation, but **I don't believe that** they are blind. If they are blind, why do they have eyes then?

Partner A: You're right! **I don't think** I'd ever thought about that.

1. Every year, more than one million earthquakes shake the earth.

2. There is no gravity in space.

3. Every hour the universe expands by 1.6 billion kilometres in all directions.

4. There is a side of the moon that is always dark.

5. There is a side of the moon that is never visible from the earth.

6. Brain cells can't regenerate.

7. The days (and nights) are getting longer than they used to be millions of years ago.

8. The Great Wall of China is the only human-made object visible from the moon.

⚞ COMMUNICATIVE ACTIVITY 3

Five Questions

Work in pairs. First, work individually to connect the words in parentheses to the sentences that follow them by using a wh- word or *if / whether*. Remember to make any changes that are needed, such as word order or punctuation. Then take turns with your partner asking each other questions by using the sentences that you made. Each person asks five questions. The student with the largest number of correct answers wins.

(I want to know) When did humankind step on the moon?

Student A: I want to know when humankind stepped on the moon.

Student B: I am not sure when humankind stepped on the moon. I think it was some time in the 1960s.

1. (Do you know) Who was Picasso?

2. (Do you think) Can you name a famous Canadian movie?

3. (Tell me) When did Canadian scientists receive a Nobel Prize for discovering insulin?

4. (I want to know) Does Venus have any moons?

5. (I wonder) How many moons does Jupiter have?

6. (I'd like to ask you) Is Gander a city in Canada?

7. (Guess) What does *gander* mean?

8. (Can you help me find out) Were Vikings actually the first Europeans to visit Canada?

9. (I'd like to know) Which Canadian city has the warmest weather in winter?

10. (Do you have any idea) Did Canada officially participate in the Iraq war?

THE SUBJUNCTIVE IN NOUN CLAUSES

Formation

Type	Example Sentence	Explanation and Meaning
future wish	I wish they <u>would</u> join us tomorrow.	*Would* is used instead of *will*. They probably <u>won't</u> join us.
present wish	I wish they <u>were</u> here now.	*Were* is used instead of *are*. They <u>aren't</u> here now.
past wish	I wish they <u>had been</u> with us yesterday.	*Had been* is used instead of *were*. They <u>weren't</u> with us yesterday.
expression of advice	He **suggested** that they <u>stay</u>.	The base form of the verb is used. Meaning: He **should** <u>stay</u>.
expression of necessity	He **ordered** that he <u>be punished</u>.	The base form of the passive verb is used. Meaning: He **must** <u>be punished</u>.

NOUN CLAUSES AFTER *WISH*

The verb *wish* can be followed by a *that* noun clause. In most cases *that* is deleted.

> I wish that I could go to the party. → I wish I could go to the party.

Wish often expresses a desire for something that is **not present**, is **unreal**, or is **not possible**. For this reason, the verb in the *that* clause is in the **subjunctive**.

For present wishes, the past tense is used in the noun clause.

> She <u>doesn't have</u> a car now. → I wish (that) she <u>had</u> a car now.

For future wishes, *would* or *could* is used in the noun clause.

> She <u>won't buy</u> a car in the near future. → I wish (that) she <u>would buy</u> a car in the near future.

> He <u>can't attend</u> the ceremony tonight. → I wish (that) he <u>could attend</u> the ceremony tonight.

For past wishes, the past perfect is used in the noun clause.

> She <u>borrowed</u> my car yesterday. → I wish (that) she <u>hadn't borrowed</u> my car yesterday.

In more formal English, the verb *was* is replaced by *were* in wish clauses.

> I wish I was there with you guys. (informal, conversational)

> I wish I were in a position to help you. (formal)

MEANING OF *WISH* CLAUSES

Wish clauses can be used to express the following three things.

1. Desire for something hard or impossible to get (at present or in the future)

   > I wish I had a million dollars.

   > I wish I could travel in time.

2. Regrets (at present or in the past)

   > Present: I wish I could come to your birthday party. Sorry I can't!

   > Past: Sorry! I wish I hadn't said all those bad things about you.

3. Complaints (usually with *would*)

   > I wish you would stop making that noise.

   > I wish he would listen to me.

THAT CLAUSES AFTER EXPRESSIONS OF NECESSITY AND ADVICE

If a *that* clause comes after a verb or an expression of advice or necessity, the verb in the *that* clause will always use the **base form** (the unconjugated form) regardless of the tense of the introductory expression.

Read the following examples:

I suggest that he go out for lunch. (*Suggest* is a verb of advice, so the verb in the *that* clause takes the base form.)

I know that he goes out for lunch. (*Know* is not a verb of advice or necessity, so the verb in the *that* clause has the third-person -*es*.)

With verbs of advice or necessity, in the negative form, we add *not* to the base form of the verb:

The judge ordered that he return to his country. → The judge ordered that he not return to his country.

EXERCISE 5

Fill in the blanks with the correct form of the verbs in parentheses.

1. Hi, Stephanie! I know it's your birthday today, so I thought I'd call and wish you a happy birthday. I wish I _____ (be) there with you now to celebrate.

2. I didn't know about your birthday party yesterday. I wish you _____ (tell) me when we met last week.

3. Tomorrow is my best friend's wedding and I won't be able to attend. I wish I _____ (go).

4. I said some very stupid things yesterday. I wish I _____ (say, negative) those things.

5. I always say stupid things without thinking. I wish I _____ (think) more before speaking.

6. He's going to say something stupid again. I wish someone _____ (stop) him.

EXERCISE 6

Decide why the speaker says each of the following sentences. Write the intention (desire, regret, or complaint) beside each sentence.

1. I wish I were in love again. _____

2. I wish you would listen to me. _____

3. I wish I could help you. _____

4. He wishes he were able to make up for his mistake. _____

5. I wish my neighbour wouldn't throw so many late-night parties. _____

EXERCISE 7

In each sentence, fill in the first blank with the correct form of the verbs of necessity or advice from the list below. Fill in the second blank with the correct form of the verb in parentheses. Use each verb of necessity or advice once. The first one has been done for you.

| advise | demand ✓ | suggest | request | propose | insist | recommend |

The customer, who was very angry, <u>demanded</u> that the manager <u>give</u> (give) her a refund.

1. The plan originally _____ that the bridge _____ (be) built

   farther away from the mall.

2. The MPs formally _____ that they _____ (meet) with the

   prime minister.

3. You want to ask for Mike's opinion? I know what he will say. He _____

   that we _____ (go) to the movies.

4. He is in his room, and he is stubbornly _____ that nobody

   _____ (go) in.

5. My professor always _____ to me that I _____ (take) a

   course in creative writing.

6. My doctor strongly _____ that I _____ (undergo,

   negative) surgery until I regain my strength.

✴ COMMUNICATIVE ACTIVITY 4

Wishes

Work in pairs. First, work individually to write nine secret personal wish sentences. These should be three desires, three regrets about the past, and three complaints with *would*. Then, try to guess what your partner wrote. You can each guess six times in each category about your partner's wishes. The partner with the most correct guesses wins the game.

Category: Complaints

Student A's secret wish: I wish my mother would stop calling me Honey.

Student B's guess: You wish your sister wouldn't use your clothes without your permission?

Student A: Wrong! Next guess?

COMMUNICATIVE ACTIVITY 5

Help, Please!

Work in pairs. Partner A uses a prompt from Column A to talk about a problem. Partner B uses an appropriate expression of advice from Column B to offer a solution or to provide advice. Switch roles after each exchange.

Partner A: I think my computer is infected with a virus.

Partner B: It is essential that you install anti-virus software and run a complete scan.

Column A	Column B
computer, virus	It is desirable that
home, purchase	It is important that
colleague, not cooperating	It is not necessary that
neighbour, noisy	It is vital that
tax, audit	It is essential that
child's classmate, bully	It is critical that
heart, surgery	It is mandatory that

BRINGING IT ALL TOGETHER

COMMUNICATIVE ACTIVITY 6

What Do You Know?

Work in pairs. First, work individually to answer the questions by filling in the answer column and then putting a check mark in the column that describes how sure you are about your answer. When you and your partner have completed your charts, exchange your books, and share your partner's answers with the rest of the class. The first two questions have been done for you.

Question	Answer	I'm Confident.	I'm Pretty Sure.	I'm Guessing.
Do aliens exist?	Yes			✓
When did the Big Bang happen?	13.75 billion years ago	✓		
What is the population of Canada?				
How large is Canada?				
Did the word Canada (*Kanata*) originally mean "village"?				
Who discovered Newfoundland and Labrador?				
Why is the NHL trophy called the Stanley Cup?				
Was Superman created by a Canadian artist?				
How should you act if you encounter a bear?				
Whose picture is on the Canadian $5 bill?				

The partner reports: My partner **guesses** <u>that</u> aliens exist. He **knows** <u>when</u> the Big Bang happened. He is **confident** <u>that</u> the Big Bang happened 13.75 billion years ago.

Reading

Read the passage and answer the questions that follow.

ARCHIMEDES' PRINCIPLE

It's the third century B.C.; we're in Syracuse, in Sicily (for centuries an important Greek outpost); and the local king, Hiero II, has reason to suspect that the royal jeweller has sneaked some silver into the new, and supposedly 100% gold, royal crown. Hiero calls in Archimedes, who for a while is stumped. He knows that gold weighs more than silver and consequently has less volume, and that the volume of a piece of

pure gold and of a crown of pure gold weighing the same amount would be the same. But how to measure the volume of a strange-shaped thing like a crown?

Then, pondering the problem one day in the tub, Archimedes realizes that a body immersed in liquid displaces exactly its own volume of that liquid. Measure the volume of the water that's spilled over the side of the tub and you've got the volume of the thing *in* the tub. At this point, Archimedes shouts "Eureka!" and runs home naked, where he puts first the piece of pure gold, then the crown said to be of pure gold, in a basin of water. The crown causes the water to rise higher, revealing itself to have a greater volume (and hence to be less dense, i.e., *not* pure gold). This reveals the jeweller to be guilty.

The story told, bear in mind that Archimedes' principle, as opposed to Archimedes' bath, applies not only to bodies immersed in water but to bodies floating on it, and not only to solids but to liquids and gases. It explains, in addition to why ships float, why balloons rise, and it warns that in determining what will and what won't sink, float, or fly away, both weight and volume must be considered, not to mention shape and position. If you can manage to remember anything here beyond "Eureka!" you might go for "specific gravity," the ratio of a given density of a solid or a liquid to the density of water (and of a gas to air), and a term that, while unknown to Archimedes, pretty much sums up what his principle winds up being all about.

Adapted from Judy Jones and William Wilson, *An Incomplete Education: 3,684 Things You Should Have Learned but Probably Didn't*.

COMPREHENSION

Complete the following sentences.

1. King Hiero suspects that _____ .

2. At the beginning of the story Archimedes is confused because he doesn't know how

_____ .

3. When Archimedes enters the bathtub he discovers that _____

    _____.

4. Archimedes proves that the crown is not made of pure gold by _____

    _____.

5. Archimedes' principle applies to both _____ and

    _____.

6. Archimedes' principle applies to solids and _____ and

    _____.

7. Archimedes' principle explains why _____ and why

    _____.

8. Archimedes' principle warns that _____.

9. Specific gravity is defined as _____.

10. The main idea of this passage is _____.

ANALYZING THE READING PASSAGE

The reading passage contains several noun clauses and reduced noun clauses. Read the passage again and underline as many of them as you can.

Listening

🔊 Track 09

THE YOUNG AND THE GENEROUS

Listen to the interview once or twice and answer the questions that follow.

COMPREHENSION

Part 1

1. What was the subject of Dr. Kiley Hamlin's study?

    _____

2. What has the study by Dr. Hamlin demonstrated?

    _____

3. How many children participated in the study?

    _____

4. How old were the children on average?

    _____

5. Why did the researchers install the bowl with the false bottom in the puppet?

    _____

6. What were the four stages (situations) created for the experiment?

    a. _____

    b. _____

    c. _____

    d. _____

7. Which of the four situations made the babies the happiest?

    _____

8. How did they measure the babies' happiness level?

    _____

9. According to Dr. Hamlin, why are human beings generous?

    _____

10. What is Dr. Hamlin's job title and where does she work?

    _____

Part 2

Listen to the interview one more time; this time, listen for the noun clause structures you learned about in this chapter. Try to find as many noun clauses as you can (there are more than 20 noun clauses), and write them on a separate sheet of paper.

Writing

Research a famous scientific principle or theory (such as the law of gravity, Newton's laws of motion, or Einstein's theory of relativity). Write the story behind the law, and explain the law in easy-to-understand language. Use the structures that you learned in this chapter as much as you can. You may refer to the reading passage in this lesson as an example. Your composition should be 250–350 words.

CHAPTER REVIEW

Summary

- Noun clauses, like other types of clauses, present complex information in a concise and effective way.

- Noun clauses are dependent clauses that act like nouns.

- Noun clauses start with *that*, *if*, *whether*, or wh- words.

- *That* is usually omitted in informal conversation or writing.

- The verbs in *that* clauses after expressions of necessity or advice appear in the subjunctive (the base form of the verb).

- Noun clauses can sometimes be reduced to infinitive form.

- The verbs in noun clauses after *wish* are usually in the subjunctive form.

- *Wish* clauses are often used to express desires, regrets, or complaints.

EXERCISE 1

The sentences below are all written incorrectly. Based on what you learned in this chapter, correct each sentence by making small changes. You may add or remove words or replace one word with another.

1. I wish that I can join my sister in Winnipeg this weekend.

2. I do not know what does Canada mean.

3. Is important that you dial 1 before international numbers.

4. You may sit whichever you want.

5. He recommended that she did not leave the country.

6. She now wishes that she visited Fredericton when she was in New Brunswick last month.

7. Do you know where is Surrey?

8. It is mandatory that he goes to Quebec City immediately.

9. Excuse me, sir! Do you know that the flight from Montreal is on time?

10. I do not know to go London.

EXERCISE 2

Combine the sentences into one.

I wish something. I want tomorrow to be a holiday. → I wish tomorrow would be a holiday.

1. I wish something. I want to fly like a bird.

   _____

2. I wish something. I didn't want to fail the course.

   _____

3. I wish something. I don't want it to be raining now.

   _____

4. I don't know. What do you want from me?

   _____

5. I don't care. Where are you going?

   _____

6. I am not sure. Is she going to be fine?

   _____

7. I know! I am sometimes wrong.

   _____

8. It is important. Employees should protect their passwords.

   _____

9. Have you decided? Do you want to leave?

   _____

10. I am sad. He is leaving the company.

    _____

11. I heard the news. Mr. Bhindi will be stepping down as president.

    _____

PART 2

8 CLAUSE
INTRODUCTION—
ADJECTIVE
CLAUSES

9 NOUN CLAUSES

10 REPORTED SPEECH

11 ADVERB CLAUSES

12 ADVERB CLAUSES
OF CONDITION

10 Reported Speech

OVERVIEW

Reporting what someone else has said is an essential skill. People use it when they tell stories or narrate an event. Students use it when they write research papers in which they have to cite experts. Reporting is also used widely in several fields, such as medicine, law, and journalism.

We can report what someone says in three major ways.

1. By repeating the exact words of the speaker inside quotation marks (direct speech):

   He said, "I do not agree with you."

2. By replacing the speaker's original perspective with our own (indirect speech):

   He said that he didn't agree with me.

3. By paraphrasing or summarizing the message, the intention, or the emotion behind the message:

   He disagreed with me.

The indirect speech method (number 2 above) often creates a noun clause (see Chapter 9).

He said **that he didn't agree with me.**

He asked **if I agreed with him.**

Warm-up 1

Work in pairs. Pose the following questions to your partner, and take notes on a separate sheet of paper when he or she answers. Then, switch roles. At the end of the exercise, report to the class what your partner said.

1. What was your childhood like? What are some of your childhood memories?

2. How do you usually spend your weekends?

3. What do you plan to do when you finish this course?

REPORTING FOR DIFFERENT SENTENCE TYPES

Formation

We face four main sentence types when reporting:

1. Statements

2. Imperatives (orders and requests)

3. Yes / no questions

4. Information questions (wh- questions)

Study the chart below to see how each type of sentence is reported.

Sentence Type	Direct Speech	Indirect Speech	Paraphrase / Summary
1. Statements	He said, "I **am** guilty."	He said that he **was** guilty.	He **confessed** his guilt.
2. Imperatives	"**Don't** walk home alone!" he said.	He told me **not to** walk home alone.	He **advised** me against walking home alone.
3. Yes / no questions	"**Are** you okay?" he asked.	He asked **if** I **was** okay.	He was **worried** about me.
4. Information questions	The policeman asked, "Where **were** you at the time of the murder?"	The policeman asked where I **had been** at the time of the murder.	The policeman **interrogated** me about my whereabouts at the time of the murder.

Warm-up 2

Work in pairs. Discuss and answer the following questions. Refer to the examples in the formation chart on the previous page.

1. How does punctuation change from direct to indirect speech?

2. In direct speech examples, what is the position of the "he said" clause? Does it appear before or after the quotation marks?

3. Why did *am* in the sentence "I am guilty" change to *was* in indirect speech (row 1 in the chart)?

4. *Don't* changes to *not to* in indirect speech for imperatives (row 2 in the chart). What do you think happens to positive imperatives in indirect speech? Change the following sentence to indirect speech:

   (direct) "Sit down!" he said. → (indirect) He asked me _____.

5. What changes happened in indirect speech for the question "Are you okay?" (row 3 in the chart)? Discuss the changes.

6. Discuss the changes for the wh- question from direct to indirect speech.

DIRECT SPEECH

PUNCTUATION

A direct speech sentence contains two main parts:

1. An introductory part containing a subject (Mike, she, they, etc.) and a reporting verb (*asked*, *said*, *inquired*, etc.)

2. The exact words we are reporting between quotation marks (" ")

The introductory phrase can come **before**, **after**, or **in the middle of** the quoted part. Pay attention to punctuation and capitalization in each of the following examples.

Mark said, "We don't like Mary."

"We don't like Mary," said Mark.

"We don't like Mary," he said.

"We don't like Mary," he said, "because she is really annoying."

"We don't like Mary," he said. "She is really annoying."

EXERCISE 1

Add punctuation and proper capitalization to the following direct speech sentences. Use the examples above as guidelines.

1. Albert Einstein once said if the bee disappears from the surface of the earth, man would have no more than four years to live.

2. Ernest Hemingway once wrote the world is a fine place and worth fighting for.

3. Who is she it was one of the young kids that asked.

4. I don't know who she is Barrow Man said she was hanging around near my stand all afternoon.

5. What are you going to do with her I said.

6. Well, right now he said she looks so gorgeous I wouldn't dare touch her. . . .

7. I'm hungry he said and I suppose she is too. Some of you nervous people who stole my flowers should buy us something to eat.

8. Get them some food Walter I said I'll pay.

Questions 3 to 8 are excerpts from David Helwig, "Something for Olivia's Scrapbook I Guess," in *Canadian Short Stories*.

REPORTING VERBS

The most common reporting verbs in English are *say* and *ask*, but sometimes other verbs add more meaning and feeling to the quotation. Try to use a variety of reporting verbs depending on what exactly you want to say. Notice the difference in meaning created by reporting verbs in the following sentences.

Anne **said,** "I don't like this." (*Say* is neutral. We don't know much about Anne's feelings.)

Anne **complained,** "I don't like this." (*Complain* shows that Anne is not happy.)

Anne **whispered,** "I don't like this." (*Whisper* shows that Anne is either shy or doesn't want others to know her opinion.)

EXERCISE 2

Replace the <u>underlined</u> reporting verbs (*said* and *asked*) in the sentences on the next page with one of the following reporting verbs below. You can use each verb once only.

| added | begged | wondered | agreed | inquired |
| shouted | replied | objected | suggested | |

1. "What will you do," <u>asked</u> the teacher, "if you fail this course?"

   "I don't know yet," <u>said</u> Jorge.

2. "Please let me go," <u>said</u> the little boy.

   "No!" the angry man <u>said</u>, "You broke my window." And then he <u>said</u>, "You should pay for it."

   "But I don't have any money," the boy <u>said</u>.

3. He <u>asked</u>, "What could we do tonight?"

   "We could go to a restaurant," she <u>said</u>.

   "You are right," he <u>said</u>.

INDIRECT SPEECH

INDIRECT SPEECH FOR STATEMENTS

In Chapter 9 (Noun Clauses), you learned that we can combine two sentences by using *that*.

I am tired. I believe it. → I believe that I am tired.

We can use the same process to change direct speech to indirect speech. This time, we have to remove the quotation marks and change the punctuation.

I say, "I am tired." → I say that I am tired.

He adds, "They all agree." → He adds that they all agree.

Changing Verbs in Indirect Speech

In the previous example, both the reporting verb (*say*) and the verb in the quotation (*am*) are in the present.

   If the reporting verb is in the **past**, we usually have to change the verb in the quotation as well when we change the sentence from direct to indirect speech. We change the verb to show that what we are reporting now was actually said in the past.

I said, "I am tired." → I said that I was tired.

In this example, *am* changed to *was* to show that I said the sentence in the past. I am not tired now. I was tired when I said that sentence.

   In this next example, agree changed to agreed because they agreed in the past:

He added, "They all agree." → He added that they all agreed.

Notice how verb tenses change in the following examples.

I said, "I write a letter." → I said that I wrote a letter.

I said, "I am writing a letter." → I said that I was writing a letter.

I said, "I am going to write a letter." → I said that I was going to write a letter.

I said, "I will write a letter." → I said that I would write a letter.

I said, "I have written a letter." → I said that I had written a letter.

I said, "I can write a letter." → I said that I could write a letter.

I said, "I may write a letter." → I said that I might write a letter.

I said, "I must write a letter." → I said that I had to write a letter.

I said, "I wrote a letter." → I said that I had written a letter.

I said, "I was writing a letter." → I said that I had been writing a letter.

Some verbs often do not change, though.

I said, "I should write a letter." → I said that I should write a letter.

I said, "I might write a letter." → I said that I might write a letter.

I said, "I had written a letter." → I said that I had written a letter.

In the following situations, the verb doesn't change in indirect speech.

1.   When we are talking about scientific **facts**, general **truths**, **sayings**, or **proverbs**:

My teacher said, "It takes the earth 365 days to travel around the sun."

My teacher said that it takes the earth 365 days to travel around the sun.

2.   When we are reporting somebody else's words immediately or within the same time frame as that of the speaker:

The prime minister said, "The government is going to live within its budget."

The prime minister said that the government is going to live within its budget.

EXERCISE 3

Change the following sentences from direct to indirect speech. Pay special attention to the **tense** of the reporting verb and to **facts**, **truths**, and **time frames**.

1.   I said, "I am deeply sorry!"

_____

2.   Bertolt Brecht was the one who believed, "Life is short and so is money."

_____

3.   That evening, we all said, "We should leave soon before it gets dark."

_____

4. In the seventeenth century, Galileo said, "The earth is not the centre of the universe."

   _____

5. On that day we all agreed, "We are lucky to have food on our table."

   _____

6. Our mother always says, "We are a lucky family because we have so many good friends."

   _____

7. Earlier today I confessed, "I am going to fail the test tomorrow."

   _____

8. Yesterday morning I said, "I will go out for lunch at noon."

   _____

 ## COMMUNICATIVE ACTIVITY 1

Tense Change Practice

Work in pairs. Student A's book is open. Student B's book is closed. Student A reads direct-speech sentences at random from the verb-tense-change examples on page 198. Student B converts them to indirect speech orally. The students switch roles. This time, Student B reads indirect speech sentences at random, and Student A orally converts them to direct speech. Students at higher levels may replace the examples in the chart with their own sentences.

Student A: I said, "I write a letter."

Student B: I said that I would write a letter.

Student B: I said that I wrote a letter.

Student A: I said, "I will write a letter."

Changing Pronouns and Possessive Adjectives in Indirect Speech

It is important to note that if you are reporting somebody else's speech, you often have to change the pronouns and possessive adjectives to show your point of view.

Notice the changes in the following example.

He said to me, "**I** <u>am</u> in **my** room watching TV when **I** suddenly <u>hear</u> **your** brother scream."

He told me that **he** <u>was</u> in **his** room watching TV when **he** suddenly <u>heard</u> **my** brother scream.

Note: *Said to* changes to *told* in indirect speech. (See the example above.)

EXERCISE 4

Change the following sentences from direct to indirect speech. Make sure to change verbs, pronouns, and possessive adjectives if necessary.

1. I said to you, "One way or another, you will tell me the truth."

   _____

2. I said to him, "You haven't said a word to me."

   _____

3. Julie said to Jeff and Ian, "I didn't see you at the meeting."

   _____

4. He said to her, "You cannot leave without my permission."

   _____

5. He said to Mom and Dad, "You know well that my sister dislikes both of you."

   _____

6. Carrie said to me, "We have your phone number on our computer at the office."

   _____

7. I said to my girlfriend, "I must leave before your parents kick me out."

   _____

8. Cindy said to Jason, "I love your desk lamp, and, one day, I am going to steal yours and leave you mine."

   _____

Changing References to Places in Indirect Speech

Another element that often changes in indirect speech is references to places.
    Look at the following pictures.

In the first picture, *here* changes to *there* because the speaker's location is different from the reporter's. In the second picture, *here* doesn't change because both the speaker and the reporter are in the same location.

Here are some general guidelines for changing place references:

here → there   this → that   these → those

EXERCISE 5

Change the following sentences from direct to indirect speech. Make sure you change verbs, pronouns, possessive adjectives, and references to places if necessary.

1. Yesterday, she said to our teacher, "I hate this school."

   _____

2. I told her then, "I will never forget these days."

   _____

3. When I was a teenager, I said to my mom, "I won't stay here in this house with you."

   _____

4. The little girl pointed to the sky and said, "I want those clouds."

   _____

Changing References to Time in Indirect Speech

If the time at which the speaker says something is different from the time at which the reporter is reporting it, references to time will often have to change too.

On Monday, Jack says, "I **will** go to Toronto **tomorrow**."

Report on Monday: Jack said that he **will** go to Toronto **tomorrow**.

Report on Wednesday: Jack said that he **would** go to Toronto **on Tuesday**.

In the first report, it is still the same day, so the verb and the adverb of time stay unchanged. The second report comes one day after Jack was supposed to leave, so *tomorrow* becomes *yesterday* or *Tuesday* to give the reader a good sense of the time. The verb changes too in the second case.

As you can see, indirect speech changes are very case specific. You have to decide how to treat each situation. However, here are some general guidelines for changing adverbs of time:

In Direct Speech		In Indirect Speech
now	→	then or immediately
today	→	that day
tomorrow	→	the day after / the next day
yesterday	→	the day before
ago	→	before
the last day / week / month / year	→	the day / week / month / year before
the next day / week / month / year	→	the following day / week / month / year

EXERCISE 6

Change the following sentences from direct to indirect speech. Make sure you change verbs, pronouns, possessive adjectives, and references to time and place if necessary.

1. "We have to leave right now," they said.

   _____

2. "He is sleeping now," she said.

   _____

3. "We will talk next week," he said.

   _____

4. Earlier today, he said, "I lost my keys yesterday."

   _____

5. Last week she said to me, "I will see you tomorrow."

   _____

6. The first time I met Fatima, she said to me, "I left my country just two weeks ago."

   _____

7. He pointed to the crowd and said, "These people have gathered here today because they are not happy."

   _____

8. On Tuesday he said, "I am going to see you later today."

   _____

✺ COMMUNICATIVE ACTIVITY 2

Role-Play

Work in groups of four. The diagram at the top of the next page shows the scene of an accident. Read the summary of the accident. One person becomes the driver of Car A; the second person becomes the driver of Car B; and the third is the witness (driver of Truck B). The last person is the police officer. The officer interviews all three drivers and then reports (in indirect speech) what each driver said.

Truck A turned left on yellow. Car A didn't see the red light because of truck A, and Car A turned on red.
Car B moved on green.
Car A hit Car B on the side.
Car B lost control, went over the median, and had a head-on collision with the side of Truck B.

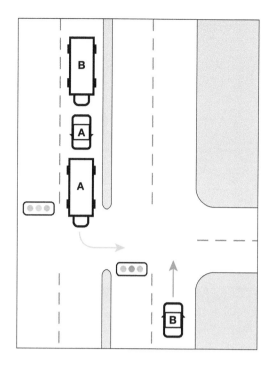

INDIRECT SPEECH FOR ORDERS AND REQUESTS (IMPERATIVES)

We usually report orders by using *tell* and requests by using *ask*.

The **imperative verb** in direct speech changes to the **infinitive** in indirect speech.

He said, "Sit down, please!" → He asked me to sit down.

Negative imperative verbs in direct speech change to **negative infinitives** in indirect speech.

He said, "Don't stare!" → He told me not to stare.

EXERCISE 7

Change the following sentences from direct to indirect speech. Some sentences contain statements and imperatives.

1. "Get out of here!" he said angrily.

2. "Don't look at me like that," he said.

3. He said, "Come a little closer toward the camera and look directly into the lens."

4. He said, "Don't walk away when I am talking to you."

5. The emergency preparedness instructor said to the students, "Get out of the building as soon as you hear the alarm. Do not use the elevators. Use the nearest stairs or exits. Once you are outside, keep at least 100 metres away from the building. Do not re-enter the building unless you are told to do so."

_____

_____

_____

_____

_____

 # COMMUNICATIVE ACTIVITY 3

Reporting Instructions

Work in pairs. You and your partner each choose one of the following topic suggestions and write instructions (in the imperative, both positive and negative) on how to do the task. Then hand your instructions to your partner to report (orally) in indirect speech. You may use Exercise 7, Question 5 above as a guideline.

Topics

- how to perform CPR
- how to drive a stick shift
- how to deliver bad news
- how to negotiate
- how to hold a baby

INDIRECT SPEECH FOR QUESTIONS

Review the section on embedded questions on pages 176–177 in Chapter 9 (Noun Clauses) before starting this section.

When we change a question from direct to indirect speech, we are embedding the question. As you learned in the previous chapter, the question changes to a statement when it is embedded. Study the following examples.

He asked, "Will you be here tomorrow?" → He asked **if I would** be **there the next day.**

He asked, "What time will you be here tomorrow?" → He asked what time **I would** be **there the next day.**

Here's what happened:

1. The question form was changed to statement (will you be → you will be).

2. (For yes / no questions only) *If* was added to the beginning of the question.

3. The verb was changed (will → would).

4. Pronouns were changed (you → I).

5. Adverbs of time (*tomorrow*) and place (*here*) were changed.

6. Punctuation was changed.

EXERCISE 8

Change the following questions into indirect speech. Imagine that the time and place have changed in all cases.

1. He asked, "How old are you?"

   _____

2. They asked, "Have you ever visited Nunavut?"

   _____

3. She asked, "Do you work full-time?"

   _____

4. Maria asked, "Whose book is this?"

   _____

5. I asked, "Did you drink any coffee today?"

   _____

6. I asked, "How much coffee did you have?"

   _____

7. She asked, "Were you at the Brandon Folk Festival last summer?"

   _____

8. Peter asked, "Will you go to the movies this weekend?"

   _____

9. Sheila asked, "What were you doing when I called?"

   _____

10. He asked, "How many resumés must I send out before I can even get an interview?"

    _____

🔆 COMMUNICATIVE ACTIVITY 4

Reporting a Conversation

Work in small groups. Each student chooses one of the following topics and prepares six questions (three yes / no and three wh- questions) on that topic. Student A poses questions for Student B to answer. Student C listens carefully and takes notes on the conversation between Students A and B. At the end of the conversation, Student C reports (in indirect speech form) both the questions of Student A and the answers of Student B to the group. Students then switch roles until all three members have had a chance to pose questions, answer questions, and report a conversation.

Topics:

- student life
- financial fitness
- sports
- health
- Canadian trivia
- careers and passions

REPORTING BY PARAPHRASING AND SUMMARIZING

In real life, people do not always follow the rules described in this chapter. In many cases, instead of reporting the exact words in a message, people report the meaning, the intention, or the feeling behind the message.

For example, this sentence

Veliborka said, "The movie was awesome."

can be reported more naturally as

Veliborka enjoyed the movie very much.

Using effective reporting verbs is perhaps the best way to summarize speech. Review the section on reporting verbs on page 196 in this chapter.

EXERCISE 9

Report the following sentences by rewording, summarizing, or paraphrasing the message. There might be more than one correct answer for each sentence.

1. "Isn't it a beautiful day?" he said.

   _____

2. He said, "Would you please pass the salt?"

   _____

3. She said, "I doubt that Parliament will ever pass such a law."

   _____

4. "God, please forgive me," she said.

   _____

5. "I don't give a damn anymore," he said.

   _____

6. The student asked her teacher, "Would it be okay if I handed in my homework late?"

   _____

 ## COMMUNICATIVE ACTIVITY 5

Summarizing a Story

Work in pairs. First, work individually, on a separate sheet of paper, to write a very short story (approximately 100 words) about something funny or sad that happened to you. Then, switch papers with your partner, and summarize your partner's story to half its original length. Finally, read your summary to your partner.

BRINGING IT ALL TOGETHER

 ## COMMUNICATIVE ACTIVITY 6

Game—Snowball Fight!

Every student in class takes a sheet of paper and writes his or her name at the top of the page. Then all students write five (direct speech) sentences on their paper (one statement, one yes / no question, one information question, one positive imperative, and one negative imperative). Students crumple their sheets and make balls out of them. They then start throwing the balls to one another for about a minute until the teacher says, "Stop!" At this point, each student should end up with a ball of paper. Students with more than one paper ball can give the extras to students without. Students open the paper balls. They have one minute to change all five sentences into indirect speech. Students then read both the original sentence and their indirect speech version. Any students with mistakes in their indirect speech sentences are eliminated from the game. In round two, the remaining students get another sheet of paper, make five more sentences, crumple them, and put them in a bag. The teacher mixes the balls and lets the remaining students each take one ball. The game continues until only one student is left. This last student is the winner.

Reading

Read the passage and answer the questions that follow.

LIFE SENTENCE FOR JEANVENNE FOLLOWING GUILTY VERDICT

A career criminal, once a member of the notorious Hole in the Wall Gang, was convicted for a second time Thursday of the "brutal execution" of a man he wrongly believed <u>ratted him out</u> on a safe-cracking job.

The jury found Andre Jeanvenne, 64, guilty of the first-degree murder of Michel Richard. The 49-year-old was found <u>stabbed</u> 18 times and shot twice in his Russell Rd. apartment on May 17, 2000.

"You were the self-appointed judge, jury and <u>executioner</u> of that innocent man who was afforded no right to a trial," Judge Colin McKinnon told the diminutive, white-haired Jeanvenne before sentencing him to life with no chance of <u>parole</u> for 25 years from his 2003 arrest.

There was no physical evidence linking Jeanvenne to the <u>grisly</u> scene.

But the jury heard Jeanvenne made damning admissions to criminal pals and undercover cops who ran a <u>sting</u> in 2002.

Jean-Claude Massie has since died but <u>testified</u> from beyond the grave on tape that he, Jeanvenne and a third man broke into Henry Amusements in Vanier in Feb. 1992, cracking the safe and netting $113,000 each.

Massie recalled Jeanvenne saying Richard—a talented shoplifter so gentle "he couldn't fight his way out of a paper bag"—had ratted him out.

A second "<u>unsavoury</u>" witness—who said Jeanvenne threatened his life three times in court—testified Jeanvenne had a .32 caliber revolver and a <u>score to settle</u> before Richard's killing. A .32 bullet was found in the body.

A third witness testified that Jeanvenne said Richard was a rat and that he'd "dumped" him because he deserved it and made chilling statements.

An undercover RCMP officer testified Jeanvenne told him Richard was a rat and when he was sure, he killed him. A second officer in the sting, which paid Jeanvenne handsomely for staged crimes, testified he said he'd killed four people.

Jeanvenne was convicted in 2005 of the murders of Richard and Donald Poulin, who was found dead from a shotgun blast by a Gloucester road in 1983.

The Ontario Court of Appeal ordered two new trials in 2010, concluding the dissimilar murders shouldn't have been tried together. A second trial in the Poulin case ended in a hung jury earlier this year.

Adapted from an article by Megan Gillis, "Life Sentence for Jeanvenne Following Guilty Verdict," *Ottawa Sun*.

COMPREHENSION

Part 1

Provide the following information about the case.

1. Defendant's name and age _____

2. Victim's name and age at the time of murder _____

3. Cause of death _____

4. Address of crime scene _____

5. The reason the victim was murdered _____

6. The name of the place the victim, the defendant, and his accomplice robbed in 1992 and the amount of money each took _____

    _____

7. The total number of witnesses who testified in court _____

8. The verdict _____

9. The reason the defendant was tried twice for the same murder

    _____

10. The year the defendant was first tried for this murder _____

Part 2

Read the passage a second time and provide the following information. You may use direct speech, indirect speech, or paraphrasing in response to the questions.

1. What did the judge say to the defendant?

    _____

2. What did Massie remember Jeanvenne saying about Richard?

    _____

3. What did the second witness say?

_____

4. What did the third witness say?

_____

5. What did Jeanvenne say to the undercover RCMP officer?

_____

6. What did he say to the second undercover officer?

_____

ANALYZING THE READING PASSAGE

The reading passage contains several instances of direct, indirect, and paraphrased / summarized speech. Read the passage again and underline as many of them as you can. Mark each type with the appropriate letter: **D** for direct, **I** for indirect, and **S / P** for summary / paraphrase.

Listening

🔊 Track 10

CATCH ME IF YOU CAN

In this clip, you will hear the story of Timothy Szabolcsi, a Canadian con man who has fooled many people.

COMPREHENSION

Part 1

Listen to the clip once and answer the following questions.

1. In which Canadian province was Timothy Szabolcsi born?

_____

2. What was the name of the city where he went to high school?

_____

3. In which city did Timothy marry and live after graduating from high school?

_____

4. Where did Tim work in the 1980s, according to his friends?

_____

5. Why did he leave the U.S. and come back to Canada in the summer of 2010?

   _____

6. Where did he start volunteering in 2010?

   _____

7. Why did the children's parents become suspicious of Tim?

   _____

8. What kind of clinic did Tim run in Garland, Texas?

   _____

9. What type of business did Tim start in BC in 2012 after disappearing from Winnipeg?

   _____

10. Where did Tim and Sheri Brown meet for the first time?

    _____

11. How much money did Sheri take out of her account to support her husband Tim?

    _____

12. What is Tim's last known address?

    _____

13. What is his most recent nickname?

    _____

Part 2

Listen to the clip again and decide whether the following statements are true (T) or false (F). If the statement is false, try to correct it.

1. In the summer of 2012 Tim called his friends from the airport and told them that he had lost his luggage and he needed a ride. _____

2. When they first met, Tim told Sheri that he was a retired Beverly Hills engineer. _____

3. Several days before their wedding, Tim told Sheri that his partners had stolen all his money. _____

4. Before they were married Sheri asked Tim if he had ever been convicted of a crime and he said no. _____

5. Tim told Sheri that he had applied to the BC College of Physicians to get his doctor's licence. _____

Complete the following statements in your own words based on what you learned in this clip. Pay attention to verbs in indirect speech form.

1. When Tim first started going by different names, Tim's friends figured that

   _____

2. CBC first got involved in Tim's case in October 2010 when concerned hockey

   parents believed that _____

3. When the parents complained to the police, the police said that there wasn't much

   they could do because _____

4. When Sheri called the BC College of Physicians, they told her that

   _____

5. After Sheri contacted Tim's old girlfriend in the US, she found out that

   _____

Writing

Work in pairs. Choose one of the following topics, and discuss the topic for about 10 minutes with your partner. Make detailed notes of what each one of you says. Outside of class, research the topic further on the Internet, and find views of experts on the topic.

Write a report on the topic defending your view (approximately 350 words). Include what you and your partner discussed, and support your point of view by including the views of the experts. Use a variety of reporting styles (direct, indirect, paraphrase) to make your writing interesting. Pay special attention to your reporting verbs.

Topics:
- a recent book, song, or movie that both you and your partner have read, heard, or watched.
- a debate on the question, "Do more prisons and tougher punishment laws reduce crime rates?"

CHAPTER REVIEW

Summary

- We can report what someone says in three ways: direct speech, indirect speech, and summary / paraphrase form. It is important to use a combination of all these styles when writing a report or a research paper to keep readers interested in your writing.

- In direct speech, we do not change any of the speaker's original words.

- In indirect speech, we make the speaker's words part of our own sentence. We keep the keywords, but change the point of view by changing pronouns, the time, and the place.

- In indirect speech, imperatives change to infinitive form; questions change to statements; and sometimes verb tenses, pronouns, and references to time and place change because we may be reporting at a later time and from a different place.

- In summary / paraphrase form, we focus on the meaning or feeling of the message and change the structure and most of the actual words.

EXERCISE 1

Change the following sentences from indirect speech or summary / paraphrase form to direct speech. Make sure to use correct punctuation and capitalization.

1. Your father told me to protect you but not to stand in your way.

   _____

2. I asked why I couldn't go to the cinema that evening.

   _____

3. She asked me if I had been living in Canada for a long time.

   _____

4. I replied that I had left my country 20 years before.

   _____

5. He asked for the salt.

   _____

6. He asked me when I planned to start.

   _____

7. I said that I would start working the following week.

   _____

8. He begged for mercy.

   _____

9. She apologized.

_____

10. The governor of the Bank of Canada announced that it had had to lower the overnight lending rate.

_____

EXERCISE 2

The following interview is between Robert Cameron, a student reporter, and Shan Li, an international student. You are the editor of the *College Times*. After reading the interview, prepare a short report based on the interview. Use a balanced mix of the three reporting methods you learned in this chapter (direct, indirect, and summary / paraphrase).

Robert: Hi. My name is Robert Cameron. I'm a reporter for the *College Times*. I was wondering if I could take a few minutes of your time and ask you a couple of questions about your experience as an international student here in Vancouver.

Shan: Sure!

Robert: Where do you come from?

Shan: I was born in mainland China, but I grew up in Hong Kong, so I'd say I come from Hong Kong.

Robert: How long have you been in Canada?

Shan: This is my third year here in Canada.

Robert: Why did you choose Canada and in particular Vancouver for your studies?

Shan: My first choice was UCLA, but I didn't know anyone in California. I have a second cousin here in Vancouver who promised to help me get settled. Also, it is very easy to travel between Hong Kong and Vancouver. On top of that, Vancouver has repeatedly been chosen as the best city in the world to live in. It is indeed a great city.

Robert: What was the biggest challenge you faced during your first year as a student?

Shan: Language was my biggest problem. I thought I had good English skills until I came here and noticed that I really didn't understand much when people talked at normal speed. It took me more than a year to really feel comfortable with English.

Robert: What do you like the most and the least about our college?

Shan: I love the college. We have a beautiful campus here, a vibrant international student community, and excellent teaching faculty. There's not much that I don't like here, but if I had to choose, I'd say the high tuition fees that I have to pay as an international student.

Robert: Do you have any advice for new international students?

Shan: Don't overestimate your level of English. Come to Canada a few months before your courses start and give yourself time to learn the real language.

Robert: Thank you for your time!

Shan: You're welcome!

11 Adverb Clauses

OVERVIEW

- Adverb clauses are subordinate (dependent) clauses; they contain a subject and a verb but cannot stand alone and need a main clause for their meaning to be complete.

- Most adverb clauses can come **before**, **after**, or **inside** the main clause. When they come before the main clause, a comma (,) follows them.

- Subordinating conjunctions are words—such as *where*, *when*, *if*, *because*—that show the relationship between the subordinate clause and the main clause.

- Adverb clauses are usually classified based on the meaning of their subordinating conjunctions.

- Adverb clauses function as adverbs; they can express different ideas, such as **time**, **manner**, **cause**, **result**, **purpose**, **comparison**, **contrast**, or **condition**.

- A different set of subordinating conjunctions is used at the beginning of the adverb clauses for each of these ideas. For example, adverb clauses of manner start with the conjunctions *as*, *if*, or *as though*, and adverb clauses of time start with such conjunctions as *when*, *before*, *after*, or *until*.

- Conditional adverb clauses are discussed in detail in the next chapter (Chapter 12).

Warm-up

Work in pairs. In the sentences below, the subordinating conjunctions are incomplete. Working together, read the sentences and add the missing letters for each conjunction. Each line represents one missing letter.

1. Some subordinating conjunctions are easier to use bec _ _ _ _ they are more common, whi _ _ others might be a bit more difficult sin _ _ you don't hear them very often in conversation.

2. Alt _ _ _ _ _ you have seen or heard almost all of these conjunctions bef _ _ _ studying this chapter, and des _ _ _ _ the fact that you might know their meaning, you probably won't be able to use some of them correctly unt _ _ you have used them several times.

3. By the t _ _ _ you finish this chapter and the next one, you should have su _ _ a good understanding of these conjunctions that you will have no trouble using them, pro_ _ _ _ _ that you keep practising _ _ much _ _ you can.

ADVERB CLAUSES OF TIME

Formation

Here are the most common subordinating conjunctions used with adverb clauses of time.
   Just like adverbs of time, adverb clauses of time tell us when the action in the main clause happens. Compare the following two sentences.

We arrived at the airport **beforehand.** (adverb of time)

We arrived at the airport **before the plane landed.** (adverb clause of time)

Subordinating Conjunctions of Time	Meaning / Usage	Example Sentence
since	use *since* to show when the action started.	Terry Fox was born in Manitoba in 1958, but he had lived in British Columbia **since** he was eight years old.
before	earlier than	**Before** he started distance running, Terry wanted to be a basketball player.

Subordinating Conjunctions of Time	Meaning / Usage	Example Sentence
while as	*while* and *as* suggest that the action is continuing	Terry took up distance running **while** he was in junior high school. On November 12, 1976, **as** Terry was driving home, he crashed into the back of a pickup truck.
after	later than	He felt some problems with his knee **after** he had the car accident.
until	to show the end of the action	Terry chose to ignore the pain in his knee **until** the basketball season ended.
as soon as	immediately after another action	**As soon as** the basketball season ended, he went to see a doctor.
when	at, during, or soon after	**When** Terry Fox was diagnosed with bone cancer, he was only 18 years old.
once	from the time when something happens	**Once** Terry found out how little money was dedicated to cancer research, he decided to run the length of Canada to increase cancer awareness.
by the time	not later than	Terry Fox had become a national hero **by the time** he reached Ontario.
as long as	to the extent that	I will never forget Terry's sacrifice **as long as** I shall live.

Note: Several example sentences in this chapter were adapted from "Terry Fox" in Wikipedia, accessed 14 August 2012.

EXERCISE 1

Fill in the blanks with the appropriate subordinating conjunction of time from the chart above. You can use each conjunction once only.

<u>After</u> Plato died, Theophrastus met and became friends with Aristotle.

1. The world will lose an enormous amount of biodiversity _____ the years pass.

2. The notion of a cell did not exist _____ the microscope was invented in the seventeenth century.

3. The pink salamander is able to reproduce _____ it even matures.

4. The nervous system makes you jerk your hand away from a hot stove almost

   _____ you have touched it.

5. _____ Charles Darwin proposed his theory of evolution, most scientists still believed the world was only a few thousand years old.

6. Sir Alexander Fleming discovered penicillin _____ he was growing cultures of bacteria in petri dishes.

7. More than 12,000,000 people have already died from AIDS _____ the beginning of this worldwide epidemic.

8. _____ HIV gets inside the body, it attacks the T-4 white blood cells.

9. _____ the human embryo reaches eight weeks, all its adult organ systems are in place and it is no longer called an embryo, but is a fetus.

10. _____ an organism remains alive, its supply of carbon-14 remains the same.

Most of the sentences in this exercise are adapted from Leonard C. Bruno, *U.X.L. Complete Life Science Resource*.

COMMUNICATIVE ACTIVITY 1

Sentence Chain

Work in pairs. Flip a coin to decide who starts the game.

Partner A makes a sentence with any of the subordinating conjunctions of time on pages 216–217. Partner B then takes the subordinate clause of Partner A's sentence and uses it as the main clause of another sentence. Partner B then completes the clause with one of the remaining conjunctions. The game continues until one of the partners is unable to make a meaningful sentence or until all conjunctions have been used.

Partner A: I came to Canada <u>after</u> I graduated from high school.

Partner B: I graduated from high school <u>before</u> I got my driver's licence.

Partner A: I got my driver's licence <u>as soon as</u> my father bought me a car.

ADVERB CLAUSES OF PLACE

The conjunction *where* is used in noun, adjective, and adverb clauses. Look at the examples below, and try to identify the clause type in each sentence.

Do you know where I live?

This is the place where I live.

There's no public transportation where I live.

The first sentence contains an embedded question (noun clause). In the second sentence, the clause modifies a noun (place) and is therefore an adjective clause. The last sentence contains an adverb clause.

Formation

Subordinating Conjunctions of Place	Meaning / Usage	Example Sentence
where	in / at / to the place in which	Terry proved that **where** there's a will, there's a way.
wherever	in every place that	**Wherever** Terry ran in Ontario, citizens cheered him on.

EXERCISE 2

Fill in each blank with *where* or *wherever*.

1. Sit _____ I can see you.

2. You may sit _____ you like.

3. He always carries his cellphone with him _____ he goes.

4. Look at _____ the sea meets the horizon.

5. Trouble follows him _____ he goes.

6. I couldn't see anything from _____ I was standing.

7. _____ ignorance is our master, there is no possibility of real peace.
    —Dalai Lama

8. A man's homeland is _____ he prospers.
    —Aristophanes

ADVERB CLAUSES OF MANNER

The two expressions *as if* and *as though*, used in adverb clauses of manner, are synonyms and are used in almost the same way.

Formation

Subordinating Conjunctions of Manner	Meaning / Usage	Example Sentence
as if as though	*as if* and *as though* describe how something seems	Terry reacted to his injury **as if** it was nothing important. Terry ran **as though** he were a healthy person.

As if and *as though* are often used after such verbs as *look*, *seem*, and *act* (or any other action verbs).

We can use the subjunctive form (past tense with a present meaning) to show that the comparison is unreal.

Read the following examples.

You look as if you **haven't had** enough sleep. (The present tense is used. The speaker means what she says.)

You look as if you **hadn't slept** for a year. (The subjunctive form is used to show that the speaker is exaggerating.)

- In **informal** English, it is possible to replace *as if* and *as though* with *like*.

  You look **like** you haven't had enough sleep.

- In **formal** English in the subjunctive form, we use *were* instead of *was*.

  He looked as if he **were** dead. (formal)

  He looked as if he **was** dead. (informal)

EXERCISE 3

Fill in the blanks with the proper form of the verbs in the parentheses, depending on the reality or unreality of the situation.

1. Are you okay? You sound as if you _____ (be) sad.

2. She looked as if she _____ (see) a monster.

3. She behaves as though she _____ (be) my mother.

4. He looks as if he _____ (be) drunk. Somebody had better drive him home.

✦ COMMUNICATIVE ACTIVITY 2

Real and Unreal

Work in pairs. Partner A chooses a subject, a verb, and a conjunction (at random) from the chart on the next page and adds any other words needed to make the first part of a sentence. Partner B completes the sentence by adding his or her own words, paying special attention to the verb (real or unreal) and changing the verb form where necessary. Switch roles after the first round and play again.

Subject	Verb	Conjunction
mother	sing	
brother	look	
it	sleep	as if
teacher	seem	as though
you	cook	
the weather	have	

Partner A: It seems as if . . .

Partner B: It seems as if **we are going to have an exam soon.**

ADVERB CLAUSES OF CAUSE

We form adverb clauses of cause when we talk about the reason something happened.

Formation

Subordinating Conjunctions of Cause	Meaning / Usage	Example Sentences
because since as	For the reason that	At first, Terry was discouraged **because** very few people were making donations. **Since** Terry Fox is considered a national hero, statues of him can be found in several cities across Canada. Fox ran with an unusual gait **as** he was required to hop-step on his good leg.
on account of the fact that / owing to the fact that / due to the fact that / in view of the fact that	*On account of the fact that* and all its synonyms are usually considered wordy alternatives for *because*. Use them only when you want to avoid repeating the other conjunctions.	**Due to the fact that** the springs in his artificial leg required extra time to reset after each step, Fox ran with an unusual gait.

- *Because* is used when the reason is **more** important than the rest of the sentence. *As* and *since* are used when the reason is **less** important than the rest of the sentence or the reason is already known.

  I quit <u>because</u> they **discriminated** against me. (Here **discrimination** is the important part.)

  <u>Since</u> they discriminated against me, I'm going to **sue** them. (Here **suing** is the important part.)

- *Since* and *as* are synonyms. *Since* is more formal than *as*.
- Longer expressions, such as *on account of the fact that* or *in view of the fact that*, are usually not recommended because they are too wordy. Use shorter versions, like *because* or *as*, where possible.

EXERCISE 4

<u>Underline</u> the most important information in the following sentences.

1. As Venus is much nearer the sun, its temperature must be higher than that of the earth.

2. Stem cell technology raises moral questions because human embryos have to be destroyed to harvest the embryonic stem cells.

3. The GPS receiver determines the lag in satellite signals, and since it knows the signal's speed, it can calculate the distance.

EXERCISE 5

Combine each of the following sentence pairs into one complex sentence by using the conjunction provided. Change pronouns to proper nouns if necessary.

1. Their car was too old. They decided to sell it. **(as)**

    _____

    _____

2. Our teacher doesn't feel very well today. She is going to dismiss the class. **(since)**

    _____

    _____

3. Our teacher doesn't feel very well today. She is going to dismiss the class. (because)

_____

_____

4. Pig flu viruses can be a big problem for people. Pigs can be infected with flu viruses from birds, other pigs, and people, creating opportunities for new virus gene combinations. (because)

_____

_____

5. The use of fossil fuels has increased. The concentration of carbon dioxide in the atmosphere is rising. (due to the fact that)

_____

_____

ADVERB CLAUSES OF RESULT

The words *so* and *such* can be used before *that* clauses. The *that* clause shows the result.

Formation

Subordinating Conjunctions of Result	Meaning / Usage	Example Sentence
so + adj. / adv. + *that* *such* + (a / an) noun + *that*	in a way that	Terry hated to lose **so** much **that** he would continue at any activity until he succeeded. Terry left **such** an impact on Canadians **that** he has been named Canada's greatest hero in several national surveys.
so that	resulting in something	The cancer spread to Terry's lungs so that he had to end his run just outside Thunder Bay in Ontario.

So is used before adjectives or adverbs. *Such* is used before nouns.

My dog was <u>so</u> **charming** that everybody fell in love with him.

My dog was <u>such</u> **a charmer** that everybody fell in love with him.

It is possible to have an adjective between *such* and the noun which follows it.

He was <u>such</u> **a charming dog** that everybody fell in love with him.

EXERCISE 6

Fill in the blanks with *such* or *so*.

1. A medication with _____ few side effects and _____ beneficial effects as those of acetylsalicylic acid is hard to find.

2. The field of oncology has experienced _____ rapid progress that it exceeds even the most optimistic predictions.

3. Learning a new language is not _____ a difficult task that many believe. All you need to do is to surround yourself with the new language _____ much that you are exposed to it constantly, _____ that you begin to think and even dream in your new language.

4. Doctors used to believe that pancreatic cancer is _____ aggressive and grows _____ quickly that screening cannot be effectively used.

ADVERB CLAUSES OF PURPOSE

We normally use a *to* infinitive to talk about our purpose.

We must buy some tools **to fix the staircase.** (normal, everyday English)

We use adverb clauses to be more emphatic. Adverb clauses are also more formal than the *to* infinitive.

A handyman must have proper tools **so that** he can do a neat repair job. (A bit more formal than the previous example. Note how the modal auxiliary *can* has been added here.)

Formation

Subordinating Conjunctions of Purpose	Meaning / Usage	Example Sentence
so that in order that for the purpose that	All three expressions are synonyms and all show intention or purpose.	Doctors had to amputate Terry's leg **so that** they could save his life. Terry Fox ran across Canada **in order that** he could draw attention to cancer research. Several memorials have been erected across the country **for the purpose that** future generations remember Terry's heroism.

- *In order that* is more formal than *so that*.
- In informal English *so* is often used without *that*.

  A handyman needs proper tools so he can do a neat repair job.

EXERCISE 7

Using the conjunctions in parentheses, change the following sentences into complex sentences with adverb clauses of purpose. Add modal auxiliaries (*can, could, may, will*) if necessary.

1. You should wake up early to get to school on time. (so that)

   _____

   _____

2. Certain conditions are needed for people to feel happy at work. (in order that)

   _____

   _____

3. Medical institutions should collect, use, or disclose personal information only to serve their patients in a better way. (for the purpose that)

   _____

   _____

ADVERB CLAUSES OF COMPARISON

The *as* + adj. / adv. + *as* structure is used when the two points of comparison have equal weight.

The *-er* / more + adj. / adv. + *than* structure is used when one of the two points of comparison has more weight than the other.

Formation

Subordinating Conjunctions of Comparison	Example Sentence
as + adj. / adv. + *as*	Can you think of any other Canadian activist **as** famous **as** Terry Fox?
-er / more / less + adj. / adv. + *than*	At one point, Terry was receiving **more** mail **than** the rest of his city combined.

- **as** + **adj. / adv.** + **as** sometimes changes to **so** + **adj. / adv.** + **as** in negative sentences.

  He is **as** old **as** he claims to be.

  He is <u>not</u> **so** old **as** he claims to be.

- The ending **-er** is used for short adjectives and adverbs. **More** is used with longer adjectives and adverbs. See Chapter 5 in *Communicating with Grammar*, Level 2, for a review of the comparative form.

EXERCISE 8

Complete the following statements by using conjunctions of comparison (*-er, more, less, as . . . as*) and adjectives.

1. Drug A is fairly effective. Drug B is very effective.

   a. Drug B is _____ Drug A.

   b. Drug A is _____ Drug B.

2. The orbital speed of earth around the sun averages about 30 km/s. The orbital speed of Venus averages 35 km/s.

   a. Earth travels around the sun _____ Venus does.

   b. Venus travels around the sun _____ earth does.

3. Galileo Galilei had an IQ of 165. Charlotte Brontë had an IQ of 165.

    a. Galileo was _____ Brontë.

    b. Bronte was _____ Galileo.

ADVERB CLAUSES OF CONTRAST

Two types of conjunctions show contrast. The first type (called "concessive") includes such conjunctions as *although*, *though*, and *even though*, which show **partial contrast**, often in the form of **surprising or unexpected information** in relation to the other half of the sentence.

> Sean went out **although** it was raining heavily. (We did not expect Sean to go out in heavy rain, but he did.)

The second type (called "adversative") includes such conjunctions as *while*, *whereas*, and *where*, which show **complete contrast** between the two clauses.

> Bill decided to go out in the rain, **while** Tanya decided to stay under the shelter. (Here Bill's behaviour is in complete contrast to Tanya's.)

Formation

Subordinating Conjunctions of Contrast	Meaning / Usage	Example Sentence
concessive: although though even though / even if despite / in spite of the fact that	Concessive conjunctions show partial contrast.	**Although** the spread of his cancer eventually forced Terry to end his quest after 143 days, his efforts resulted in a lasting, worldwide legacy. **Though** he stood only five feet tall, Terry made the school's basketball team. Terry was determined to continue playing basketball, **even if** he was the last substitute on the team. **Despite the fact that** it was a hot summer, Terry continued to run 42 kilometres per day.
adversative: while whereas / where	Adversative conjunctions show complete contrast.	Terry felt he was born to be a basketball player, **while** his coach felt he was better suited to be a distance runner. Terry learned that recent medical advances had improved his chance of survival to 50%, **whereas** a couple of years earlier his chance would only have been 15%.

- *Although*, *though*, and *even though* are very close in meaning. *Though* is less formal than *although*. *Even though* is more emphatic than *though* and *although*.
- Among adversative conjunctions, *where* is the least formal and *whereas* is the most formal.

EXERCISE 9

In the sentences below, remove *but* and add *although* or *while* in the appropriate sentence position based on contrast type. Change the punctuation if necessary.

It was raining, **but** the children kept playing outside. (concessive)

Although it was raining, the children kept playing outside.

The children kept playing outside, **but** their parents ran inside. (adversative)

The children kept playing outside, **while** their parents ran inside.

1. He is not looking for a job, **but** he is receiving very tempting offers.

   _____

2. Maryam wants to go to college, **but** her parents want her to go to university.

   _____

3. Rachel is a Jew, **but** her husband is a Buddhist.

   _____

4. I will go to see this movie, **but**, in general, I don't like horror movies.

   _____

Note: For adverb clauses of condition, refer to Chapter 12.

REDUCING ADVERB CLAUSES

Certain types of adverb clauses can be reduced (shortened) to adverb phrases or participle clauses. Also, we can sometimes express the idea in the adverb clause in the form of a preposition + noun structure (prepositional phrase).

The Formation chart gives you an overview of the process.

Formation

Type	Example Sentence	Explanation
adverb clause	**While I was going home,** I saw an old friend.	The regular adverb clause of time is followed by main clause. The subject (I) is the same in both clauses.
adverb phrase	**While going home,** I saw an old friend.	The subject and the verb *be* in the adverb clause are deleted. This can be done only if the two subjects are the same.
participle clause	**Going home,** I saw an old friend.	The conjunction, the subject, and the verb *be* are deleted. This can be done only if the two subjects are the same.
prepositional phrase	I saw an old friend **on my way home.**	The complex sentence is changed into a simple sentence. The idea in the adverb clause is instead expressed through a preposition + noun structure.

We can reduce adverb clauses to adverb phrases and participle clauses only when the subject of the adverb clause is the same as the subject of the main clause.

ADVERB PHRASES

Some adverb clauses (such as clauses of time or concession) can be often reduced to adverb phrases.

Here are the steps to change an adverb clause to a phrase:

1. Make sure the subjects of both clauses in the sentence are the same.

2. Delete the subject of the adverb clause and the verb *be* (*am, is, are, was, were*). If the verb is not from the *be* family, change the verb to the *-ing* form. If the verb is negative, add *not* before the verb.

3. If the deleted subject was a proper noun (e.g., *Tom, Mary, Emily*) and the subject of the main clause was a pronoun (e.g., *he, she, they*), change the pronoun into the proper noun.

    I ran out of breath **while I was jogging.** (Delete the subject and *was.*)

    I ran out of breath **while jogging.**

    I bought a carton of milk **before I came home.** (Delete the subject and change *came* to *coming.*)

    I bought a carton of milk **before coming home.**

Although ~~Tom was~~**n't prepared, he** delivered an excellent speech. (Delete *Tom* and *was*, keep the negative adverb *not*, and change *he* in the main clause into *Tom*.)

Although not prepared, Tom delivered an excellent speech.

EXERCISE 10

Change the adverb clause in each sentence below into an adverb phrase. If the change is not possible, write "N/A" ("not applicable").

1. He fell asleep while he was driving.

   _____

2. He fell asleep while I was driving.

   _____

3. I will take a shower after I go home.

   _____

4. Before you blow the candles, you should make a wish.

   _____

5. When she is not teaching, Carol writes children's stories.

   _____

6. I have had a horrible cough since I came back from Mexico.

   _____

7. Though Jerry was still weak after his surgery, he went to his friend's funeral.

   _____

8. Once the kids are ready, we will leave.

   _____

PARTICIPLE CLAUSES

Participle clauses are formed similarly to adverb phrases, but the conjunction is also deleted. Participle clauses are more formal than both adverb clauses and adverb phrases, and are mostly used in writing.

As Carl was **jogging in the forest,** he saw a big black bear.

Jogging in the forest, Carl saw a big black bear.

Because I didn't have **enough money,** I accepted the first job that I was offered.

Not having enough money, I accepted the first job that I was offered.

EXERCISE 11

In the following sentences, reduce the adverb clauses into participle clauses.

1. Once they reach their first goal, they will set higher ones.

   _____

2. As we had run almost out of gas, we decided to stop at the next gas station.

   _____

3. Because she knew she wouldn't be able to sleep on the plane, Karen downloaded some movies on her iPad.

   _____

4. Since André didn't know anyone at the meeting, he busied himself with some brochures.

   _____

PREPOSITIONAL PHRASES

It is sometimes also possible to reduce an adverb clause by changing the clause into a prepositional phrase (preposition + noun).

Here are examples of some of the most common patterns.

The outdoor party was cancelled **due to the fact that the weather was bad.** → The outdoor party was cancelled **due to bad weather.**

Terry continued to run **in spite of the fact that it was hot.** → Terry continued to run **in spite of the hot weather.**

We went home **after we left the party.** → We went home **after the party.**

Her doctor sent her to a specialist **so that she could be tested more thoroughly.** → Her doctor sent her to a specialist **for more thorough tests.**

He left the party **because he had a bad headache.** → He left the party **because of his bad headache.**

As soon as he graduates, he will travel around the world. → **Upon graduation,** he will travel around the world.

Although he is constantly in pain, he is in good spirits. → **Despite his constant pain,** he is in good spirits.

EXERCISE 12

Change the adverb clause in each of the following sentences into a prepositional phrase.

1. She didn't cry after she was born.

   _____

2. I decided to stay home because it was raining heavily.

_____

3. He went out although it was hot.

_____

4. As soon as he arrived, he headed for the summit.

_____

5. In spite of the fact that there was a big snowstorm, the lost boy survived a night in the Rockies.

_____

6. I saw an accident while I was going to school.

_____

BRINGING IT ALL TOGETHER

 ## COMMUNICATIVE ACTIVITY 3

Co-write a Story

Work in pairs. Partner A writes a complex sentence containing an adverb clause and passes the sentence to Partner B. Partner B adds to the sentence with another adverb clause. When you both feel the sentence is long enough, end the sentence and start a new sentence. The new sentence must be the continuation of the same story. Continue doing this until you have a complete story of about 500–600 words. Any pattern you learned in this lesson is allowed (adverb clauses, reduced adverb clauses, prepositional phrases, etc.). Repeated conjunctions are also allowed.

Partner A: Although I did not feel well, I went outside.

Partner B: Although I did not feel well, I went outside **so that I could get some fresh air.**

Partner A: Although I did not feel well, I went outside so that I could get some fresh air **as I hadn't been outside since I got sick the week before.**

Reading

Read the passage on the next page and answer the questions that follow.

HOW TO CURE HICCUPS

Hiccups have <u>bedeviled</u> people since the first caveman shoved too big a hunk of woolly mammoth into his <u>gullet</u>. Singultus, as it is medically known, results from an irritation of the diaphragm, usually caused by indigestion. Phrenic nerve fibers discharge in response, resulting in the <u>spasmodic</u>, painful contractions of the diaphragm. Air is sucked in, then the windpipe abruptly closes (Hic!). Hiccups have no beneficial purpose, though they do argue for taking smaller bites and chewing your food slowly.

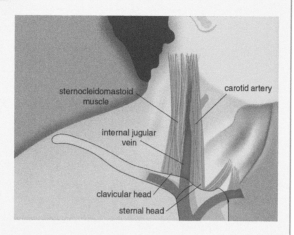

. . . Thomas Assmar, of Jewett City, Connecticut, invented a supposedly miraculous hiccup-curing machine that sufferers would stand on while drinking water and be <u>tossed</u> up and down 92 times a minute. It is claimed that everybody who tried it was cured—as many as 100 people in all—but the machine has been lost since Assmar died in 1978. Except for Assmar's inventions, for hundreds of years hiccups cures have been pretty much the same (hold a sugar cube or <u>glob</u> of peanut butter in your mouth, drink water through a handkerchief, stand on your head, breathe through a paper bag, munch on a wedge of lime, etc.). But if you suffer from frequent attacks of the hiccups, you have probably tried all of these remedies and found them wanting. Fortunately, medical science has weighed in on the problem.

Instead of a folk remedy, try the Hughes/Green hiccups cure, invented by former hiccups sufferer Dave Hughes, of Redwood Valley, California: (1) Pour a tall glass of water. (2) While holding your breath and pinching your nose closed, repeatedly take sips of water until you feel like you are drowning, then stop. (3) Inhale deeply and breathe normally. The hiccups should be cured. Hughes believes this technique works by depriving the spasmodic muscles of oxygen, causing them to stop the hiccuping reflex.

For more stubborn cases, try icing down the nerve fibers that are responsible. It turns out the ideal places to interrupt the hiccups are the sides of the neck. In order to stop the hiccups, use the method developed by S. Gregory Hipskind, M.D., of Bellingham, Washington. Find your Adam's apple (for women, this point is about 2 inches [5 centimetres] directly below the chin). Move back until you are above your clavicle (the big protruding bone at the base of your neck). You should be just behind the sternocleidomastoid muscles, well back of and below your carotid arteries. Apply ice cubes to each side until the hiccuping stops.

In really serious cases, your doctor can give you a shot of nefopam, an anti-shivering medication that is highly effective, or baclofen, a muscle relaxant. If those injections don't work, nimodipine, a calcium channel blocker that <u>inhibits</u> muscle contractions, has been shown to cure even the most <u>intractable</u> cases of the hiccups.

If all else fails, consider the last-resort, successful cure of the former hiccup world-record holder, Jack O'Leary of Los Angeles, who hiccupped an estimated 100 million times during an eight-year <u>bout</u>: a prayer to St. Jude, the patron saint of lost causes.

Adapted from John T. Walbaum, *The Know-It-All's Guide to Life: How to Climb Mount Everest, Cure Hiccups, Live to 100, and Dozens of Other Practical, Unusual, or Just Plain Fantastical Things.*

COMPREHENSION

1. What is singultus?

   _____

2. What causes hiccups?

   _____

3. What happens when phrenic nerve fibres discharge?

   _____

4. How did Assamar's machine work?

   _____

5. What happened to Assamar's machine?

   _____

6. What were the folk remedies for hiccups before Assamar's machine was invented?

   _____

   _____

7. What was the Hughes/Green cure? How did it work?

   _____

   _____

8. Explain how to stop hiccups by using Hipskind's method.

   _____

   _____

9. Who is the hiccups world record holder? How long did he hiccup?

   _____

   _____

10. What is the general tone of this passage? How do you know?

    _____

    _____

ANALYZING THE READING PASSAGE

The reading passage contains several instances of adverb clauses. Read the passage again and <u>underline</u> as many of them as you can. Then, identify each clause's type.

Listening

◀)) Track 11

MARATHON OF HOPE

Listen to the audio and answer the questions that follow.

COMPREHENSION

Part 1

1. Where did Terry Fox start his Marathon of Hope?

   _____

2. Where did his marathon end?

   _____

3. Who restored Terry Fox's van?

   _____

4. What happened to the van after Terry's death? Who finally found it? (Retell the whole story.)

   _____

   _____

   _____

5. What does each of the speakers remember about Terry's marathon?

   _____

   _____

   _____

6. What are the birth dates of each of the speakers? (Carol and Alex)

   _____

7. Why didn't the Fox family like the first Terry Fox movie?

   _____

8. Who is Dean Karnazes? Why is he mentioned in this clip?

   _____

ADVERB CLAUSES   235

9. What was the problem with Terry's artificial leg?

_____

10. In which province did Terry face problems? What was the nature of the problems?

_____

Part 2

Listen to the clip one more time, and find as many adverb clauses and reduced adverb clauses as you can. Copy the clauses on a separate sheet of paper and identify their type.

Writing

Research the life of Terry Fox. Write a short biography (400–500 words) focusing on his cancer, his run, and his legacy. Use adverb clauses or reduced adverb clauses where you can. You may use the examples in the formation tables as guidelines.

CHAPTER REVIEW

Summary

Function / Type	Subordinating Conjunctions
time	since, before, while, as, after, until, as soon as, when, once, by the time, as long as
place	where, wherever
manner	as if, as though
cause	because, since, as, on account of the fact that, owing to the fact that, due to the fact that, in view of the fact that
result	*so* + adj./adv. + *that*, *such* + (*a/an*) noun + *that*, so that
purpose	so that, in order that, for the purpose that
comparison	*as* + adj./adv. + *as*, *-er/more/less* + adj./adv. + *than*
contrast	**concessive:** although, though, even though, even if, despite / in spite of the fact that **adversative:** while, whereas, where

Adverb clauses can add important information about the action or state in the main clause. For example, depending on the conjunctions used, they can show **where**, **when**, **how**, or **why** the action in the main clause occurred.

Adverb clauses can come **after** (very common), **before** (common), or **inside** (very rare) the main clause.

Adverb clauses are sometimes reduced (shortened) to become more concise or to create variety.

We can reduce an adverb clause to

- an adverb phrase (While he was going home → While going home)
- a participle clause (While he was going home → Going home)
- a prepositional phrase (As soon as he graduates → Upon graduation)

EXERCISE 1

Some conjunctions, such as *since*, *while*, *as*, and *so*, have more than one meaning and are used in more than one type of adverb clause. Read the following sentences, and decide what type of adverb clause (time, purpose, cause, etc.) each contains.

1. I have been living in this town **since** I was born. _____

2. **Since** I have been living here all my life, I sometimes come across my childhood friends. _____

3. Yesterday, I saw my best friend from high school **while** I was walking home.

   _____

4. I remember he wanted to be an engineer, **while** I wanted to be an artist.

   _____

5. He left town after high school **so that** he could study civil engineering.

   _____

6. He said he felt **so** homesick **that** he had to quit school and come back home.

   _____

7. **As** he had nothing else to do after coming back, he started painting.

   _____

8. **As** he said this, I looked at his hands and clothes and noticed some dried drops of paint. _____

9. To make a long story short, soon his work attracted **so** much attention **that** he

    decided to become a full-time artist. _____

10. The ironic part is that I am now a computer engineer. Life is not **so** predictable

    as we might think, is it? _____

EXERCISE 2

Change each of the following compound sentences into a complex sentence by removing the coordinating conjunction (such as *and, so, but, or, yet*) and adding a subordinating conjunction from the list below. There might be more than one correct answer for some sentences; however, you can use each conjunction once only. Rearrange sentence elements if necessary.

since	after	because	as soon as
although	as	while	even though

He was tired, **so** he went to sleep. → He went to sleep **because** he was tired.

1. He came in, **and** I immediately closed the door.

    _____

2. They came in first, **and** then I closed the door.

    _____

3. You know I did it, **so** I cannot deny it.

    _____

4. We studied hard for the test, **yet** we didn't pass.

    _____

5. I want to be an artist, **but** my brother wants to be a doctor.

    _____

6. I am a full-time student, **so** I cannot hold a full-time job.

    _____

7. He did not agree to have surgery, **so** he died.

    _____

8. Next Monday is a holiday, **but** I still have to go to work.

    _____

Adverb Clauses of Condition

OVERVIEW

- Conditional clauses are adverb clauses and follow the same rules as adverb clauses you learned about in the previous chapter.

- There are two main types of conditional sentences: real conditions (the condition is real and possible) and unreal conditions (the condition is not real or possible).

- Like all other unreal situations in English (e.g., wishes), the subjunctive is used in unreal conditions.

- Besides *if* (the most common conjunction), there are several other subordinating conjunctions of condition, such as *unless*, *in case*, and *provided that*.

Warm-up 1

Work in pairs. Read the list of subjects of selected quotations from famous people. Discuss the meaning of the quotations that follow. Then, match each of the general subjects with the corresponding quotation. Check your dictionary for the meaning of any words you do not know. The first one has been done for you.

| ~~history~~ | spunk | candour | self-sufficiency | self-confidence | doubt |

history   Cleopatra's nose: if it had been shorter, the whole face of the earth would have been different.
—Blaise Pascal

(Meaning: Egyptians at the time considered a large nose to be a sign of beauty and wisdom.)

_____ If you happen to have a wart on your nose or forehead, you cannot help imagining that no one in the world has anything else to do but stare at your wart, laugh at it, and condemn you for it, even though you have discovered America.
—Fyodor Dostoyevsky

_____

_____ If you want a thing done well, do it yourself.
—Napoleon Bonaparte

_____

_____ If we are strong, our character will speak for itself. If we are weak, words will be of no help.
—John F. Kennedy

_____

_____ If you tell the truth, you don't have to remember anything.
—Mark Twain

_____

_____ We are not certain, we are never certain. If we were, we could reach some conclusions, and we could at last, make others take us seriously.
—Albert Camus

_____

Warm-up 2

Read the quotations one more time. This time, underline the verbs in the conditional sentences: <u>one line</u> for the verbs in the *if* clause and <u>two lines</u> for the verbs in the main clause. Discuss the relationship between the verb tenses in the two clauses. The first one has been done for you.

Cleopatra's nose: if it <u>had been</u> shorter, the whole face of the earth <u>would have been</u> different.

REAL CONDITIONS

Conditional sentences can be divided into two main categories: real conditions and unreal conditions.

Real conditions refer to situations that happened before, are true at present, or will probably happen in the future. In this category of conditions, the conjunction *if* sometimes has a similar meaning to *when*.

In those days, **if** I received any extra money, I spent it on books.

In those days, **when** I received any extra money, I spent it on books.

In real conditions, as in other adverb clauses, we can have almost any normal combination of subordinate and main clause tenses.

Formation

The following chart contains some of the most common verb tense combinations in real conditions.

Tense Combination	Explanation	Example Sentence
present + present	This structure is mostly used to convey facts. This is often called the "zero conditional" or "factual conditional."	If you **wash** your hands too often, your skin **becomes** too dry.
present + future	This is the most common combination in the real condition category. This is often called the "first conditional" or "predictive conditional" (because it predicts what will happen in the future when a condition is met).	If you **study** hard enough, you **will pass** the test.
present + imperative	This combination is used to provide instructions in the event something happens (first conditional.)	If Ken **calls**, **tell** him to call back in half an hour.
past + future	In this case, the condition is set in the past and the result appears in the future (first conditional.)	If he **left** Toronto only half an hour ago, he **won't make** it to Kingston in time for our meeting.
past + past	In this type, both the condition and the result are in the past (first conditional.)	Even if he **knew** the dangers, he probably **didn't care**.

PRESENT + PRESENT (ZERO CONDITIONAL)

This structure is usually used to convey general timeless truths, scientific facts, or habitual activities.

The most common tense in zero conditionals is simple present, although it is also possible to use progressive forms.

If the temperature is increased, the ice melts. (simple present)

If the ice is melting, it means the temperature is increased. (present progressive)

EXERCISE 1

Fill in the blanks with the appropriate present tense form of the verbs below.

yield	continue	stand	cease	increase

1. If the body loses water, the concentration of plasma in the body _____.

2. If one kidney _____ to function, the body is able to survive with the activity of the other.

3. Why don't your stomach contents flow out of your mouth if you _____ on your head?

4. If parents _____ to the child's wishes each time he cries, it quickly becomes obvious to the child that this is the most successful means of getting what he or she wants.

5. If vitamin B12 deficiency _____ for a long time, symptoms, such as numbness and tingling in the feet, develop.

COMMUNICATIVE ACTIVITY 1

Facts, Facts, Facts

Work in pairs. Complete each of the following zero conditional clauses with a logical or scientific result clause.

If you boil water long enough, . . .

If you boil water long enough, it turns into steam.

1. If you drink too much pop, . . .

   _____

2. If you stare at the sun with unprotected eyes, . . .

   _____

3. If two sentences are joined by coordinating conjunctions (*and, or, but*), . . .

   _____

4. If sulphuric acid is stored in a metal container, . . .

_____

5. If we add up the three interior angles of any triangle, . . .

_____

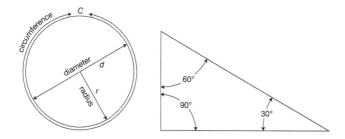

6. If the diameter of a circle is multiplied by pi (3.1416), . . .

_____

PRESENT + FUTURE (FIRST CONDITIONAL)

This structure shows the possible results of **present** or **future** conditions.

If you <u>save</u> more today, you <u>will live more comfortably</u> in the future. (future result of present condition)

If you <u>arrive</u> early tomorrow, we <u>will go</u> to the museum. (future result of future condition)

EXERCISE 2

Fill in the blanks with the appropriate form of the verbs in parentheses to complete the quotations below. Pay special attention to negative and passive verbs.

"If you _____ (build) a better mousetrap, you _____ (catch) better mice."
—George Gobel

"If you <u>build</u> a better mousetrap, you <u>will catch</u> better mice."
—George Gobel

1. "If you _____ (program, negative) yourself, life _____ (program) you!"
   —Les Brown

2. "If the blind _____ (lead) the blind, both _____ (fall) into the ditch."
   —Matthew 15:14

3. "If you _____ (know, negative) where you are going, any road

   _____ (get) you there."
   —Lewis Carroll

4. "If you _____ (do) good, good _____ (do, passive)

   to you; but if you _____ (do) evil, the same _____
   (measure, passive) back to you again."
   —*Fables of Bidpai*

5. "Do what you feel in your heart to be right—for you'll be criticized anyway. You

   _____ (damn, passive) if you _____ (do), and damned
   if you don't."
   —Eleanor Roosevelt

PRESENT + OTHER MODALS

Although *will* is the most common modal in first conditional structures, it is also possible to use other modals.

   If you enjoy tennis, you **might** also enjoy badminton.

   If you wait too long, you **may** lose great opportunities.

   If you haven't already done so, you **should** get your flu shot as soon as possible.

   If you are planning to go to the United States, you **must** get a passport.

   If you want, you **can** join us for a cup of coffee.

   If you have two cottages, you **could** rent one to make some money.

EXERCISE 3

Circle the modal that best completes each sentence.

1. If you are a good boy, I (should / could / might) buy you a bar of chocolate.

2. If you need money, I (should / could / might) lend you some.

3. If you are taking any other medication, you (should / could / would) tell your surgeon.

4. If they give me a chance, I (must / may / can) be able to solve their problem.

5. How (must / may / can) you be happy if you don't have any money?

6. You (must / should / might) place a child in a child seat if he or she is three years of age or younger.

PRESENT + IMPERATIVE (FIRST CONDITIONAL)

This structure is used to give advice, instructions, or commands in case of present or future conditions.

> If you don't secure the ladder, you will fall down.

EXERCISE 4

Complete each sentence with your own instructions (in either the positive or the negative imperative) based on each condition.

> If you get to school late, _____.
>
> If you get to school late, **don't enter the classroom.**

1. If you need my help, _____

2. If you are a handyman, _____

3. If you cannot find a good job that matches your personality, _____

_____

4. When driving on icy roads, if you see an obstacle on the road ahead,

_____

5. If you are a first responder at the scene of an accident, _____

_____

 COMMUNICATIVE ACTIVITY 2

If . . .

Work in pairs. Make an *if* clause (in present tense), and have your partner complete the condition with an imperative result statement. Switch roles after four sentences. Try to do the exercise orally first; if you find it too difficult, you may write your clause on a separate sheet of paper and pass it to your partner.

> **Partner A:** If you exercise but don't follow a balanced diet, . . .
>
> **Partner B:** If you exercise but don't follow a balanced diet, don't expect to lose weight.

PAST + FUTURE AND PAST + PAST (FIRST CONDITIONAL)

Past + future and past + past patterns are also possible real condition structures, although they are not very common.

> If she lost your address on her way here, she won't make it to the party on time.
>
> If they asked him to do something, he always found a way to do it wrong.

EXERCISE 5

Match the numbered conditions on the left with lettered results on the right.

_____ 1. If he didn't participate in the elections last time, . . .	a. he spent it on fancy cars.
_____ 2. If he found some free time, . . .	b. he spent it at his cottage.
_____ 3. If he had any money, . . .	c. he probably won't be in good mood today.
_____ 4. If he had a headache last night, . . .	d. he won't be able to understand this book.
_____ 5. If I ever had any good memory skills, . . .	e. I lost them all after my head injury.
_____ 6. If he started learning Arabic only a month ago, . . .	f. he probably won't vote this year either.

UNREAL CONDITIONS

Unreal conditions refer to situations that did not happen or will probably never happen. Since the situation is unreal or imaginary, the subjunctive is used.

Formation

Here are the most common patterns for unreal conditions.

Tense Combination	Example Sentence	Explanation
past + *would*	If I **had** enough money, I **would buy** a car now.	This applies to conditions that are not true now or will not be true in the future. I don't have money and I won't buy a car. (This is often called the "second conditional.")
past perfect + *would have*	If I **had studied** hard, I **would have passed** the test last semester.	This applies to a past condition that was not fulfilled. I didn't study, and I didn't pass the test. (This is often called the "third conditional.")
past perfect + *would*	If I **had saved** my money before, I **would live** more comfortably now.	This is about a past condition that did not materialize. Therefore, the effect is not felt today. I did not save money in the past. Therefore, I do not have a comfortable life now. (This is a "mixed conditional.")

Although *would* is the most common modal in unreal conditions, it is also possible to use other modals, such as *could* or *might*.

PAST + *WOULD* (SECOND CONDITIONAL)

In the second conditional, the past tense in the *if* clause does not indicate past time. It shows a present or future condition that is unlikely to happen.

- In the *if* clause, many types of past tenses (simple, progressive) and *could* can be used.

- In the result clause, besides *would* (to predict), we can use *could* (to show possibility) or *might* (to show uncertainty).

- In formal English, instead of *was* in the *if* clause, we use *were*.

   If she were living in Toronto these days, she would understand what I mean.

   If I had more time, I could learn a new skill.

   If you could win the lottery, you might be able to buy a house in Vancouver one day.

EXERCISE 6

Using the modals *would*, *could*, or *might*, complete the following clauses in your own words.

1. I wish I'd win the lottery. If I had a couple of million dollars, _____

   _____ .

2. I wish I were immortal. If I could live forever, _____ .

3. I wish I had psychic powers. If I could see the future, for instance, _____

   _____ .

4. I wish I could travel to the past. If I were able to travel to any time period in the

   past, _____ .

5. I wish I were the leader of my country. If I had a leader's powers, _____

   _____ .

❖ COMMUNICATIVE ACTIVITY 3

What Would You Do?

Work in pairs. Take turns asking and answering the following questions. Partner A asks the first question. Partner B answers, starting his or her answer with *if*. Partner B asks the next question.

If you were to spend the rest of your life in the company of only one person, who would you choose and why?
If you had to be reincarnated as an animal in your next life, which animal would you choose and why?
If you had to name the all-time best song, which would you choose and why?
If you could acquire one superpower, which power would you choose and why?
If you could hold a one-hour conversation with any person who is no longer alive, who would you choose and why?
If you could change one thing about yourself, what would it be and why?

PAST PERFECT + *WOULD HAVE* (THIRD CONDITIONAL)

The third conditional shows how things might have been different in the past if something had happened in a different way. In other words, the third conditional discusses a condition that never happened in the past.

> **If I had installed burglar alarms, the thieves wouldn't have robbed my house.** (I didn't install the alarm and they robbed my house.)

EXERCISE 7

Using the modals *would have*, *could have*, or *might have*, complete the following clauses in your own words. Compare your answers with those of your classmates.

1. If Hitler hadn't been born, _____.

2. If dinosaurs hadn't become extinct, _____.

3. If North America had been discovered in the twentieth century, _____ _____.

4. If penicillin had been discovered in the Middle Ages, _____ _____.

5. If the 9/11 attacks had never happened, _____ _____.

COMMUNICATIVE ACTIVITY 4

What Would You Have Done?

Work in pairs. Flip a coin to decide who starts the game.

The winner of the coin toss (Partner A) makes a conditional sentence about the past. Partner B takes the main clause of Partner A's sentence and uses it as the *if* clause of another conditional sentence, which he or she completes. The game continues until one of the players is unable to make a meaningful sentence. Repetitions are not accepted.

Partner A: If I had been born 20 years earlier, I wouldn't have come to Canada.

Partner B: If I hadn't come to Canada, I wouldn't have met my husband.

Partner A: If I hadn't met my husband, I wouldn't have married him.

You may use the following questions for inspiration:

- What would have happened if you had been born a different gender?
- What would have happened if you had been born in a different country or of a different race?
- What would have happened if you hadn't been born at all?
- What would have happened if you had or hadn't made a certain mistake?

PAST PERFECT + *WOULD* (MIXED CONDITIONAL)

The mixed conditional explores how a different condition in the past would change some situation in the present.

If I hadn't eaten so much at lunch, I wouldn't feel so bloated now. (I ate too much in the past and I feel bloated now.)

EXERCISE 8

Using the modals *would*, *could*, or *might*, complete the following clauses in your own words to discuss the effect of the past condition on the present.

If I hadn't learned about mixed conditionals, _____ now.

If I hadn't learned about mixed conditionals, I wouldn't be able to write this sentence correctly now.

1. If the telephone hadn't been invented, today _____

   _____ .

2. If Facebook hadn't been created, we _____

   _____ today.

3. If Canadian and British troops hadn't won the Anglo-American War of 1812,

   Canada _____ today.

4. If the Chinese had discovered and settled North America before the Europeans, today _____.

5. If Justin Bieber's mother hadn't posted his songs on YouTube, _____ _____ today.

⚜ COMMUNICATIVE ACTIVITY 5

Past and Present

Work in pairs. Discuss some of the things each of you did or didn't do in the past and how those things affect your present. Use mixed conditionals when possible.

SUBORDINATING CONJUNCTIONS OF CONDITION

Several other subordinating conjunctions besides *if* can appear in conditional sentences. However, *if* is the most common conjunction of conditions, especially in unreal conditions.

Formation

The following chart gives you a list of the most common subordinating conjunctions besides *if*.

Subordinating Conjunction	Explanation	Example Sentence
unless	*Unless* is similar in meaning to *if not*. It emphasizes a negative condition.	See you tomorrow, **unless** you decide to come by tonight.
on condition that	*On condition that* means *only if* and is normally used in **formal** situations.	He agreed to confess **on condition that** they gave him legal protection.
as long as / so long as	*As / so long as* means *only if* and is normally used in **informal** or conversational situations.	I'll **go so long as** you go with me.
provided / providing (that)	*Provided / providing (that)* is a synonym of *if* in real conditions.	I will buy your car **provided that** you give me a discount.

in case (that)	*In case* is normally used when we talk about **precautions**, when the possibility of the condition happening is weak.	I'll leave you a note **in case** I decide to go early.
in the event (that)	*In the event that* is similar to *in case that*.	Call this number **in the event that** you need help.
whether . . . or not	*whether . . . or not* is used to show that something is true in either of two cases or conditions. *Whether . . . or not* is similar in meaning to *even if*.	I am going with you **whether** you like it **or not**.

EXERCISE 9

Rewrite each sentence below by using the subordinating conjunction in parentheses.

1. The bank will give you the mortgage **if** you have a 25 percent down payment. (provided that)

   _____

2. **If** there is**n't** a miracle, he won't survive. (unless)

   _____

3. I don't mind giving you the money **only if** you promise to pay it back in a week. (as long as)

   _____

4. **If by any chance** you need that book, I'll have it with me. (in case)

   _____

5. I will tell you what I think **only if** you promise not to tell anyone else. (on condition that)

   _____

6. Our meeting will be postponed **if** more than two of the participants cannot be present. (in the event that)

   _____

7. **Even if** we **don't** agree, he is going to do it any way. (whether . . . or not)

   _____

BRINGING IT ALL TOGETHER

 ## COMMUNICATIVE ACTIVITY 6

Newspaper Search

Work in pairs. Your teacher will give you a newspaper. Look for all the conditional structures you learned in this chapter. <u>Underline</u> any that you find, and cross each type off the following list. The pair that has crossed off the most types wins the game.

zero conditional	third conditional	past + past
first conditional	present + imperative	mixed conditional
second conditional	past + future	

Reading

Read the passage and answer the questions that follow.

WHAT IF EVERYONE LOOKED ALIKE?

Question: Life surely would be confusing if we couldn't tell who is who. But could this actually happen in the normal course of events?

Answer: As long as humans continue to reproduce sexually, their <u>offspring</u> will acquire genes from both sets of parents and will not be identical to either one. Even if the original population of humans were extremely uniform genetically, over time <u>mutations</u> would tend to increase the diversity in the gene pool, and the result would be different-looking people.

Q: But as different races and ethnic groups intermarry and raise children, won't humanity tend to produce people that look more and more alike?

A: Not at all. If different races should intermarry extensively, there might be far fewer people with the physical characteristics now associated with one particular race, but the diversity in the gene pool would be as extensive as before.

Q: So if in the future everyone looked alike, I suppose we are talking about some cloning experiment carried to the ultimate extreme, with the only permitted offspring being the clones of say, "Our Great Leader."

A: That seems to be the most likely possibility. If everyone were cloned from one person, we would all be as close as identical twins and would probably think and act very much alike, as well as look alike. It seems likely that society would be <u>regimented</u> to an incredible degree with little room for individuality.

Q: It sounds as if you're describing a colony of ants rather than a human society.
A: That's right. In fact, the reason why ant colonies are so <u>cohesive</u> is precisely because all the worker ants are clones produced by a single queen. If everyone is everyone else's identical twin, each individual puts the welfare of the colony ahead of its own.

Q: Aside from regimentation and loss of individuality, what other consequences would there be if everyone were identical clones?
A: One of the advantages of genetic diversity is that when environmental conditions change, a species can readily adapt to its changing environment. Genes that correspond to characteristics better suited to the new environment are more likely to get passed down to future generations. For example, moths whose coloration closely matches that of trees in their area are less likely to become a tasty meal for birds. In nineteenth-century England, when trees in some areas became increasingly <u>soot</u>-covered, it was the darker-coloured moths that survived and outbred their lighter-coloured <u>brethren</u>—even though initially nearly all the moths were light-coloured. The lesson is that species having a completely <u>homogeneous</u> genetic background would be extremely <u>vulnerable</u> to environmental changes.

Q: But ants in a colony seem to have little difficulty adapting to their environment, despite their genetic uniformity. Why would the situation be any different for people?
A: Of course, each ant colony is cloned from its own queen. Different colonies have somewhat different genetics, and these differences allow some ant colonies to adapt better to their environment than others. The first life forms on Earth reproduced <u>asexually</u>. It seems likely that the reason nature invented sex in the first place was to give organisms a better ability to adapt to changing environments.

Adapted from Robert Ehrlich, *What If You Could Unscramble an Egg?*

COMPREHENSION

1. Why does sexual reproduction make humans look different from one another?

   _____

2. What is the most probable result of widespread interracial marriages?

   _____

3. What is one scenario in which identical humans are possible?

   _____

4. Why are ant colonies so cohesive?

   _____

5. What is the most important advantage of genetic diversity?

   _____

6. Why are moths mentioned in this passage?

_____

7. Why can ants adapt to the environment despite their genetic uniformity?

_____

8. What was the first method of reproduction on earth?

_____

9. Why did nature invent sex?

_____

10. What is the main conclusion we can draw from this reading passage?

_____

ANALYZING THE READING PASSAGE

The reading passage contains several instances of conditional sentences. Read the passage again. Complete the following *if* clauses by providing the result clause.

1. If everyone were cloned from one person, _____

_____ .

2. If we couldn't tell who is who, _____

_____ .

3. If everyone were identical clones _____

_____ ?

4. If different races should intermarry extensively, _____

_____ .

5. If in the future everyone looked alike, _____

_____ .

6. Even if the original population of humans were extremely uniform genetically,

_____ .

7. If everyone is everyone else's identical twin, _____

_____ .

Listening

🔊 Track 12

WHAT IF THE ASTEROID NEVER HIT?

In this clip, from the CBC Radio One program *Quirks and Quarks*, you will hear a discussion about what the world would be like today if the asteroid that killed the dinosaurs had never hit the earth.

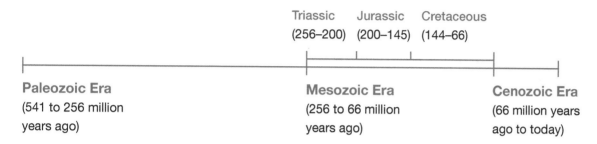

Triassic   Jurassic   Cretaceous
(256–200)   (200–145)   (144–66)

Paleozoic Era
(541 to 256 million
years ago)

Mesozoic Era
(256 to 66 million
years ago)

Cenozoic Era
(66 million years
ago to today)

COMPREHENSION

Part 1

Bob MacDonald, the host of the program, asks his guest, Dr. David Evans, several questions. Listen to Bob's questions and match the first half of the question on the left with the second half on the right. The wording of the questions might be slightly different from what you hear in the clip.

Pterodactylus, an
avian dinosaur

_____ 1. What would the world be like

_____ 2. What do you suppose would have happened

_____ 3. What state were the dinosaurs at

_____ 4. Do you think that dinosaurs would still

_____ 5. Do you think that they would have evolved

_____ 6. How would mammals have done

Tyrannosaurus (T-Rex),
a non-avian dinosaur

a. into something more than you see as the classic T-Rex?
b. if the asteroid had missed the earth?
c. if the giant asteroid that wiped out the dinosaurs had missed the earth?
d. if the dinosaurs were still around?
e. be around today?
f. just before the asteroid struck?

Mammals

monotremes
(egg laying)
e.g., platypus

marsupials
(pouch birth)
e.g., kangaroo

placentals
(live birth)
e.g., human

Listen to the clip again and decide whether the following statements are true (T) or false (F) according to Dr. Evans' responses. If the statement is false, try to correct it.

1. Avian dinosaurs (dinosaurs that could fly) went extinct about 66 million years ago. _____

2. If the asteroid hadn't hit the earth, there's a good possibility that dinosaurs would still be around today. _____

3. If the dinosaurs had survived, they wouldn't be much different from their earlier forms today. _____

4. The dinosaurs were on the decline even before the asteroid struck the earth. _____

5. Mammals shared their world with dinosaurs for over a hundred million years. _____

6. Large mammals coexisted with dinosaurs. _____

7. If the dinosaurs hadn't died they would be living alongside humans today. _____

8. Most of the mammals that we see today in the major orders didn't radiate until after the asteroid wiped out the big dinosaurs. _____

Part 3

On a separate sheet of paper, answer the following questions in your own words based on what you learned in this clip.

1. What happened to non-avian dinosaurs after the asteroid struck?

2. What do you think happened to avian dinosaurs?

3. Name the earliest period during which we could find the ancestor of today's mammals.

4. What would mammals be like today if the asteroid hadn't killed the dinosaurs?

5. What is Dr. Evans' job? (Name two positions).

6. How can you send your science questions to this radio program? (Give the exact address.)

Writing

Write a short two-paragraph response to each of the following questions. Use the appropriate type of conditional sentences in your responses. Consider each situation from at least two different perspectives or with two different outcomes. Explain the reasons for your responses.

1. What new advances in technology do you predict in the next 10 years if we progress at the current rate?

2. If you could change two things in the world right now, what would you change and why?

3. What would possibly have happened to early humans if they hadn't discovered fire?

4. How would your life be different today if your parents had made some choices in their lives differently?

CHAPTER REVIEW

Summary

- Since conditional clauses are actually adverb clauses, they behave in the same way as adverbs.

- If the conditional clause precedes the main clause, a comma is needed. No comma is needed if the conditional clause follows the main clause.

  If I see you, I will tell you.

  I will tell you if I see you.

- Conditional clauses, like adverb clauses, can be reduced.

  Unless a sign specifies differently, you are permitted to make a right turn at red lights after a complete stop. → Unless specified differently, you are permitted to make a right turn at red lights after a complete stop.

  If you do not have a valid passport, you cannot enter the United States. → Without a valid passport, you cannot enter the United States.

  See Reducing Adverb Clauses on pages 228–229.

- Different conjunctions (e.g., *if, unless, in case*) can be used to form conditional sentences.

- Real conditions have more verb combination varieties than unreal conditions, which are restricted to the subjunctive.

EXERCISE 1

Fill in the blanks with the correct tense of the verbs in parentheses. There might be more than one correct answer in some cases.

1. He could have passed the test if he _____ (study) harder.

2. If the Americans had won the War of 1812, Canada most likely _____ (be) part of the United States today.

3. He was always mean to me in those days. Even if he knew the answer, he never

   _____ (tell) me.

4. He is mean to me. Even if he had any money, I don't think he _____ (give) any to me.

5. If you have ever travelled to Vancouver, you _____ (know) that it rains a lot there.

6. If you are a responsible citizen, you _____ (vote) in the federal elections.

7. What would you do if you _____ (be) me?

8. If I _____ (be) in Pierre Trudeau's shoes, I would have dealt with the Quebec Crisis differently.

9. _____ (talk, negative) to me unless you have something worthwhile to say.

10. If 2 + 2 makes 4, then 2 × 2 _____ (make) 4 too.

EXERCISE 2

The following sentences are all written incorrectly. Based on what you learned in this chapter, correct each sentence by changing the words or the punctuation. There might be more than one way to correct some sentences.

1. If we had been given a chance, we would help you yesterday.

2. If we had any money, we would have lent you some.

3. If I see him, I would tell him.

4. If I would have seen him, I could have helped him.

5. If he knew me why didn't he say anything?

6. You will fail unless you don't study harder.

7. I would give you some money provided that I had any.

8. If I had worked harder, I would have had more money today.

9. If she does not get immediate help, she should die.

10. Pure water would always boil if it reaches 100 degrees Celsius at sea level.

Part 2 Review

Self-Study

OVERVIEW

The self-assessments in this unit give you a chance to review and reinforce the grammar points from Part 2 (Chapters 8–12).

Check your knowledge and if you find areas that need more attention, go back to the appropriate chapter and review the material.

EXERCISE 1

Add correct punctuation to the following sentences.

1. After 1935 economic conditions began to improve slowly in Canada yet federal politicians did little to help the recovery

2. While the contributions of Canadians to the Second World War were significant the conflict raised serious issues at home

3. Tommy Douglas the premier of Saskatchewan from 1944 to 1961 is recognized as the father of the Canadian health care system

4. Tommy Douglas once said Man can now fly in the air like a bird swim under the ocean like a fish he can burrow into the ground like a mole Now if only he could walk the earth like a man this would be paradise

5. But what about you he asked

EXERCISE 2

Fill in the blanks with the best connector from the following list. You can use each connector once only.

while	which	before	as soon as	so
when	of whom	after	as many as	as
who	since	where	because	

1. On August 23, 1711, _____ 950 people drowned when the British ships preparing to attack Quebec sank.

2. On May 13, 1873, 60 men died during a coal mine fire in Westville, Nova Scotia. It took two years _____ all the bodies were recovered.

3. On May 26, 1896, a bridge in Victoria, British Columbia, collapsed _____ a streetcar was passing over it. Fifty-five people were killed in that accident.

4. The worst coal mine disaster in Canadian history happened in 1914 in Hillcrest, Alberta, _____ 189 men died in an explosion.

5. Halifax was the scene of Canada's worst human-made disaster in 1917, _____ a French munitions ship collided with a freighter. More than 1,600 people were killed and 9,000 injured in the explosion.

6. In 1958 in Vancouver, design errors in a bridge led to its collapse, killing 18 people two _____ were responsible for the design errors.

7. In 1971, a bar in Montreal was set on fire by three angry patrons _____ had been kicked out of the bar. The fire killed 37 people.

8. In 1977, a fire broke out at the police headquarters in Saint John, New Brunswick. The fire was _____ hot that the locks on prison cell doors were melted. Twenty prisoners were killed in that fire.

9. In 1985 an Air India flight from Montreal crashed in the Atlantic _____ a bomb went off on board. Of the 329 victims in this terrorist attack, 280 were Canadians.

10. In 1989, gunman Marc Lepine shot himself _____ killing 14 women and wounding 13 others at Montreal's l'École Polytechnique. Lepine left a letter claiming the female students had to be killed _____ they were all feminists.

11. On September 2, 1998, a Swissair plane, _____ was en route from New York City to Geneva, developed problems. The plane crashed off the coast of Nova Scotia _____ the pilot was trying to dump fuel over the Atlantic Ocean. Many residents in the nearby communities went to help the survivors _____ they heard the crash but all 229 people on board were killed.

EXERCISE 3

Using the following conjunctions, combine each pair of sentences to form a complex sentence. Make the second sentence a subordinate (adjective, adverb, or noun) clause. You may change the position of clauses or put one clause inside the other one.

whether	whereas	whose	although
before	whom	if	because
while	which		

1. Margaret Atwood and Yann Martel are Canadian novelists. Both of them received the Man Booker Prize.

    _____

    _____

2. The Fathers of Confederation deliberated for two years. They finally selected Canada as the name for the new Dominion.

_____

_____

3. Has Canada decided? Will it participate in the next summit or not?

_____

_____

4. The War of 1812 occurred between the army of the British Empire in North America and that of the United States. Neither of the armies won the war.

_____

_____

5. Some newspapers do not issue a digital version. Others do not issue a print version and are solely available in digital format.

_____

_____

6. Canadians spend more than $300 million a year on over-the-counter cold remedies. None of the over-the-counter cold remedies can cure a cold.

_____

_____

7. Jack Layton died of cancer in August 2011. The NDP became the official opposition under Layton's leadership.

_____

_____

8. Major John Richardson, the first native-born Canadian novelist, died of starvation in New York City. He couldn't make a living as an author and was too proud to beg for food.

_____

_____

9. A naturalized Canadian can serve as the prime minister of Canada. Only a natural-born American can serve as president of the United States.

_____

_____

10. Do you know? Do tree squirrels hibernate in winter?

_____

_____

EXERCISE 4

Change the following sentences from direct into indirect or paraphrased reported speech. There is more than one way to change some of the sentences.

1. He asked, "What are you trying to do?"

_____

2. Jenny said, "Do you think the bus will stop in Banff tomorrow?"

_____

3. The meteorologist said, "It often snows in Ontario in November."

_____

4. The meteorologist said, "It is snowing here in Toronto now."

_____

5. My friend said, "Close your eyes and make a wish. Don't look until I tell you."

_____

6. Khaled said, "I would like to have some privacy please."

_____

7. Bita said, "May I ask you a question?"

_____

8. The boy said, "My mom gave me an iPad for my birthday yesterday."

_____

9. Trevor said, "Wow! What a beautiful day!"

_____

10. My sister said, "I might call you later tonight."

_____

EXERCISE 5

(Circle) the letter of the best answer.

1. I really hope I _____ the mid-term test tomorrow.
   a. pass
   b. passed
   c. would pass
   d. would have passed

2. I wish I _____ the mid-term test tomorrow.
   a. pass
   b. passed
   c. will pass
   d. could pass

3. He could probably have passed the mid-term test if he _____ ready for it.
   a. were
   b. was
   c. had been
   d. has been

4. If he had had more time, he _____ more.
   a. would study
   b. could have studied
   c. could be studying
   d. would be studying

5. He looked as if he _____ for a long time.
   a. hasn't slept
   b. hadn't slept
   c. didn't sleep
   d. wouldn't sleep

6. You look as though you _____ sleep.
   a. need
   b. needed
   c. had needed
   d. will need

7. "Ma'am, you wouldn't treat me like this if I _____ your father's dog."
   —*King Lear*
   a. had been
   b. am
   c. would be
   d. were

8. He said that my car wasn't ready and that the tires _____.
   a. need to change
   b. need to be changed
   c. needed to change
   d. needed to be changed

9. After the dentist had examined her teeth, he recommended that _____ an immunologist.
   a. she consults
   b. she consult
   c. she would consult
   d. she consulted

10. _____ the second-largest country in the world, Canada has a relatively small population.
    a. Despite it is
    b. In spite being
    c. Despite of being
    d. In spite of being

11. I _____ you would stop singing. It's annoying.
    a. hope
    b. wish
    c. hoped
    d. wished

12. _____ you do, don't call him early in the morning.
    a. However
    b. Whatever
    c. Whenever
    d. Whichever

13. It is _____ day for jogging.
    a. so a perfect
    b. as if a perfect
    c. such a perfect
    d. like a perfect

14. This is the person upon _____ I depend the most.
    a. who
    b. that
    c. which
    d. whom

EXERCISE 6

Unscramble the following words and make them into sentences.

1. I could / he could / I said / talk / meet / me / to him / then, / after lunch / or

   _____

2. he said / he had / he would / me / outside / lunch / after / that / meet / finished

   _____

3. the truth / your reaction/ had known / wouldn't have told / I / you / I / if

_____

4. visa / nationalities / Canada / to / in order to / need / to get / don't / travel / a / some

_____

5. the teachers' requests / the teachers / the union / the directors / to address / demanded / that / meet with

_____

6. five chapters / this chapter / most / which / of / grammatical points / learned / in / in the / last / reviewed / we / you

_____

EXERCISE 7

Which choice is **not** correct or clear? (Circle) your answer.

1. a. While Milan was speeding, a police officer was following him.
   b. While speeding, a police officer was following Milan.
   c. A police officer followed Milan as he was speeding.
   d. A police officer was following Milan while he was speeding.

2. a. You cannot buy this house without the required down payment.
   b. If you do not have the required down payment, you cannot buy this house.
   c. Unless you have the required down payment, you can buy this house.
   d. You can buy this house provided that you have the required down payment.

3. a. You look like you didn't sleep for a century.
   b. You look as if you hadn't slept for a century.
   c. You look as though you didn't sleep much last night.
   d. You look like you didn't sleep much last night.

4. a. If I knew the answer, I'd give it to you.
   b. If I would know the answer, I'd give it to you.
   c. If I had known the answer, I'd have given it to you.
   d. If I had known the answer, I might have given it to you.

5. a. He is the man that I told you about.
   b. He is the man whom I told you about.
   c. He is the man which I told you about.
   d. He is the man I told you about.

6. a. I usually like the cars that run faster.
   b. I usually like the cars run faster.
   c. I usually like faster cars.
   d. I usually like fast-running cars.

APPENDIX A: STATIVE VERBS

Stative verbs are verbs that refer to a state (no action takes place), whereas dynamic or action verbs describe an action (they require the subject to do something). When a verb describes a state, we normally do not use it in progressive form.

Compare the verbs *hear* (stative, no action) and *listen* (action) in the examples below:

I am listening to you now. (I'm actively doing something.)

I hear you now. (I'm not doing anything, but whether I like it or not, I hear you.)

~~I am hearing you now.~~ (not normally used with *-ing*)

Stative verbs usually express **senses**, **emotions**, **mental states** (thoughts and opinions), **ownership / relationship**, or **measurements**. Here are the most common stative verbs by category.

senses	see, hear, smell, taste, feel, appear / look
emotions	love, hate, like, dislike, desire, want, need, prefer, appreciate, seem, deserve, sound
mental states	believe, imagine, suppose, think, know, remember, recognize, understand, doubt, mean, wonder
ownership / relationship	own, belong, have, contain, consist, involve, include, depend
measurements	measure, weigh, equal, cost, fit

Some of the verbs above have more than one meaning and can sometimes be used as action verbs. When using progressive forms, always check to make sure there is action involved:

He's smelling the flowers. (action)

These flowers smell awful! (state)

He is looking through the window. (action)

He looks (seems) tired. (state)

I am thinking about the problem. (action)

I think (believe) I'm sick today. (state)

She is seeing a new guy. (going out with a new boyfriend)

She sees him now. (He is visible to her.)

He is measuring the window. (action)

The window measures a metre wide. (state)

APPENDIX B: COMMON IRREGULAR VERBS

Base Form	Simple Past	Past Participle
arise	arose	arisen
be	was, were	been
beat	beat	beaten
become	became	become
begin	began	begun
bend	bent	bent
bet	bet	bet
bind	bound	bound
bite	bit	bitten
bleed	bled	bled
blow	blew	blown
break	broke	broken
bring	brought	brought
build	built	built
burst	burst	burst
buy	bought	bought
catch	caught	caught
choose	chose	chosen
come	came	come
cost	cost	cost
cut	cut	cut
deal	dealt	dealt
dig	dug	dug
do	did	done
draw	drew	drawn
drink	drank	drunk
drive	drove	driven
eat	ate	eaten
fall	fell	fallen
feed	fed	fed
feel	felt	felt
fight	fought	fought
find	found	found
fly	flew	flown
forbid	forbade	forbidden
forget	forgot	forgotten
forgive	forgave	forgiven
freeze	froze	frozen
get	got	gotten
give	gave	given
go	went	gone

Base Form	Simple Past	Past Participle
grind	ground	ground
grow	grew	grown
hang	hung	hung
have	had	had
hear	heard	heard
hide	hid	hidden
hit	hit	hit
hold	held	held
hurt	hurt	hurt
keep	kept	kept
kneel	knelt	knelt
know	knew	known
lay	laid	laid
lead	led	led
leave	left	left
lend	lent	lent
let	let	let
lie	lay	lain
lose	lost	lost
make	made	made
mean	meant	meant
meet	met	met
mistake	mistook	mistaken
pay	paid	paid
put	put	put
prove	proved	proven / proved
quit	quit	quit
read	read	read
ride	rode	ridden
ring	rang	rung
rise	rose	risen
run	ran	run
say	said	said
see	saw	seen
sell	sold	sold
send	sent	sent
set	set	set
shake	shook	shaken
shine	shone	shone
shoot	shot	shot

Base Form	Simple Past	Past Participle
show	showed	shown
shrink	shrank	shrunk
shut	shut	shut
sing	sang	sung
sink	sank	sunk
sit	sat	sat
sleep	slept	slept
slide	slid	slid
speak	spoke	spoken
speed	sped	sped
spend	spent	spent
spin	spun	spun
split	split	split
spread	spread	spread
spring	sprang	sprung
stand	stood	stood
steal	stole	stolen
stick	stuck	stuck
sting	stung	stung
stink	stank	stunk

Base Form	Simple Past	Past Participle
strike	struck	struck
swear	swore	sworn
sweep	swept	swept
swim	swam	swum
swing	swung	swung
take	took	taken
teach	taught	taught
tear	tore	torn
tell	told	told
think	thought	thought
throw	threw	thrown
understand	understood	understood
upset	upset	upset
wake	woke	woken
wear	wore	worn
win	won	won
wind	wound	wound
withdraw	withdrew	withdrawn
write	wrote	written

APPENDIX C: PREPOSITIONS AFTER VERBS, ADJECTIVES, AND NOUNS

absent from: He was absent from work today.

accused of: She accused him of cheating.

accustomed to: She is accustomed to cold weather.

acquainted with: I'd like to get acquainted with her.

addicted to: I'm addicted to chocolate.

afraid of: I'm afraid of flying.

agree with / about / (up)on: He agreed with me about exchanging information, but we couldn't agree on the time or the place.

angry at / with somebody: She was angry with herself for her stupid decision.

angry about / over / for something: Are you still angry over the new regulations?

annoyed with somebody: Are you still annoyed with me?

annoyed about / by / at something: Are you still annoyed about last night?

apologize to somebody for something: I apologized to them for my behaviour.

apply to, for: I applied to that university for film studies.

approval from somebody for something: I received approval from my boss for the trip to New York.

approve of: I don't approve of your decision.

argue with somebody about / over something: He always argues with me about money.

arrive in, at: We arrived in the country at noon and arrived at our hotel at 2:00 pm.

ashamed of: You should be ashamed of yourself!

associated with: He was not associated with the crime.

an attack on: This is an attack on liberty.

aware of: Were you aware of this problem?

bad at: I'm really bad at math.

believe in: I do not believe in ghosts.

belong to, in: This bag belongs to me. He is so old he belongs in a museum.

blame for: I don't blame you for the accident.

blessed with: He is blessed with two beautiful children.

bored with, by: He was bored by the lecturer. He was bored with the lecture.

capable of: He is capable of defending himself.

care about, for: I care for you. I don't care about money.

certain about / of: Are you certain about what will happen?

change to / in: Did you notice any change in his behaviour?

clever at: He is so clever at math.

cluttered with: My room is cluttered with paper.

committed to: I am committed to your cause.

compare with: She does not like to be compared with her older sister.

compare to: She compared his snoring to the sound of a chainsaw.

complain to somebody about / of something: I complained to him about the noise.

composed of: The essay is composed of five paragraphs.

concerned about: I am concerned about this.

congratulate / congratulations on: I congratulated him on his success.

connected to: He is connected to the net.

consist of: The question consists of two parts.

content with: I'm content with my answer.

(in) contradiction to: My answer was in contradiction to his expectation.

contribute to: I contributed to the article.

convinced of: I am convinced of his innocence.

coordinated with: I coordinated everything with my colleague.

count on / upon: I count on you and your help.

covered with: The cake was covered in chocolate.

crash into: The car crashed into the house.

crowded with: The road was crowded with buses.

decide on / upon: We decided on a solution.

dedicated to: She is dedicated to her job.

demand for: There is a demand for his product.

depend on / upon: He depends on me.

dependent on: I'm dependent on him.

independent of: I'm independent of them.

devoted to: I'm devoted to them.

different from: This is different from that.

difficulty in: I had difficulty (in) speaking.

disappointed in / with: I'm disappointed in myself.

discriminated against: They discriminated against the Aboriginal peoples.

discuss with: I can discuss it with them.

distinguish from: You can't distinguish this one from the next.

divide into: The cake was divided into four parts.

divorced from: She was divorced from him.

dream about / of: I dreamed of you.

dress in: She was dressed in red.

be done with: I'm done with you and your crazy ideas.

emphasis on: There was an emphasis on economy.

be engaged in, to: He is engaged to his girlfriend now. The two parties are engaged in talks.

be envious of: I am envious of you.

be equipped with: His car is equipped with anti-theft technology.

escape from: You cannot escape from the truth.

example of: This is an example of stupidity.

excel in: He excelled in music.

be excited about: He is excited about his new job.

be exhausted from: He is exhausted from hard work.

excuse for: There is no excuse for such behaviour.

be exposed to: They were exposed to radioactive material.

be faithful to: The movie was faithful to the novel.

be familiar with: I am not familiar with that concept.

famous for: She is famous for her beautiful voice.

fed up with: I am fed up with grammar.

feel like: I feel like learning something else.

fight for / against, with: I fight with my comrades against injustice and for equality.

be filled with: She was filled with joy.

be finished with: I am finished with him.

fit for: He is fit for this job.

focus on: We should focus on more important issues.

be fond of: I am fond of grammar.

forget about: let's forget about him.

forgive for: I forgive you for what you did.

be friendly to / with: She was very friendly with Jane.

be frightened of / by: They were frightened of strangers.

be furnished with: The office was furnished with leather chairs.

be gone from: Joy is gone from our lives.

good at: I'm good at math.

be grateful to somebody for something: I am grateful to you for your help.

be guilty of: He was guilty of theft.

happy about, with: I am quite happy with the way things are and I'm happy about the results.

hide from: You cannot hide from me.

hope for: I am full of hope for those kids.

increase in: There was an increase in interest rates.

be innocent of: He was found innocent of that crime.

insist (up)on: I insist on eating healthy.

be interested in: I am interested in trying new things.

introduce to: Let me introduce you to my friend.

be involved in: He was involved in illegal activities.

be jealous of: I am jealous of you.

keen on: I am keen on learning a new language.

key to: He is the key to solving this mystery.

keep from: They kept him from the truth.

be known for: The director was well known for his latest romantic comedy.

lack of: There was a lack of understanding between us.

lacking in: The story was lacking in emotion.

laugh at: I laughed at his jokes.

be limited to: We are limited to three choices only.

be located in: The store is located downtown.

look forward to: I look forward to seeing you.

be made of / from: Shoes are made of leather. Butter is made from milk.

be married to: They married 20 years ago and they are still happily married to each other.

nice to: It was nice to hear from him.

object to: She objected to my reasoning.

opposed to: They were opposed to her.

participate in: He did not participate in the riots.

patient with: They were patient with me.

pay for: I paid for the ticket.

pleased with: I am pleased with the results.

polite to: He was polite to her.

pray for: She prayed for him.

prepared for: They were prepared for the disaster.

prevent from: Facebook prevented me from adding friends.

prohibit from: They prohibited me from talking about the case.

protected from: My computer is protected from cyber attacks.

proud of: She was proud of her achievements.

provide with: They provided him with food and water.

qualified for: He qualified for the program.

reason for: There is a reason for everything.

recover from: He recovered from illness.

related to: He is related to the king.

relevant to: This is not relevant to our discussion.

rely (up)on: I rely on you.

remembered for: He was remembered for his benevolence.

remind of / about: Flowers remind me of her. Remind me about the party, okay?

replace with: The old model was replaced with a more improved one.

rescue from: He was rescued from the fire.

respect for: I have a lot of respect for you.

respond to: He responded to my email.

responsible for: I am responsible for security.

satisfied with: I am satisfied with the result.

scared of / by: I am scared of dogs.

search for: They searched for him.

shocked at / by: I was shocked by all the noise.

shout at: He shouted at me.

similar to: This is similar to that one.

smile at: He smiled at her.

speak to / with: I spoke with him.

specialize in: They specialize in cyber security.

spend on: They spend a lot of money on clothes.

stare at: Don't stare at me.

stop from: He was stopped from leaving the United States.

subscribe to: I subscribed to the magazine.

substitute for: Substitute sugar for healthier options.

succeed in: They succeeded in finishing the game.

success in: I owe my success in life to my father.

suffer from: He suffered from migraines.

sure about / of: I am not sure about this.

surprised at / by: He was surprised at the results.

take advantage of: We took advantage of the opportunity.

take care of: We took care of that issue.

take part in: They took part in the negotiations.

talk about / of: They always talk of peace.

terrified of / by: I was terrified by the consequences.

thank for: I thank you for your time.

think about / of: I always think about them.

throw at / to: They threw stones at me. He threw the ball to me.

tired of / from: I'm tired of you. I'm still tired from the trip.

typical of: This is typical of them.

upset with: Are you upset with me?

used to: I am used to doing this.

vote for: I vote for change.

wrong with: What's wrong with you?

worried about: Are you worried about something?

APPENDIX D: ACTIVE AND PASSIVE VERB FORMS

Present Tenses

	Active	Passive
simple	He writes a book.	A book is written.
progressive	He is writing a book.	A book is being written.
perfect	He has written a book.	A book has been written.
perfect progressive	He has been writing a book.	N/A

Past Tenses

	Active	Passive
simple	He wrote a book.	A book was written.
progressive	He was writing a book.	A book was being written.
perfect	He had written a book.	A book had been written.
perfect progressive	He had been writing a book.	N/A

Future Tenses

	Active	Passive
simple	He will write a book.	A book will be written.
progressive	He will be writing a book.	N/A
perfect	He will have written a book.	A book will have been written.
perfect progressive	He will have been writing a book.	N/A

Other Forms

	Active	Passive
going to	He is going to write a book.	A book is going to be written.
modals	He can write a book.	A book can be written.
perfect modals	He could have written a book.	A book could have been written.
gerunds	I'm in the process of writing the book.	The book is in the process of being written.
perfect gerunds	What's the possibility of his having written such a book?	What's the possibility of such a book having been written by him?
infinitives	He is begging to write this book.	This book is begging to be written.
perfect infinitives	He is supposed to have written the book.	The book is supposed to have been written by him.

N/A: The structure is not common in modern English.

APPENDIX E: MODALS AND THEIR FUNCTIONS

Modal Auxiliary	Meaning and Use	Example Sentences
Simple Modals		
will	the future friendly request	I will do it soon. Will you pass the salt please?
would	past habit	When I was a kid, I would always check under the bed before sleeping.
	polite request desire (usually with *like*) hypothesis (conditional)	Would you please pass the salt? I would like to travel more. What would you do if you were me?
shall	polite suggestion legal obligation	Shall we go? All items shall be returned immediately.
should	advice strong probability	You should take good care of yourself. The show should be over by now.
ought to	advice	You ought to take more care.
can	ability casual request permission typical possibility	Can you breathe? Can you help me please? You can call me any time. Cats can have up to eight kittens.
could	past ability polite request possibility	She could sing perfectly when she was five. Could you come closer? He could be anywhere.
may	polite request permission probability	May I open the door? You may kiss the bride now. It may get cold there.
might	possibility	I might be able to help.
must	necessity logical certainty	You must get 50 percent to pass this test. He must be crazy!
Perfect Modals		
will have	future perfect (actions completed by a certain time in the future)	He will have graduated by next fall.
would have	past unreal condition or situation	He would have called if you had asked, but you never asked him, so he didn't call.
should have / ought to have	advice not taken	You should have closed the door, but you didn't.
may have	probability in the past	He may have been there.
could have	possibility in the past unreal past possibility	He could have done it. He had the means. You could have broken your neck. You're lucky you didn't.
might have	possibility in the past unreal past possibility	He might have left already. You might have broken your neck. You're lucky you didn't.
must have	logical certainty in the past	He must have left home by now. I am pretty sure he is not home.

GLOSSARY

Word or Term	Definition	Chapter	Page
abolish	to get rid of	5	90
acquit	to pronounce not guilty	3	52
acumen	the ability to make quick and wise decisions	7	133
asexually	without sex	12	253
baronet	a member of British nobility	7	133
bedevil	to cause problems or discomfort for you over a period of time	11	233
blood transfusion	putting new blood in the body	2	30
bout	a period of illness; period of suffering	11	233
brethren	old-fashioned word for brothers	12	253
cohesive	connected in a way that it makes a uniform whole; united	12	253
compatible	well-matched; consistent	1	13
complacent	feeling so confident or satisfied that you may think no further action is necessary	1	13
conjure up	bring (images) to one's mind; evoke	8	166
controversial	causing public disagreement or strong opinions	6	109
coyly	in a shy manner	4	72
crumpled	crushed or creased paper	8	166
dejected	hopeless and sad	3	52
discrimination	unfair and prejudiced treatment of a person	8	166
entrepreneurial	business-minded	7	133
executioner	the person who executes (kills) criminals	10	208
exploit	take unfair advantage of a person or a situation	6	109
feat	an impressive and sometimes dangerous achievement	8	166
ferry (v.)	to carry people or goods across water	8	166
filthy	very dirty	6	109
flaw	a small weakness or imperfection	8	166
flirt	to behave playfully toward someone to show sexual or romantic desire	4	72
float	to stay on the surface of water (or other liquids)	9	187
foul	unpleasant; very bad	3	53
frankness	being honest and outspoken	1	13
glob	a small (usually round) amount of liquid or soft food	11	233
gratify	to make happy or satisfied	3	52
grisly	violent and bloody (used to describe death or murder)	10	208
gullet	the tube that connects your mouth to your stomach; esophagus	11	233
hag	an ugly old woman	3	53
heroine	a female hero	1	14
hilarious	very funny	6	110
homogeneous	all of the same or similar type	12	253
immerse	to throw into water (or other liquids)	9	187
inclination	a tendency to behave in a particular way	5	90
inhibit	to prevent something from happening	11	233
insane	crazy	7	133
interference	the act of involving yourself in other people's business	6	109
intractable	uncontrollable; difficult to stop	11	233

Word or Term	Definition	Chapter	Page
jollity	feeling jolly and happy	3	52
legacy	something that someone has achieved and survives after his or her death	7	133
maiden	a girl or woman who is not married	3	52
makeshift	something made with whatever is available; improvised	5	91
mandate	period of time a politician stays in power	1	13
mutation	a change in the basic genetic structure of living organisms	12	252
offspring	an animal's baby or babies	12	252
outpost	a small town away from other towns, formed as a military camp or trade centre	9	187
parole	conditional release from prison	10	208
patent (v.)	to register an invention officially to prove you own its rights	2	30
pesky	annoying	2	30
platonic	referring to a relationship without sex	4	72
ponder	to think deeply about a problem	9	187
prosperity	being successful and having a lot of money	6	109
rat out	to inform on your colleagues, associates, friends, etc., to betray them by disclosing their wrongdoings	10	208
regimented	strictly disciplined and organized	12	252
repel	to keep someone or something away	2	30
repression	controlling and restricting a group of people by force	8	166
sabotage (v.)	to damage intentionally	4	73
sanction	to order or give permission officially	3	52
sanitation	conditions related to people's health and cleanliness	6	109
settle a score	hurt someone because he or she hurt you in the past; to take revenge	10	208
shrewd	making clever decisions and judgments	7	133
skeptical	having doubts	4	72
slum	an area of the city where poor people live in very bad conditions	6	109
sneak	to put, add, or bring something secretively or unlawfully	9	187
soot	black powder produced as result of burning	12	253
sovereignty	control	3	52
spasmodic	happening for short periods and not often	11	233
spring up	to appear suddenly	6	109
stab	to push a knife into someone's body	10	208
sting	a police undercover operation to catch criminals, usually by pretending to be one of them	10	208
strive	to try hard	5, 6	91, 109
stumped	confused	9	187
subtle	indirect or complicated	4	73
testify	to make a statement or provide evidence (usually in a court of law)	10	208
torpedo	a rocket that is fired from a ship or a submarine	7	133
toss	to throw	11	233
unsavoury	unpleasant	10	208
verbalize	to say in words; to express	4	72
vulnerable	easy to hurt or attack	12	253
wink at	close and open one eye quickly as a sign; blink; force to go away by blinking	6	109